What Works with Women Offenders

What Works with Women Offenders

Edited by
Rosemary Sheehan, Gill McIvor
and Chris Trotter

WILLAN
PUBLISHING

Published by

Willan Publishing
Culmcott House
Mill Street, Uffculme
Cullompton, Devon
EX15 3AT, UK
Tel: +44(0)1884 840337
Fax: +44(0)1884 840251
e-mail: info@willanpublishing.co.uk
website: www.willanpublishing.co.uk

Published simultaneously in the USA and Canada by

Willan Publishing
c/o ISBS, 920 NE 58th Ave, Suite 300
Portland, Oregon 97213-3786, USA
Tel: +001(0)503 287 3093
Fax: +001(0)503 280 8832
e-mail: info@isbs.com
website: www.isbs.com

First published 2007

ISBN-978-1-84392-239-1 paperback
ISBN-978-1-84392-240-7 hardback

British Library Cataloguing-in-Publication Data

A catalogue record for this book is available from the British Library

Typeset by GCS, Leighton Buzzard, Beds
Printed and bound by TJI Digital, Trecerus Industrial Estate,
Padstow, Cornwall

Contents

Preface and acknowledgements

Monash University, Australia, hosted the inaugural conference 'What works with women offenders: A cross-national dialogue about what are effective responses to female offenders' at the Monash Centre in Prato, Italy, 20–22 June, 2005. This innovative, international conference in Tuscany brought together a range of people who work with, and have an interest in helping, women offenders. They included academics, practitioners and policy contributors from a range of European, North American and Australasian countries. The conference provided the opportunity for dialogue between representatives of different national systems both about their system responses to female offenders and about the programmes they have developed for women who offend. In the context of dramatic increases in the imprisonment of women across western jurisdictions, the aim of this dialogue was to examine what responses work best in alleviating the problems that contribute to women's offending and imprisonment, and what interventions offer the best opportunity for rehabilitation. Particular attention was given to issues of the health and mental health of women prisoners; the role of addiction in women's offending; families and parenting roles; education and work opportunities; political and societal responses to women offenders; and, the effectiveness of interventions that have been developed in response to offending and women.

The idea for the conference grew out of research undertaken in Victoria, Australia, by Rosemary Sheehan and Chris Trotter, that asked women in prison, and at intervals after their release, what services and supports helped them manage during, and after, prison. Gill McIvor undertook a parallel, though more limited, study of women leaving prison in Scotland. Women who go to prison have a range of social and personal problems and are likely to require significant amounts of support both while in custody on release. Given that the risk of reoffending is strongly influenced by the social situation and circumstances women return to on release, our research set out to identify what services provided the most effective support to the women and were more likely to reduce their risk of reoffending on release. It became clear that the challenges posed by women offenders in Scotland and Victoria were very similar and were shared by other women in other countries that had similarly witnessed significant increases in female incarceration.

This book arose out of the Prato conference, convened by Rosemary Sheehan. The book is made possible by the generous support of Brian Willan and Willan Publishing, whose interest in criminology has greatly encouraged this venture. Our thanks go also those who participated in the conference and who contributed to the writing of this book, providing a unique cross-national perspective on women offenders and giving attention to an important social and political issue.

Rosemary Sheehan, Gill McIvor and Chris Trotter

List of figures and tables

Figures

Tables

Notes on contributors

Dr Monica Barry is Research Fellow in the Department of Applied Social Science, University of Stirling, Scotland.

Professor Marianne Berry is Professor of Social Welfare, School of Social Welfare, University of Kansas, USA.

Catherine Flynn is undertaking her doctoral studies in the Department of Social Work, Monash University, Victoria, Australia.

Dr Loraine Gelsthorpe is Reader in Criminology and Criminal Justice at the Institute of Criminology, University of Cambridge, England.

Kelly E. Knight contributed to this book whilst a Research Associate in the field of psychological research with the National Council on Crime and Delinquency, in Oakland, California, USA.

Shabnam Javdani contributed to this book whilst a Research Associate with a background in psychology working at the National Council on Crime and Delinquency, in Oakland, California, USA.

Dr Nancy Loucks is an independent criminologist based in Scotland.

Professor Gill McIvor is currently Professor of Criminology in the Department of Applied Social Science at Lancaster University,

Lancaster, England. She was previously the Director of the Social Work Research Centre at the University of Stirling, Scotland.

Tracie McPherson is Programme Coordinator for the *Women 4 Work* programme conducted by Melbourne Citymission, a non-government agency that provides services for people on the margins of society, Victoria, Australia.

Dr Margaret Malloch is Senior Research Fellow at the Scottish Centre for Crime and Justice Research at the University of Stirling, Scotland.

Dr Sally Malin was Griffins Society Visiting Research Fellow 2003–4 at the London School of Economics. She is currently the Chair, Barnet Primary Care Trust, London, England.

Valerie Monti-Holland is Transnational Co-ordinator, SOVA (Supporting Others through Volunteer Action) Women into Work Moving On, EQUAL Project in Sheffield, England.

Professor James Ogloff is Professor of Clinical Forensic Psychology at Monash University and Director of Psychological Services Forensicare, Victorian Institute of Forensic Mental Health, Australia. Prior to this appointment he was Professor of Law and Forensic Psychology, Simon Fraser University, and Director of Mental Health Services, British Columbia Corrections, Canada.

Caroline O'Keeffe is Research Manager at the Hallam Centre for Community Justice, Sheffield Hallam University, Sheffield, England.

Sue Pearce is Assistant Director in the Thames Valley Probation Area for the National Probation Service for England and Wales, based in Bicester, England.

Professor Judy L. Postmus is Assistant Professor in the School of Social Work at Rutgers University, New Brunswick, New Jersey, USA.

Professor Paul Senior is Director of the Hallam Centre for Community Justice at Sheffield Hallam University, Sheffield, England.

Associate Professor Margaret Severson is a member of Faculty in the School of Social Welfare at the University of Kansas, Lawrence, Kansas, USA.

Associate Professor Rosemary Sheehan teaches undergraduate and postgraduate students in the Department of Social Work, Monash University, Victoria and holds a Governor-in-Council appointment to the Children's Court of Victoria to conduct alternative dispute resolution conferences.

Fabiana Silva is a Research Associate at the National Council on Crime and Delinquency in Oakland, California.

Associate Professor Chris Trotter teaches in the Department of Social Work, Monash University and is the Director of the Monash Criminal Justice Research Consortium, Victoria, Australia.

Dr Christine Tye is Senior Psychologist with Forensicare, the Victorian Institute of Forensic Mental Health, Victoria, Australia.

Dr Angela Wolf is Senior Researcher with the National Council on Crime and Delinquency in Oakland, California, USA.

Introduction

Rosemary Sheehan, Gill McIvor and Chris Trotter

Increasing numbers of women are now being incarcerated in prisons throughout the world (Home Office, 2004; National Offender Management Service, 2005; Scottish Executive, 2006; Frost, Greene and Pranis, 2006). The number of women in prison as a percentage of overall prison figures remains low: around 6% in the UK, Canada, Australia and New Zealand, 7% in the USA, although these percentages may vary in individual countries. However, in most countries, the number of women in prison has increased dramatically in recent years, significantly outstripping increases in the number of male prisoners and with particular consequences for minority ethnic, black and aboriginal women, who constitute disproportionate levels of female prison populations in many countries including Canada, Australia, the UK and the USA.

Harsher responses to offending and a shift away from responses that tended to give women probation or short terms of imprisonment have contributed to this dramatic increase in women in prison (Frost, Greene and Pranis 2006; Chesney-Lind 2002). These trends have significant consequences not only for the women, but also for their families and their communities. Women who enter the criminal justice system very often struggle financially, have low levels of education and have few social supports. They are women who are likely to have experienced trauma and abuse, commencing as children, and who suffer from physical and mental health problems as well as substance abuse issues. They are women who are more likely than men in the criminal justice system to be the sole support and caregivers for their children. Their absence places significant strain on their children and their families, many of whom will have already suffered from instability associated with parental substance abuse, mental health problems and associated criminal activity (Sheehan and Levine 2004). Children with a mother in prison may experience fragmented care arrangements, have little contact with their mothers, and feel shamed and fearful about their mother's circumstances and what will happen in the future. Chesney-Lind (2004) notes that women attempting to reunify their families after prison face significant barriers; the lack of housing, income, job skills and employment history, and community disapproval make reintegration into the community particularly difficult for women.

Women's pathways into prison often reflect a history of child abuse. There is a significant association between childhood sexual abuse and violence and subsequent problems such as alcohol and drug abuse, involvement in prostitution and living with male partners who are involved in criminal activity (Frost, Green and Pranis 2006). Women may become caught up in the criminal activity of their male partner and themselves experience criminal consequences.

Imprisoning women does not solve the problems that underlie their involvement in the criminal justice system (Frost, Greene and Pranis 2006). Greater attention needs to be paid to developing alternative responses that offer appropriate support and intervention to address women's underlying problems and reduce reoffending. However, services and interventions must be gender-responsive (Bloom, Owen and Covington 2003), build self-esteem, strengthen women's social and familial support networks, and enhance their access to education and employment opportunities. Such interventions need to provide women with strategies to cope with the stresses they face, and take account of women's family responsibilities, if they are to be successful. Frost, Greene and Pranis (2006) believe that sentencing reforms and greater public investment in effective drug treatment and gender-responsive services are necessary to help women reduce their offending, maintain their care of their children and remain integrated into the broader community.

Appropriate action is therefore required at different stages in the criminal justice process. First, at the sentencing stage, to ensure that greater use is made of appropriate community-based disposals, especially those that provide links into drug and other services that allow the problems that contribute to women's offending to be addressed. Second, further attention needs to be given to services and supports that imprisoned women require while they are serving their sentences, to minimise the harmful effects of custodial sentences upon them. Third, greater attention needs to be paid to post-release services, to provide housing and income support or employment, and support for women resuming their parenting role. For example, many women struggle to secure adequate housing, and this stands in the way of them resuming the care of their children.

This book sets out to explore these themes, by seeking better to understand the nature, circumstances and causes of female offending and by identifying effective responses to women who offend. Importantly, given the recent large increases in women's imprisonment that have promoted academic, policy and practice concerns are an international phenomenon, this book – and the conference upon which it was based – sought contributions from across jurisdictions with a view to sharing knowledge and experience and enabling policy and practice in different countries to be informed by experiences elsewhere.

The first three chapters seek to identify the extent and nature of female offending, the factors that appear to be associated with women's involvement in offending and how female offending is responded to by criminal justice systems. In Chapter 1, Gill McIvor (Scotland) focuses on the nature of female offending in different jurisdictions by considering the rate, frequency, seriousness and types of offences for which women are convicted and how this differs from men. Comparative trends in female imprisonment are also examined and reasons for the unprecedented rise in the imprisonment of women are considered. The chapter concludes by considering policy initiatives that have been introduced in several countries to reduce offending by and imprisonment of women, drawing in particular upon experience in Scotland.

Chapter 2 by Monica Barry (Scotland) considers the reasons for young women's involvement in offending, their reasons for continuing to offend and the factors that appear to be associated with their subsequent decisions to desist. As previous studies have also shown, drug misuse and involvement with offending partners were frequently cited as pathways into offending by women, who soon came to regard any benefits offending bestowed as being far outweighed by the costs. Desistance among women was often associated with the assumption of family and other personal responsibilities (which, in turn, helped to support women's efforts to become drug-free). Basing her analysis upon the concepts of capital, generativity and responsibility-taking, she argues that women's desistance from offending may be understood in terms of their having achieved opportunities both to accumulate and expend capital that are both real and sustainable.

Chapter 3 by Loraine Gelsthorpe (England) discusses gender and sentencing, highlighting the complex ways in which gender and sentencing interact, she draws upon Garland's 'culture of control' and Carlen's concept of 'carceral clawback' in explaining the increasingly harsh treatment of women by the criminal justice system. Reflecting upon the accumulating evidence that women's 'criminogenic needs' are in certain respects different from those of men and upon the development of gender specific interventions that are underpinned by knowledge of women's pathways into offending, needs and styles of engaging, she argues that equality of treatment of men and women should not necessarily mean sameness of treatment and that procedural justice is likely to be enhanced if due diversity and difference are duly recognised and addressed.

Chapter 4 by Margaret Severson, Judy Postmus, Marianne Berry (USA) examines of the concepts of risk and need in the context of women and offending, with particular reference to the needs of women in prison. Looking specifically at the experiences of victimisation and abuse among incarcerated and non-incarcerated women, their study found higher levels of prior victimisation as children and adults and more severe forms of violence among the women who were in prison. The imprisoned women also had histories characterised by greater material and social deprivation, a higher incidence of drug and/or alcohol problems and lower levels of social support. Importantly, they found that the services that women who had been abused most valued – those focused upon providing practical as opposed to emotional support – also tended to be those they were less likely to receive.

In Chapter 5, Margaret Malloch and Nancy Loucks (Scotland) highlight the high incidence of drug misuse among female offenders and discuss contemporary responses to women in the criminal justice system with drug and/or alcohol problems, including the importance of resources that acknowledge the broader contexts of women's lives. Their chapter focuses in particular on the development in Scotland of an innovative residential and daycare project (218) aimed at offering the courts an alternative to female imprisonment while ensuring that women's needs were met in an holistic way. This required the co-operation of staff from different agencies and with distinctive professional backgrounds, including the provision of support from both health and addiction workers to enable women to address problematic substance use. Women who attended 218 were very positive about the service, believing that it addressed their needs and most women reported reductions in drug and alcohol use, reductions in offending and improvements in health and well-being.

Chapter 6 by Sue Pearce (England) discusses the development of offending behaviour programmes for women in prison and in the community in England and Wales in the context of programme accreditation. While the majority of programmes that have been accredited employ cognitive behavioural methods to change offenders' attitudes and behaviour, emerging evidence that women who offend have different needs and different routes into offending from men suggests that programmes that have been developed for male offender populations cannot simply be adapted to make them suitable for women. Importantly, she argues that in developing provision of this type, account also needs to be taken of women's heterogeneity and of relevant external factors that may impact adversely on the ability to make available gender appropriate provision. Chapter 7 by Chris Trotter (Australia) examines the role of probation and parole in responding to the needs of women who offend and considers, in particular, whether women are helped more and do better after prison (including avoiding re-offending) if they are supervised on parole. While concluding that in broad terms similar principles may underpin effective community supervision of men and women, it is argued that female offenders may benefit more from the support provided by a relationship-oriented style of supervision and from an holistic approach to the difficulties they face.

The focus of the following two chapters is upon health problems experienced by female offenders. In Chapter 8, Jim Ogloff (Canada and Australia) and Christine Tye (Australia) outline the prevalence and nature of mental illness among women offenders in prisons and in the community. It identifies the high incidence of mental health problems among, in particular, female prisoners and reviews what needs to be in place to effectively respond to the mental health needs of women who offend.

Chapter 9 by Angela Wolf (USA) discusses the health problems that confront imprisoned women and the strategies that have been adopted to address their often serious health needs. In it she identifies the high incidence of health problems among female prisoners (including sexually transmitted disease and mental health problems) in comparison both with non-incarcerated women and imprisoned men and how imprisonment can further impact in various ways upon female prisoners' well-being and health. Although the implications for the provision of health services to women in prison are still emerging, the chapter concludes by outlining strategies that might facilitate women's access to relevant services and contribute to improvements in their health.

Children and child care responsibilities can be a source of concern for women who are subject to community disposals (for example arranging suitable childcare to attend appointments). However this is an issue of considerable significance for women who are imprisoned. Chapter 10 by Rosemary Sheehan and Catherine Flynn (Australia) considers the experiences of women prisoners and their children, including how women in prison maintain their links with their children and the issues women face on their return to the community in terms of their resumption of family connections and parenting role.

The following three chapters in this volume consider how some of the other practical barriers that prevent women's effective integration in the community may be addressed. Chapter 11 by Paul Senior, Caroline O'Keeffe and Valerie Monti-Holland (England) examines how education programmes, such as literacy, life skills or vocational training, contribute to reduced reoffending for women prisoners or offenders on community-based orders. Chapter 12 by Tracie McPherson (Australia) considers the relationship between employment and offending and the extent to which employment assistance can contribute to reintegration and reduced offending. In Chapter 13, Sally Malin (England) presents a comprehensive account of research that examines the pivotal role of housing and associated support for women after prison, providing a cross-national perspective on how these services support the reintegration into their communities of women who offend.

Chapter 14 concludes this book by discussing the themes which have been developed in the book and comes to some conclusions about what does and what does not work for women offenders and suggests a way forward.

Within criminology and criminal justice, women's offending has historically received relatively scant attention in comparison with offending by men. As the contributions to this volume demonstrate, women's offending is less common that offending by men, usually not of a serious nature and rarely results in serious harm. Despite this, more and more women are being imprisoned and for longer periods of time and the social and personal consequences of imprisonment for women can be particularly acute. International developments in policy and in practice (including the development of gender responsive interventions and strategies) reflect a growing concern to limit the unnecessary use of women's imprisonment and to provide – whether in prison or as an alternative – services, interventions and resources that are better able to meet their needs. We hope that this book, by adding to the growing, though still relatively small, literature on the characteristics, circumstances and needs of female offenders contributes to and encourages ongoing discussion and debate.

References

Bloom, B., Owen, B. and Covington, S. (2003) *Gender-responsive Strategies: research, practice and guiding principles for women offenders*. Washington, DC: National Institute of Corrections.

Chesney-Lind, M. (2002) 'Criminalising Victimisation: The unintended consequences of arrest policies for girls and women', *Criminology and Public Policy*, November, 81–90.

Chesney-Lind, M. (2004) *The Female Offender: Girls, women and crime* (2nd ed.) Thousand Oaks, CA: Sage Publications.

Frost, N., Greene, J. and Pranis, K. (2006) *HARD HIT: The growth of imprisonment of women, 1997–2004*. New York: Institute on Women and Justice, Women's Prison Association.

Home Office (2004) *Statistics on Women and the Criminal Justice System 2003*. London: Stationary Office.

National Offender Management Service (2005) *Population in Custody, July 2005*. London: Home Office.

Raeder, M. (1995) 'The Forgotten Offenders: The effect of sentencing guidelines and mandatory minimums on women and their children'. New York: Vera Institute of Justice *Federal Sentencing Reporter*, 8, 3 (December).

Scottish Executive (2006) *Prison Statistics Scotland, 2005/06*. Edinburgh: Scottish Executive.

Sheehan, R. and Levine, G. (2004) 'Parents As Prisoners: Maintaining the parent-child relationship', *15th ISPCAN Congress*, 19–22 September, Brisbane, 2004.

Chapter 1

The nature of female offending

Gill McIvor

Introduction

This chapter discusses the types of offences women are involved in and how their offending compares (in terms of its rate and seriousness) with offending by men, highlighting the relatively minor nature of the offences most commonly committed by women. However, there is evidence that how criminal justice systems respond to offending by women has changed in recent years. In particular, western jurisdictions have witnessed a dramatic increase in women's imprisonment (in terms of both the numbers of women imprisoned and the sentenced female prison population) that has far outstripped any such increases in the imprisonment of men. This chapter will argue that the observed increases in women's imprisonment cannot be attributed to increases in the severity of female offending but appear instead to reflect more punitive responses by the courts to offending by women. Recognising the harmful effects of imprisonment upon women and their families (and its ineffectiveness in reducing the risk of further offending), some jurisdictions have, with varying degrees of success, developed strategies aimed at encouraging greater use of community-based disposals. The Scottish experience will be drawn upon to illustrate how, despite policy commitments to improve the range and quality of resources available to female offenders in the community, the trend toward carceral expansion cannot easily be reversed.

Women's offending

The incidence of female offending

Perhaps the most striking feature of offending by women is its relative infrequency in comparison with offending by men. Across different jurisdictions, women represent a relatively small proportion of those convicted and sentenced by the courts. For example, in England and Wales, women represented only 19% of those cautioned by the police or convicted of an offence (referred to as 'known offenders') in 2002 (Home Office 2003) and 19% of defendants who were convicted of an offence in 2005 (Home Office 2006). In 2006 more men than women were convicted of all categories of indictable offences, with the exception of cruelty to or neglect of children (where 59% of those convicted were female).

With respect to summary offences, in 2005 women were more likely than men to have been convicted of Education Act offences (not sending children to school) and non-payment of a television licence (where 73% and 63% respectively of those convicted were women) (Home Office 2006). With the exception of 'offences by a prostitute' (where 99% of defendants were women) it is obvious that offending that is predominantly committed by women in England and Wales is connected very much to the domestic sphere. The fact that women's offending is also, in general, less serious than offending by men is illustrated by the finding that women represented only 15% of those convicted of indictable (that is, more serious) offences in 2005 but 20% of those convicted summarily (that is, of less serious offences) (Home Office 2006).

Similarly, in Scotland, men accounted for 84% of all convictions in 2004/5. More men than women had a charge proved against them in almost all crime and offence categories, the only exception being 'other crimes of indecency' where women accounted for 70% of offences, these being mainly related to prostitution. Unlike in England and Wales, however, similar proportions of those convicted of both crimes and offences[1] in Scotland in 2004/5 were women (Scottish Executive 2006a).

Looking to other jurisdictions, a similar pattern pertains. For instance, in the United States, local data collated centrally by the FBI indicated that female offenders represented 23% of all arrestees (Federal Bureau of Investigation, 2004) while data from the Bureau of Justice Statistics showed that 17% of those convicted of felonies

2

in 2002 were women (Durose and Langan 2005). In Canada 15% of adult court cases in 2002–3 involved a female accused (McCutcheon 2003) while in New Zealand, male offenders accounted for 82% of all cases that resulted in conviction in 2004 (for which the gender of the offender was known) with female offenders accounting for 18% of cases (Lash 2006). In Australia, defendants who were prosecuted in 2004–5 were overwhelmingly male, with this being particularly true of those convicted in the higher courts, where 88% were male (and 12% female). As in other jurisdictions, proportionally more women were prosecuted in the lower courts (22% of cases) (Australian Bureau of Statistics 2006a).

Even though the gap between male and female offending (in terms of the percentages who report having committed illegal acts) is smaller when self-reported offending is considered (e.g. Graham and Bowling 1995; Flood-Page et al. 2000) boys are still more likely than girls to report having committed all but the least common offences (Triplett and Myers 1995; Jamieson et al. 1999). Young men also report engaging in different types of offences more frequently than young women and are much more like to report committing more serious offences (Jamieson et al. 1999).

Offences committed by women

The most recent data for England and Wales (Home Office 2006) indicate that women are disproportionately represented among those convicted of thefts from other people, employers and shops, for fraud, police assault, Education Act offences, social security offences, offences by prostitutes, non-payment of fares on public transport and non-payment of television licences.[2] Numerically, the most common offences for which women were convicted in 2005 were (in descending order): failure to pay for a television licence, driving while disqualified, shoplifting, non-payment of fares on public transport, common assault, offences under the Education Act and failing to surrender to bail (Home Office 2006).

A broadly similar picture is found in Scotland where, aside from prostitution, the categories in which women formed a higher than average proportion of those convicted in 2004–5 included fraud (37%), shoplifting (29%), non-payment of a television licence (69%) and 'other non-sexual crimes of violence' (42%) which includes neglect or maltreatment of children (Scottish Executive 2006a). In that year, the most common offences in respect of which women were convicted were failure to pay for a television licence, shoplifting, breach of the peace, assault (including resisting arrest), driving while disqualified and speeding.

Data for Canada indicate that in 2002–3 men were disproportionately over-represented among those who appeared in court for crimes against the person, criminal code traffic offences and crimes against property. While still representing the minority of those appearing in court, women accounted for a significant proportion of accused charged with prostitution (43% of cases), fraud (29%) and theft, including shoplifting (28%) (McCutcheon 2003). In New Zealand, women are disproportionately represented among those convicted of crimes against property, which includes shoplifting and fraud and under-represented among those convicted of offences involving violence (Lash 2006).

In Australia the most common offences in respect of which both men and women were convicted in 2004–5 were intention to cause injury and drug offences. Gender differences were evident with regard to sexual assaults and deception and related offences, the former being markedly more common among men (14% of those adjudicated compared with 2% of women) and the latter more common among women (18% of those adjudicated compared with 6% of men). The most common offences for both men and women sentenced in magistrates' courts were road traffic and 'motor vehicle regulatory offences'. Thereafter the most common offences among male defendants were public order offences (21%) and Acts intended to cause injury (15%). Among women, offences of theft and related offences (25%) and public order offences (15%) were next most common (Australian Bureau of Statistics 2006a).

Additional data for the state of Victoria indicate that the most common categories of offences for women sentenced in the higher (Supreme and County) courts in 2002–3 were robbery and cultivating/manufacturing/trafficking drugs, especially among younger women in their twenties. Conviction rates for deception (fraud) were also relatively high for women, especially those between 30 and 39 years of age. Women accounted for 13% of all those sentenced (Victoria Department of Justice 2004).

Overall, therefore, this brief comparative analysis suggests that women's offending is less common and less serious than offending by men. These differences in patterns of male and female offending suggest that although there may be certain commonalities, it is likely that the pathways into offending by men and women are different and that different theoretical explanations for male and female involvement in crime are required.

Explanations for offending: pathways and needs

Women's offending challenges traditional theoretical explanations of crime which were developed essentially to explain offending by men. This has resulted in the development of theoretical explanations for women's offending that have focused upon a range of biological, psychological and sociological factors and which increasingly have incorporated feminist analyses to locate women's offending within patriarchal structures and wider socio-structural influences (Gelsthorpe 2004). Increasingly, attention is being paid to identifying the factors which appear to be related to women's pathways towards crime. For example, in the UK, Farrington and Painter (2004) found that socio-economic factors (such as low social class, low family income, poor housing and large family size) and child-rearing practices (such as low levels of praise by the parents, harsh or erratic discipline, poor parental supervision, parental conflict, and low paternal interest in children and in their education) were better predictors of offending among women than among men.

An understanding of how women become involved in crime can be gained from the accounts of women themselves or from the analysis of the experiences and characteristics of women drawn into the criminal justice system. These analyses suggest that women's offending is often rooted in poverty and deprivation (for example, stealing to provide for children) or problems relating to substance misuse. Female offenders frequently have experiences of abuse, psychological problems (including depression and low self-esteem) and past or present involvement in abusive personal relationships (Chesney-Lind 1997; Loucks 2004; Rumgay 2000). What is less clear, however, is whether and in what ways these experiences contribute to women's offending. Whilst the links between poverty and drug use and crime may be understood at a simplistic level in essentially utilitarian terms, the relationships between women's histories of abuse and their involvement in criminal activity are less clearly discerned (e.g. Dowden and Andrews 1999).

It is now recognised that women are likely to have different 'criminogenic needs' from men (Hedderman 2004a) because their routes into offending and reasons for offending are often different (Jamieson *et al.* 1999). Experiences of physical and sexual abuse appear to be more specific (though not unique) to women (Hollin and Palmer 2006). Others – such as criminal history, unemployment and substance misuse – appear to pertain to both men and women. However, even if certain factors appear to be *associated* both with

5

women's offending and with offending by men, it not necessarily the case that the way in which these factors intersect with offending is similar for men and women. For example, analysis of data from the Drug Use Careers of Offenders (DUCO) study in Australia (Makkai and Payne 2003; Johnson 2004) suggests that drug use may play a different role in the development of male and female offending, with men more likely than women to report having engaged in offending prior to their first use of drugs (Australian Institute of Criminology 2005). This is consistent with Jamieson et al.'s (1999) finding that the offending of young women in their late teens and early twenties in Scotland was usually drug related. Many young women in that study reported having been initiated into drug-use by their male partners and having begun committing offences to finance their (and often their partner's) use of illicit drugs. This being so, they considered desistance from offending to be unlikely unless their drug problems were addressed.

Gender and desistance from crime

Traditionally, criminological interest has focused upon when and why young people start offending, with a view to both understanding the aetiology of crime and identifying methods of preventing young people from becoming involved in committing offences. Offending is, essentially, an age-related phenomenon and most young people – male and female – eventually 'grow out of crime'. In recent years, however, increasing attention has been paid to the processes associated with desistance from offending: how and why people eventually stop committing crimes (e.g. Burnett 1992; Leibrich 1993; Graham and Bowling 1995; Rex 1999; Maruna 2001; Farrell 2002). An enhanced understanding of the processes that accompany or promote the cessation of offending may, it is argued, inform the development of more effective interventions with young people who have already begun to offend (McNeill 2003, 2006).

Although research on desistance has concentrated primarily upon men, a few studies have included both sexes (e.g. Graham and Bowling; 1995; Leibrich 1992; Maruna 2001; Uggen and Kruttschnitt 1998) or have focused solely upon women (e.g. Sommers et al. 1994; Katz 2000). There is evidence that young women, who are of course less likely to offend in the first place, desist sooner than young men (Graham and Bowling 1995; Jamieson et al 1999; Flood-Page et al. 2000). Moreover, while it appears that in some respects the *process* of desistance may be similar for young men and women – with the familiar themes of maturation, transitions, changed lifestyles and relationships being pertinent for both groups – there are also important gender differences (McIvor *et al.* 2004). For example, Jamieson *et al.* (1999), in their study of desistance among young people in Scotland, found that young women were more likely than young men to cite moral as opposed to utilitarian rationales for stopping offending and were more likely to emphasise the importance of relational aspects of this process (Gilligan 1982). The latter included the views of parents, experiences of victimization, the assumption of parental responsibilities and dissociation from offending peers. Young men, on the other hand, more often emphasized personal choice and agency in their decisions not to offend. This clearly has implications for the types of interventions that are likely best to engage with and support male and female desistance from crime (see also Barry, Chapter 2 in this book).

Trends in the use of female imprisonment

Female offending is, therefore, less frequent, less serious and more transient than offending by men. As a consequence, women who offend represent a relatively small proportion of those imprisoned by the courts, though there is some evidence that the imprisonment rate of women is higher in countries in which women have higher social-economic status (Heitfield and Simon 2002).

Despite women's offending being largely of a non-serious nature, one of the most striking phenomena in recent years has been the dramatic increase in western jurisdictions in the numbers of women imprisoned, resulting in female prison populations reaching unprecedently high levels. For instance, in the United States (see Frost *et al.* 2006), the number of imprisoned women stood at its highest recorded level in 2003, having increased in average by 5% per annum since 1995, higher than the 3.3% average annual growth in the male prison population. In 2002–3 the number of women who received prison sentences of one year or more increased by 4.2% compared with a 1.9% increase in the numbers of similarly sentence men. While women comprised 5.7% of all prisoners in 1990, by 2003 this had risen to 6.9%. Moreover, as is the case with men, black and Hispanic women are vastly over-represented in the state and federal prison population (Harrison and Beck 2004).

In England and Wales the average number of women in prison increased from 1,577 in 1992 to 4,299 in 2002 (an increase of 173%

compared with an increase of 50% in the average male population) while the percentage of women in the prison population increased from 3.4% to 6.1% over the same period. In 2002 the main offence groups in respect of which women were imprisoned were drug offences (41%), violence against the person (16%) and theft and handling (14%). 71% of women imprisoned in 2002 received sentences of less than one year (Home Office 2003).

More recent data reveal a continuing trend, with 4,370 women in custody in England and Wales in December 2005. While the female prison population increased by 3% between December 2004 and December 2005, the male population increased by only one per cent. Over this period, the highest increases were among young women under 18 years of age (20%) and those aged between eighteen and twenty years (16%), while the adult (twenty-one years and over) female population rose by one per cent. Between December 2004 and December 2005 the largest proportionate increase in receptions to prison was in female young adults which increased by 15%, while female untried receptions increased by 14% over that period (compared with a 6% increase in male untried receptions) (National Offender Management Service 2006).

In comparison with men, women in Scotland are less likely to be imprisoned for violent crimes and sexual crimes and are more likely to receive a custodial sentence for crimes of dishonesty and crimes involving the possession or selling of drugs. In 2004/5 adult female prisoners (that is, those aged 21 years and over) were most likely to have been imprisoned for other thefts (primarily shoplifting), drug offences, petty assaults and breaches of the peace. The mean prison sentence imposed on adult women was 212 days (compared with 303 days imposed in respect of adult men). More than two-thirds of adult women who received a prison sentence (71%) were sentenced to less than six months in custody: with 50% remission they would be released after serving a maximum of three months assuming that no remission was forfeited while they served their sentence. The most common offences resulting in imprisonment of young women (aged 16–20 years) were other thefts, petty assaults and serious assaults. However, the mean sentence length imposed was only 193 days and 69% received a sentence of less than 6 months (Scottish Executive 2006b).

The data for Scotland indicates a steady increase in the daily female prison population from 189 women in 1996/7 to 332 in 2004/5. Over that period the number of daily sentenced prisoners increased from 143 to 248 (an increase of 73%) while the number of remand prisoners rose from 46 to 84 (an increase of 83%). The increase in the daily female population applies equally to young women and adults, though the average male sentenced young offender population actually *decreased* steadily over the same period. Overall, the percentage of women in the daily prison population increased from 3% to 5% between 1996/7 and 2004/5, with the percentage of the daily sentenced population increasing from 3% to 4.5% and the percentage of the daily remand population growing from 4.5% to 7%. However further analysis suggests that the numbers of women *given* custodial sentences has not increased markedly: there were, for example, 1,268 receptions in 1996/7 and 1,312 in 2004/5 with the number of receptions fluctuating somewhat in between. Rather, the number of women remanded in custody prior to conviction or sentence has increased steeply (from 1,009 in 1996/7 to 1,807 in 2004/5) and, although it fell in 2004/5, the average length of sentence imposed on women has also risen sharply (from 172 days in 1996/7 to a high of 276 days in 2002/3) (Scottish Executive 2006b).

In Australia in 2006, 7% of the prison population was female and the imprisonment rate for men (308 prisoners per 100,000 adult male population) was thirteen times more than the imprisonment rate for women (23 prisoners per 100,000 adult female population) (Australian Bureau of Statistics 2006b). It appears that women are less likely to receive a custodial sentence than men when sentenced in the higher and magistrates' courts and are more likely when sentenced in the higher courts to have a custodial sentence fully suspended (Australian Bureau of Statistics 2006a). However, over the previous ten years the number of female prisoners increased by 90% (from 964 at 30 June 1996 to 1,827 at 30 June 2006), while the number of male prisoners increased by only 39% (from 17,229 to 23,963) over the same period. In the state of Victoria there was a 76% increase in the average number of female prisoners in between 1995–2001 (Victoria Department of Justice 2001), despite it being acknowledged to be the most liberal Australian state with regard to the sentencing of offenders.

In Australia similar proportions of male and female prisoners in 2006 had been incarcerated for an offence/charge of homicide (10% of males, 11% of females) and acts intended to cause injury (18% of males, 17% of females). However, men were more likely than women to have been imprisoned for sexual assault (12% compared with 1% of women) and robbery and extortion (10% compared with 7%). Women, on the other hand, were more likely to have received a custodial sentence for deception (9% compared with 3% of men),

9

theft (11% compared with 5% of males) and illicit drug offences (14% compared with 10%) (Australian Bureau of Statistics, 2006b).

Canada witnessed a 57% increase in the number of women admitted to federal jurisdiction between 1994–5 and 2004–5. Although women still represent a small proportion of those given prison sentences, this increased from 3.2% of admissions in 1994–5 to 5.0% of admissions in 2004–5 (Public Safety and Emergency Preparedness Canada, 2005). In New Zealand, 11% of cases resulting in a custodial sentence in 2004 involved female offenders. However the female sentenced prison population had increased by 113% over the previous ten years while the male sentenced population rose by only 30% over the same period (Lash, 2006). Between 1994 and 2003 the sentenced female prison population in New Zealand increased by 91% (Spier and Lash, 2004). There was, moreover, a 387% growth in the female remand population over the decade to 2004, while the male remand population increased by 147% between 1995 and 2004 (Lash, 2006).

There are five key messages to derive from this brief comparative analysis of women's imprisonment. First, it is clear that, although numerically they are still very much in the minority, women constitute an increasing proportion of prison populations. Secondly, the increase in the rate of imprisonment of women is greater that the rate of increase in the imprisonment of men. Thirdly, the increase in female imprisonment appears to be greater among younger women. Fourthly, female prison populations are generally increasing at the same time as there is either no increase or a decrease in the numbers of women convicted by the courts: in other words, there is little evidence that the growing incarceration of women reflects a significant change in levels or patterns of female crime.

Finally, where such predictions are available, the use of imprisonment for women is estimated to continue increasing and to do so at a greater rate of increase than the imprisonment of men. For example, the Justice Department in New Zealand estimated that the female sentenced prison population would increase by 15% while the male population would increase by 12% between 2003–4 and 2010 (New Zealand Ministry of Justice, 2004).

The causes and consequences of women's increasing imprisonment

In Scotland, there is no evidence that women are proportionately more likely to be convicted of crimes and offences that they were ten years ago: the number of women convicted per 100,000 population (10) was identical in 1995/6 and in 2004/5 and, indeed, decreased between 1998 and 2003 (Scottish Executive, 2006a) when the use of imprisonment with women and the Scottish female prison population were rising at unprecedented levels. In England and Wales too, although the number of women convicted of offences increased between 1992 and 2002, the numbers of known male offenders (that is, those convicted and cautioned) actually *decreased* to a similar extent over the same period. This suggests not that there had been an increase in the numbers of women arrested but, rather, that fewer of those who were arrested were cautioned rather than having their case taken to court (Home Office, 2004).

Further Home Office analysis suggests that the rise in sentenced prison receptions for women was being driven by a more severe response to less serious offences, with the rate of increase of women being given a custodial sentence being higher at the magistrates' court than at Crown Court (Home Office, 2004). Hedderman (2004b) similarly concluded from her analysis of sentencing trends that while *some* of the increase in the numbers of women imprisoned in England and Wales might be accounted for by the fact that more women were appearing before the courts, the scale of the increase, coupled by a lack of evidence that women were committing more serious offences and the observation that the use of custodial sentences was increasing across all offence types suggested instead that sentencing by the courts – especially the magistrates courts – was becoming more severe.

Evidence from New Zealand also suggests that increases in women's imprisonment cannot be accounted for by the courts dealing with more serious female offenders. An increase in the numbers of women imprisoned following the introduction of the Sentencing Act 2002 (which aimed, among other things, to ensure that sentencing takes account of the gravity and seriousness of offending and the culpability of the offender) appeared to have occurred in the absence of any change in the average seriousness of cases resulting in conviction (New Zealand Ministry of Justice, 2004).

Could, as Carlen (2003a), has suggested, the increased tendency to imprison women reflect the growing influence of risk assessment in the criminal justice sphere? Drawing upon Hudson's (2002) argument that 'welfare' needs have been redefined as psychological needs and that the latter have, in turn, been equated with the risk of reoffending, Carlen suggests that women are increasingly likely to be perceived as presenting a risk of reoffending and are, therefore, more at risk of being given a custodial sentence. Carlen further argues that the proliferation of prison programmes and in-prison reforms may

11

persuade sentencers that imprisonment can be beneficial in its effects, especially for those who are deemed to be 'at risk'. In a similar vein, prisons may be viewed by the courts as a means of providing women (and perhaps to a lesser extent men) a period of 'respite' from longstanding drug misuse and its personal and physical problems. Yet, as Tombs and Carlen (2006) have argued, the resources that have been introduced into prisons, such as anti-addiction programmes, would be much more effective in a non-custodial setting.

The types of offences for which women are imprisoned and the lengths of sentences they receive would suggest that most in fact present little 'risk' to society. However the personal and social costs of being imprisoned – and the economic costs to society – can be immense. Studies of imprisoned women conducted in the United States (Owen and Bloom 1995), Canada (Shaw 1994; Blanchette 1997), Australia (Edwards 1995) and the UK (Morris *et al.* 1995; Loucks 1998) support a general conclusion that 'imprisoned women are usually marginalised women sharing characteristics that are devalued by society' (Bloom *et al.* 1995: 132).

The backgrounds of women in prison are characterised by experiences of abuse, drug misuse, poor educational attainment, poverty, psychological distress and self-harm. While men often share many of these characteristics, problems amongst female prisoners are generally much more acute and their offending presents less of a threat to public safety (Loucks 1998). Female prisoners are more likely than male prisoners to have a history of physical or sexual abuse (Stermac *et al.* 1991) and are more likely to self-harm (Leibling 1992). Imprisonment often serves to weaken or destroy women's existing ties to the community, including ties with their children (Caddle and Crisp 1997). A recent independent inspection of Cornton Vale prison in Scotland, while commending the progress that had been made in improving the physical estate and opportunities for prisoners, nonetheless concluded that much still had to be done and questioned what the prison could do for the very damaged women who were sent to it by the courts (HM Inspectorate of Prisons 2005).

Despite clear evidence that female prisoners have a range of social and personal problems and are likely to require significant amounts of support on release (Dauvergne-Latimer 1995), relatively little is known about the services accessed by and support available to women following a prison sentence. Previous research into the resettlement of prisoners has focused largely or exclusively upon men, though there is evidence that female ex-prisoners have considerable needs (Morris *et al.* 1995; Blanchette and Dowden 1998) and that they have more needs than similarly sentenced men (Blanchette and Dowden 1998). The quality of support available to ex-prisoners is central to their successful reintegration in the community and the avoidance of further personal, social and economic costs associated with continued reoffending (Petersilia, 2000). Yet there is growing evidence that women have limited information about services that are available in the communities to which they return and that little attention is paid to women's need for access to the structural determinants of social justice (such as appropriate housing and employment) when they are released from prison (Davies and Cook 1999; Carlen, 2003a; Hannah-Moffat, 2003).

Policy responses to women's imprisonment

The dramatic growth in women's imprisonment in recent years has resulted in increased policy attention to this issue. At one level, this has resulted in reform within prisons themselves and in the relationships between prisons and community alternatives, with Carlen (2003b) proposing that changes in women's imprisonment have typically been scandal-driven (as in Scotland – see below), aimed at legitimating the prison itself or in response to an underlying set of principles (such as a recognition of women's gender-specific needs). At another level this has resulted in the development of gender-responsive policies and practices in which the emphasis is placed upon the provision of services and resources that are better able to meet the needs and circumstances of women who offend. While the remainder of this chapter focuses specifically upon policy developments related to women's imprisonment in Scotland, initiatives that have been taken forward in two other jurisdictions are also briefly considered to provide some comparative perspective on how this issue is being addressed.

In 2000 the government in England and Wales undertook a consultation on a Strategy for Women Offenders, the outcomes of which were published in September 2001. A result of the consultation (and the government's response to it) was the establishment in 2004 of the Women's Offending Reduction Programme (WORP) that brought together key stakeholders (such as the National Probation Service, Prison Service, Youth Justice Board, National Treatment Agency, Drug Strategy Directorate, Department of Health, Department for Constitutional Affairs, Court Services and other Home Office Units) to develop a more co-ordinated response to the characteristics and needs of female offenders (Home Office 2004; National Offender Management Service, 2005). Its purpose was defined as being to 'reduce women's offending and the number of women in custody, by providing a better tailored and more appropriate response to the particular factors which have an impact on why women offend' (Home Office 2004:5). The key priorities of the programme were identified as being to make community programmes and interventions more appropriate and accessible for women; meeting women's mental health needs; dealing with substance misuse; building the evidence base to identify the approaches that work best with female offenders; and communicating, training and providing guidance on gender issues (Home Office, 2004). As Gelsthorpe (Chapter 3 in this book) notes, one outcome of the WORP has been the establishment of pilot Women's Offending Action Teams in two regions of the country, aimed at providing a multi-agency response to female offenders' needs.

The Department of Justice in Victoria (Australia) published a four-year strategy in 2005 to address the increase in female prisoners (Victoria Department of Justice 2005). The strategy includes provision for women in the community, such as bail accommodation and improved practical support for women on community orders, though many of the key proposals relate to women who are *imprisoned* (such as improvements to in-prison facilities, the provision of sexual assault counselling advocacy and support services, an intensive mental health support unit, debt management advice, improved training and employment opportunities and extended post-release support). Other elements of the strategy include providing the judiciary with information about the effectiveness of sentencing options for women and providing training for community corrections staff in the preparation of court reports on and supervision of female offenders.

In Scotland, political interest in female offending and responses to it increased in the late 1990s following a tragic series of seven suicides at Cornton Vale (Scotland's only dedicated female prison) over a period of 30 months. Only two of the women who died had been convicted: the other seven had been remanded in custody awaiting sentencing or trial. Although no single reason for the suicides emerged from the subsequent fatal accident enquiries, it appeared that a history of drug abuse and withdrawal problems shortly after being incarcerated were shared by many of the women who died. As a result of the suicides a review of the use of custody and community disposals for female offenders was commissioned by the Chief Inspectors of Social Work and Prisons. The resulting report concluded that 'the backgrounds of women in prison are characterised by experiences of abuse, drug misuse, poor educational attainment, poverty, psychological distress and self-harm' (Scottish Office 1998: 13) and that:

> Almost all women offenders could be safely punished in the community without major risk of harm to the general population. A few are in prison because of the gravity of their offence but the majority are there because they have not complied with a community disposal. (Scottish Office 1998: 42)

The report ('A Safer Way') contained a number of recommendations aimed at improving the conditions within which imprisoned women are detained and reducing the use of imprisonment for woman in Scotland (such as increased bail provision, the development of a unitary fine system in which the level of penalty imposed is related to ability to pay, the increased use of community-based disposals and the development of a dedicated resource for female offenders in Glasgow which had a particularly high level of female imprisonment). The report also recommended that the daily prison population in Cornton Vale should be reduced from over 176 to 100 and that no young women under eighteen years of age should be held in prison by the year 2000.

An outcome of 'A Safer Way' was the establishment in August 1998 of an Inter-Agency Forum to develop services for female offenders in Glasgow which included representatives of criminal justice agencies as well as organisations employed in areas of health, housing, employment and drugs rehabilitation. The Forum's recommendations included exploring the possibility of a daily court for women, providing additional resources to enable women to address their drug use, building upon and expanding existing diversion strategies at all stages in the system and the creation of 'Time Out' Centres, to provide a wide range of residentially or non-residentially based support services for women. Its work was subsequently taken forward by a ministerial group charged with turning the forum's proposals into practical measures which reported in 2002 (by which time a further two women had committed suicide in Cornton Vale). This report – 'A Better Way' (Scottish Executive, 2002) – concluded that greater emphasis should be placed upon alleviating the social circumstances that lead some women to offend, intervening early to ensure that women's needs can be met without recourse to imprisonment, promoting the use of the full range of community disposals (including the 'Time Out' Centre advocated by the Inter-Agency Forum) and shifting the penal culture away from punishment and towards rehabilitation and 'treatment', with a particular emphasis upon the development of gender-responsive provision (Bloom *et al.* 2003).

Despite the considerable policy interest in female offending in Scotland (the impetus for which, as Carlen [2003b] observes, has been both scandal-driven and principled) the Scottish female prison population has, as was demonstrated earlier in this chapter, continued to rise, leading Tombs (2004) to argue that reductionist policy initiatives are unlikely to be effective unless the morality of imprisoning vulnerable women is brought to the fore and unless clear action is taken to reduce the number of prison spaces available. Similarly, the Scottish Consortium on Crime and Criminal Justice (2006) – an umbrella organisation of voluntary sector providers – has recently called for a strategic effort to reduce women's imprisonment involving all parts of the criminal justice system. However, one positive outcome of the increased policy attention to women's offending was the establishment in 2003 of the 218 Time Out Centre in Glasgow. Providing a range of residential and non-residential, holistic gender-appropriate services, the success of the 218 Centre in providing a community-based alternative to custody for women involved in offending in Glasgow has been documented in Loucks *et al.* (2006) and is discussed by Malloch and Loucks in chapter five of this book.

A key policy challenge lies in identifying how aspects of best practice that have been encapsulated in 218 can be introduced in other parts of the country in which a dedicated facility such as the 218 Centre would not be feasible in terms of either capacity or cost. However, a more pressing challenge lies in convincing sentencers that most women who appear before the courts do not present a risk to public safety and that custodial sentences, however short, are likely to exacerbate rather than ameliorate the problems experienced by already vulnerable women. Given that the availability of community-based disposals appears insufficient in itself to persuade the courts to make greater use of them, is a more radical solution required in which the prison is 'decentered' (Hannah-Moffat, 2001) and a presumption of community alternatives brought to the fore? Would, for example, legislating against the use of short prison sentences (as has occurred, for instance, in Western Australia) help to stem the flow of women into prison or would it simply result in longer custodial sentences being imposed?

Conclusions

The imprisonment of women is increasing across western jurisdictions not, it seems, because more women are committing serious crime, but because more women are involved in relatively minor offending – often drug-related – for which increasingly harsh penalties are being imposed. Immarigeon (2006:iv) has observed in his introduction to a recent compendium of articles on women and girls in the American criminal justice system:

> At the start of the 21st century ... women offenders and prisoners have perhaps reached the tipping point where they can no longer be shunted aside, left managed – just adequately or at least silently – by staff and officials at individual facilities or offices...By now, it is increasingly accepted that the treatment of women and girls in the criminal justice system should never again be an afterthought.

As the preceding discussion will have made clear, these observations apply equally to other western jurisdictions which, like the USA, have witnessed inexorable increases in the numbers of women in prison. Recognising that the problem exists is an important first step. The greater challenge, however, is identifying and putting into effect policies and practices that provide alternatives to imprisonment for the many women across different jurisdictions who are imprisoned and vulnerable but who could scarcely be regarded as posing a significant threat to the communities in which they live.

Notes

1 Contraventions of the law in Scotland are divided for statistical purposes into crimes and offences, crimes generally being more serious.
2 Categories with very small overall numbers have been excluded here.

References

Australian Bureau of Statistics (2006a) *Criminal Courts Australia, 2004–5,* http://www.abs.gov.au/AUSSTATS/abs@.nsf/Lookup/ 62E9BAFF94DAD459CA2568A9001393FE?OpenDocument

Australian Bureau of Statistics (2006b) *Prisoners in Australia, 2006,* http://www.abs.gov.au/ausstats/abs@.nsf/1020492cfcd63696ca2568a1002477b5/8d5807d8074a7a5bca256a6800811054!OpenDocument

Australian Institute of Criminology (2005) 'Gender difference in the sequence of drug use and crime', *Crime Facts Info No 90.* Canberra, ACT: Australian Institute of Criminology.

Blanchette, K. (1997) *Risk and Need Among Federally Sentenced Female Offenders.* Correctional Service of Canada.

Blanchette, K. and Dowden, C. (1998) 'A profile of federally sentenced women in the community: Addressing needs for successful integration', *Forum on Corrections Research,* (10) 1: Correctional Service of Canada.

Bloom, B., Immarigeon, R. and Owen, B. (1995) 'Editorial introduction', *Prison Journal,* 75 (2): 131–4.

Bloom, B., Owen, B. and Covington, S. (2003) *Gender-Responsive Strategies: Research, practice and guiding principles for women offenders.* Washington DC: National Institute of Justice.

Burnett, R. (1992) *The Dynamics of Recidivism.* Oxford: University of Oxford Centre for Criminological Research.

Caddle, D. and Crisp, D. (1997) *Imprisoned Women and Mothers,* Home Office Research Study 162. London: Home Office.

Carlen, P. (2003a) 'A strategy for women offenders? Lock them up, programme them ... and then send them out homeless', *Criminal Justice Matters,* 53: 36–7.

Carlen, P. (2003b) *Reforming Women's Imprisonment; Models of change,* paper presented at ESRC Future Governance Workshop, Vienna and Budapest.

Carlen, P. and Tombs, J. (2006) 'Reconfigurations of penality: The ongoing case of the women's imprisonment and reintegration industries', *Theoretical Criminology,* 10 (3): 337–60.

Chesney-Lind, M. (1997) *The Female Offender: Girls, women and crime.* Thousand Oaks, CA: Sage.

Dauvergne-Latimer, M. (1995) *Exemplary Community Programs for Federally Sentenced Women: A literature review.* Ontario: Correctional Service of Canada.

Davies, S. and Cook, S. (1999) 'Neglect or punishment? Failing to meet the needs of women post-release', in S. Cook and S. Davies (eds) *Harsh Punishment: International experiences of women's imprisonment.* Boston: Northeastern University Press.

Dowden, C. and Andrews, D.A. (1999) 'What works for female offenders: A meta-analytic review,' *Crime and Delinquency,* 45 (4): 438–52.

Durose, M.R. and Langan, P.A. (2005) *State Court Sentencing of Convicted Felons 2002,* Washington DC: Bureau of Justice Statistics, http://www.ojp.usdoj.gov/bjs/pub/pdf/sc0202st.pdf

Edwards, A. (1995) *Women in Prison,* Sydney: New South Wales Bureau of Crime Statistics and Research.

Farrall, S. (2002) *Rethinking What Works With Offenders: Probation, social context and desistance from crime.* Cullompton: Willan Publishing.

Farrington, D.P. and Painter, K. A. (2004) 'Gender differences in offending: Implications for risk-focused prevention', *Home Office Online Report 09/04*, http://www.homeoffice.gov.uk/rds/pdfs2/rdsolr0904.pdf

Federal Bureau of Investigation (2004) *Crime in the United States, 2003*, Washington DC: FBI, http://www.fbi.gov/ucr/03cius.htm

Flood-Page, C., Campbell, S., Harrington, V. and Miller, J. (2000) *Youth Crime: Findings from the 1998/99 Youth Lifestyles Survey*, Home Office Research Study 209. London: Home Office.

Frost, N., Greene, J. and Pranis, K. (2006) *HARD HIT: The Growth of Imprisonment of Women, 1997–2004*. New York: Institute on Women and Justice, Women's Prison Association.

Gelsthorpe, L. (2004) 'Female offending: A theoretical overview', in G. McIvor (ed.) *Women Who Offend*. London: Jessica Kingsley.

Gilligan, C. (1982) *In A Different Voice*. Cambridge MA: Harvard University Press.

Graham, J. and Bowling, B. (1995) *Young People and Crime*. London: Home Office.

Hannah-Moffat, K. (2001) *Punishment in Disguise: Penal governance and federal imprisonment of women in Canada*. Toronto: University of Toronto Press.

Hannah-Moffat, K. (2003) 'Getting women out: The limits of reintegration reform', *Criminal Justice Matters*, 53: 36–7.

Harrison, P.M. and Beck, A.J. (2004) *Prisoners in 2003: Bureau of Justice Statistics Bulletin*. Washington, DC: US Department of Justice.

Hedderman, C. (2004a) 'The "criminogenic" needs of women offenders', in G. McIvor (ed.) *Women Who Offend*. London: Jessica Kingsley.

Hedderman, C. (2004b) 'Why are more women being sentenced to custody?', in G. McIvor (ed.) *Women Who Offend*. London: Jessica Kingsley.

Heitfield, H. and Simon, R.J. (2002) 'Women in Prison: A comparative analysis'. *Gender Issues, Winter*, 53–75.

HM Inspectorate of Prisons (2005) *HM and YOI Cornton Vale – Inspection 2–3 February 2005*. Edinburgh: Scottish Executive.

Hollin, C. and Palmer, E. (2006) 'Criminogenic need and women offenders: A critique of the literature', *Legal and Criminological Psychology*, 11 (2): 179–195.

Home Office (2003) *Statistics on Women and the Criminal Justice System*. London: Stationary Office.

Home Office (2004) *Women's Offending Reduction Programme: Action Plan*. London: Home Office.

Home Office (2006) *Criminal Statistics 2005 England and Wales*. London: Home Office.

Hudson, B. (2002) 'Gender issues in penal policy and penal theory', in P. Carlen (ed.) *Women and Punishment: The struggle for justice*. Cullompton: Willan.

Immarigeon, R. (2006) (ed.) *Women and Girls in the Criminal Justice System: Policy issues and practice strategies*. Kingston, NJ: Civic Research Institute.

Jamieson, J., McIvor, G. and Murray, C. (1999) *Understanding Offending Among Young People*. Edinburgh: The Stationery Office.

Johnson, H. (2004) 'Key findings from the Drug Use Careers of Female Offenders study', *Trends and Issues in Crime and Criminal Justice No. 289*. Canberra, ACT: Australian Institute of Criminology.

Katz, R.S. (2000) ' "Explaining girls" and women's crime and desistance in the context of their victimization experiences: A developmental test of strain theory and the life course perspective', *Violence Against Women*, 6 (6): 633–60.

Lash, B. (2006) *Conviction and Sentencing of Offenders in New Zealand 1995–2004*. Wellington, New Zealand: Ministry of Justice.

Leibling, A. (1992) *Suicides in Prison*. London: Routledge.

Leibrich, J. (1993) *Straight to the Point: Angles on giving up crime*. Dunedin, New Zealand: University of Otago Press.

Loucks, N. (1998) *HMPI Cornton Vale: Research into drugs and alcohol, violence and bullying, suicides and self-injury, and backgrounds of abuse,* Scottish Prison Service Occasional Paper 1/98. Edinburgh: Scottish Prison Service.

Loucks, N. (2004) 'Women in prison', in G. McIvor (ed.) *Women Who Offend*. London: Jessica Kingsley.

Loucks, N., Malloch, M., McIvor, G. and Gelsthorpe, L. (2006) *Evaluation of the 218 Centre*. Edinburgh: Scottish Executive Social Research.

Makkai, T. and Payne, J. (2003) 'Key findings from the drug use careers of offenders (DUCO) study, *Trends and Issues in Crime and Criminal Justice No. 237*. Canberra, ACT: Australian Institute of Criminology.

Maruna, S. (2001) *Making Good: How ex-convicts reform and rebuild their lives*. Washington, DC: American Psychological Association.

McCutcheon, A.C. (2003) *Adult Criminal Court Statistics 2002–3*. Ottawa: Statistics Canada.

McIvor, C., Murray, C. and Jamieson, J. (2004) 'Is Desistance from Crime Different for Women and Girls?', in R. Immarigeon and S. Maruna (eds) *After Crime and Punishment: Pathways to offender reintegration*. Cullompton: Willan Publishing.

McNeill, F. (2003) 'Desistance-Focused Probation Practice'. In W-H Chui and M. Nellis (eds) *Moving Probation Forward: Evidence, arguments and practice*. Harlow: Pearson Longman.

McNeill, F. (2006) 'A desistance paradigm for offender management', *Criminology and Criminal Justice*, 6 (1): 39–62.

Morris, A., Wilkinson, C., Tisi, A., Woodrow, J. and Rockley, A. (1995) *Managing the Needs of Female Prisoners*. London: Home Office.

National Offender Management Service (2005) *Population in Custody, July 2005*. London: Home Office.

National Offender Management Service (2005) *Women's Offending Reduction Programme: Annual review 2004–2005*. London: Home Office.

National Offender Management Service (2006) *Offender Management Caseload Statistics Quarterly Brief: October to December 2005 England and Wales*. London: Home Office.

New Zealand Ministry of Justice (2004) *Forecasts of the Male and Female Sentenced Prison Populations, 2004*. Wellington: New Zealand Ministry of Justice.

Owen, B. and Bloom, B. (1995) 'Profiling women prisoners: Findings from national surveys and a California sample', *The Prison Journal*, 75 (2): 165–85.

Petersilia, J. (2000) *When Prisoners Return to the Community: Political, economic and social consequences*. Washington DC: US Department of Justice.

Public Safety and Emergency Preparedness Canada (2005) *Corrections and Conditional Release Statistical Overview*. Ottawa: Public Safety and Emergency Preparedness Canada.

Rex, S. (1999) 'Desistance from offending: Experiences of probation', *The Howard Journal of Criminal Justice*, 38 (4): 366–83.

Rumgay, J. (2000) 'Policies of neglect: Female offenders and the probation service', in H. Kemshall and R. Littlechild (eds) *User Involvement and Participation in Social Care*. London: Jessica Kingsley.

Scottish Consortium on Crime and Criminal Justice (2006) *Women in Prison in Scotland: An unmet commitment*. Edinburgh: Scottish Consortium on Crime and Justice Research.

Scottish Executive (2002) *A Better Way: The report of the ministerial group on women's offending*. Edinburgh: Scottish Executive.

Scottish Executive (2006a) *Criminal Proceedings in Scottish Courts 2004/5*. Edinburgh: Scottish Executive.

Scottish Executive (2006b) *Prison Statistics Scotland 2005/06*. Edinburgh: Scottish Executive.

Scottish Office (1998) *Women Offenders – A Safer way: A review of community disposals and the use of custody for women offenders in Scotland*. Edinburgh: Scottish Executive.

Shaw, M. (1994) 'Women in prison: A literature review', *Forum on Corrections*.(6) 1, Canadian Department of Corrections.

Sheehan, R., Trotter, C. and McIvor, G. (2006) *Women After Prison*. Melbourne: Monsah University School of Social Work.

Sommers, I., Baskin, D.R. and Fagan, J. (1994) 'Getting out of the life: Crime desistance by female street offenders', *Deviant Behavior*, 15 (2): 125–49.

Spier, P. and Lash, B. (2004) *Conviction and Sentencing of Offenders in New Zealand: 1994 to 2003*. Wellington, New Zealand: Ministry of Justice.

Stermac, L., MacLean, H. and Loucks, A. (1991) *Treatment Needs of Female Offenders*. Correctional Service of Canada.

Tombs, J. (2004) 'From "A Safer to A Better Way": Transformations in penal policy for women', in G. McIvor (ed.) *Women Who Offend*. London: Jessica Kingsley.

Triplett, R. and Myers, L.B. (1995) 'Evaluating contextual patterns of delinquency: gender-based differences', *Justice Quarterly*, 12: 59–84.

Uggen, C. and Kruttschnitt, C. (1998) 'Crime on the breaking: gender differences in desistance', *Law and Society Review*, 32 (2): 339–66.

Victoria Department of Justice (2001) *Statistical Overview of the Victorian Prison System 1995/1996 to 2000/2001*. Melbourne: Victoria Department of Justice.

Victoria Department of Justice (2004) *Victorian Higher Courts Sentencing Statistics 2002–3*. Melbourne: Victoria Department of Justice.

Victoria Department of Justice (2005) *Better Pathways: An integrated response to women's offending and reoffending*. Melbourne: Victoria Department of Justice.

Chapter 2

The transitional pathways of young female offenders: towards a non-offending lifestyle

Monica Barry

Introduction

This chapter explores young women's reasons for starting and stopping offending, notably during the transition to adulthood. It argues that the concept of capital – and how it is accumulated in the transition to adulthood – is crucial in understanding young women's propensity or otherwise to offend and concludes with an exploration of the value of expenditure of capital in the transition towards a non-offending lifestyle.

The fact that women spend less time committing fewer and less serious crimes than men has had little influence on criminological thought until recently. Because women account for a minority of all crimes committed, criminologists have been misled into assuming they can learn little from female criminal activity and Cain (1996) has argued that male offending tends therefore to be the yardstick against which *all* offending is measured. Women tend only to get 'occasional walk on parts' in criminological studies of this kind (Scraton 1990: 18): the young male offender is the norm, and the young female offender becomes the anomaly. As Brown (2005) comments: '*one* crime problem has become *the* crime problem'.

One in six known young offenders is a woman (Muncie 1999) but self-reported crime figures put women more on a par with their male counterparts in relation to minor offending at least (Jamieson *et al.* 1999; Sommers *et al.* 1994). Thus, whilst crime may be – unofficially – as much an activity for women as for men, women's offending is either less visible or less likely to result in official action. However, when detected in crime, women are more likely to heed early warnings from the police and criminal justice system (Cavadino and Dignan 1997) and hence more likely to desist sooner than men.

Although undertaken less often, women's offending tends not to differ significantly from men's, but still their offending is seen as mundane and trivial in comparison to men's (Burman 2004). It is perhaps a myth to suggest that women offenders are mainly involved in shoplifting and prostitution as a result of poverty or economic marginality, since often the types of offences they commit are no different from those committed by men (Brown 2005; Heidensohn 1994; Morris 1987). However, women's reasons for starting offending may differ from men's reasons and impact on the types of offences they commit. For example, women tend to start offending later than men if drug use is a problem, and such offending will tend to be acquisitive – for example, fraud, shoplifting or theft – to fund a habit (Katz 2000). Women are also more likely to start offending because of a relationship with an offender or drug user (Uggen and Kruttschnitt 1998) or because of an abusive relationship where they are pressurised into offending (Barry 2006; MacDonald and Marsh 2005), but again this is mainly acquisitive crime to fund their partner's or their own drug habit.

Power and powerlessness in transition

This chapter develops the notion of young women's greater likelihood of an early transition to adulthood and a law-abiding lifestyle through the lens of Pierre Bourdieu's concepts of capital (1977; 1986). Bourdieu utilises four concepts of capital (social, economic, cultural and symbolic) to explain how individuals gain power through social action:

Social capital is valued relations with significant others. To Bourdieu, social capital includes not only social networks but also 'sociability' – 'a continuous series of exchanges in which recognition is endlessly affirmed' (1986: 250). For young people, social capital is less stable by dint of their transitional status. Whilst for many young women, the family is the main source of social capital, social relationships are also developed within the school milieu or with boyfriends, although such friendships tend to lack continuity at that age.

Economic capital is the financial means to not only the necessities but also the luxuries of everyday living. Bourdieu stresses the dominance of economic capital because such capital can be transmitted, preserved and rationally managed (Bourdieu 1990). However, it would seem that economic capital is not readily attainable for many children and young people, given their transient status, their confinement to full-time education and their resulting segregation from the adult labour market.

Cultural capital is legitimate competence or status and comes from knowledge of one's cultural identity (e.g. styles and modes of presentation); from the acquisition of cultural goods; and through educational and other qualifications. To Bourdieu, cultural capital is not easily acquired or transmitted and does not lend itself readily, therefore, to the relatively short (in terms of the life cycle) transition period between childhood and adulthood. However, for young women, cultural capital can be acquired through body image or motherhood.

Symbolic capital, to Bourdieu, is an overarching resource that brings prestige and honour gained from the collective, legitimate and recognised culmination of the other three forms of capital (Bourdieu 1989). Symbolic capital can be gained within the peer group for young people, notably by offending – the kudos and reputation gained from being a successful offender or having money and consumables as a result.

Poverty and marginalisation are well known influences on one's propensity to offend. McRobbie (1991: 37) has described working-class girls in particular as 'one of the most powerless sectors of society', not least because in the transition to adulthood, young women tend to have neither the protection of their families nor responsibilities within the wider society. However, they do tend to have responsibilities within the home (to parents, partners or children) which may give them greater, albeit often unrecognised, status in the transition to adulthood. The youth phase in the life cycle, however, holds little status generally for young people and there are few support systems to guide them, structurally or emotionally, towards adulthood (Barry 2006). Nevertheless, Graham and Bowling (1995), amongst others, have found that young women often make a smoother and faster transition to adulthood than their male counterparts. Whilst they found young women to be more successful at making the transition

25

from childhood to adulthood on leaving school (in terms of leaving home, forming stable relationships and becoming more economically and socially independent), young men are less likely to successfully make that transition until well into their twenties, partly because of greater peer pressure. Graham and Bowling (1995) suggest that men are more likely to desist from offending if they remain within the parental home into their twenties, whereas female offenders, on the other hand, are much more likely to stop offending on leaving home, leaving school and forming their own family units.

In terms of the concept of capital, there have been several ways identified in the study described below that young people could accumulate capital through offending. These were: offending for friendships; offending for money; offending for kudos/street credibility; and offending for self-esteem. The findings from this study, however, highlight certain gender-related discrepancies between the sample's rationale for offending, with friendships, money and self-esteem being key reasons for the women offending, and kudos/street credibility being the key factor for the men. Likewise it will be seen from this study that the women stopped offending for different reasons than the men – with *actual* commitments to their homes, families and relationships being particularly influential in their stopping offending, whereas the men only had *potential* – and therefore less influential - commitments to employment and raising a family as the impetus to stopping offending.

The Scottish desistance[1] study

Whilst reconviction data are often used to examine whether people have stopped offending, increasingly qualitative studies of people's own narratives and views of offending and non-offending are now being examined to better understand the processes involved (Barry 2006; Farrall and Bowling 1999; Farrington 1997; Jamieson *et al.* 1999; Maruna 2001; Shover 1996). The narratives reported here are from a study of young people's experiences and perceptions of starting and stopping offending which was undertaken by the author throughout Scotland, as doctoral research, between 2000 and 2001. Its main aims were to explore previously persistent young offenders' perceptions of why they start offending, continue offending over a period of time and stop offending, whether there were gender differences emerging from the analysis, and whether there was a common thread between their reasons for starting, continuing and stopping offending.

All of the men in the sample were accessed through an intensive probation project operating in various parts of Scotland, but because women tend not to be given intensive probation in Scotland; only seven of the female respondents could be accessed this way. The remaining thirteen young women were contacted via probation officers in various local authorities. The young people ranged in age from 18 years to 33 years, with the women tending to be older than the men at interview. The men were more likely to live with their parents or a partner, whereas the women were more likely to live on their own or with their children. The 40 respondents – 20 young men and 20 young women – all came from socio-economic backgrounds that restricted their opportunities for stable employment, adequate housing and social identity. The sample is unusual in that it comprises 40 young people who had been heavily involved in offending in the past but also includes a combination of persisters and desisters as well as an equal gender mix.

Compared to many other studies of starting or stopping offending, this sample consisted entirely of young people who had been high-tariff, serious offenders for a substantial part of their offending lives. The mean average number of previous offences for the men was 38 years and for the women 18.5 years. There was no significant difference in the mean average number of years that they had been offending to date, as this was ten years for both sexes. Interestingly, from Home Office statistics compiled in 2001, it would seem that 83% of female offenders and 60% of male offenders offend for less than one year, whilst three per cent of female offenders and 25% of male offenders offend for over 10 years (cited in Burman 2004). This highlights the high-tariff characteristics of the sample under study.

Four-fifths of the young people in this study started offending as 'children' (i.e. at the age of fifteen or under), their reasons being mainly because of a lack of attention or love, to seek encouragement or recognition, to earn money or as a (latent) reaction to (past) traumas in their lives. Many came from families marred by death, illness, separation and transience, and many felt unloved or uncared for as a result. Indeed, the school setting may have offered these young people respite from marginalisation or familial neglect or abuse and gave them an opportunity to create a social identity for themselves. This research gave this group of young people an opportunity to describe and explain how and why they became involved in crime, and will hopefully go some way towards developing a greater understanding of youth offending more generally.

The men were more likely to start offending earlier than the women, although the most common age for starting was twelve to fifteen for both sexes. According to both self-reported and official records on this sample's offending histories, as well as starting offending later than the men, the women were also more likely to stop offending later. This does not fit readily with perceived wisdom in trends in women's offending, but it could be that these women desisted later than the men because of more entrenched drug problems, and also the fact that they were recruited via probation officers who had had recent involvement with them as clients.

Women's rationale for starting offending

The main influence on both the young men and the young women in the onset phase of offending was the fact that their peers were offending and they wanted to be seen as part of that friendship group. Having friends was a crucial source of social capital as they moved away from the influence of the family and into the school environment, and having a reputation as an offender also gave them symbolic capital. However, the women were more likely to start offending specifically for the attention of usually a male partner who was offending, but also the attention of older peers, because this gave them social and symbolic capital:

> [My first boyfriend] was a drug dealer and I admired him ...
> I fancied him and I thought he was cool because everybody respected him, and all the people my age respected me because I was mucking about with this person (23-year-old female).

> No one cared. That's what I thought. There wasn't very much for me at that time. It was just me and me alone. And then I started getting in with the wrong crowd, older lassies... I was acting big... it was an ego boost (25-year-old female).

The young women were also more likely to be influenced to take drugs by partners who were themselves using drugs – not least if those partners wanted the women to help them raise the money to feed a drug habit. This often resulted in the women becoming not only dependent on drugs but also dependent on those relationships with drug-using partners for love and attention, however violent they became:

I got forced into it. Basically my boyfriend turned round and said do you love me? I said aye, I love you. He said, if you love me, try this. I said I don't want to. And he said he'd batter me if I didn't (21-year-old female).

I just knew I needed to [offend] ... If I didn't, I knew I would get battered from him at the end of the night... He'd hit me, fling cups at my head and ashtrays and slap me if I didn't get the things I was told to get. So he was making money off me but giving me the speed that he was dealing. After being at the court and that, I knew I still had to go and steal (23-year-old female).

Although sociability and relationships were the main impetus for these young women starting offending, they were also much more likely than the men to see the monetary advantages of offending (for consumables, clothes and drugs), whereas the men were more likely to see the personal advantages of relieving boredom and keeping in with one's friends. For the women, the social, economic and symbolic capital accruing from offending was more apparent in the starting phase, as one woman explained about why she started offending at the age of seventeen:

[Shoplifting] gave me confidence. I felt going with somebody else's cheque book and getting all dressed up and going in [to a shop], I could spend what I wanted, they treated me well because they thought I had enough money. They had a different outlook ... It was like a power trip (29-year-old female).

Drug or alcohol use – for recreational purposes initially – was seen as one of the main influences in both men and women's rationale for starting offending – sixteen of the twenty men and eighteen of the twenty women suggested drugs or alcohol as the precipitating factor in their offending. Drugs and alcohol were often seen as vehicles towards gaining other sources of capital – notably social and symbolic – through the 'companionability' of experimenting with drugs/alcohol or trying to impress their friends by conforming to their activities. However, once drug or alcohol use became problematic, there was a noticeable shift in their reasons for continuing to offend, much more so for the women. Ongoing offending and drug-taking were no longer sociable or pleasurable activities but became routine and solitary activities – a vicious cycle of offending to get money for drugs:

> I didn't realise it was killing me. I didn't think there was anything wrong with me but it got to a point every day you wake up, you do the same thing, you get up, you've the clothes on you had on from the night before, you get up, you find where you're going to get money from, you'd walk for miles and miles, you'd climb a mountain for a tenner [ten pounds] at the top of it and you'd walk back down it again and buy yourself a bag [of heroin]. You wouldn't eat. The only thing you would eat was chocolate. If you never had money for chocolate... you'd steal a bar of chocolate to keep your sugar level up (21-year-old female).

Offending may have brought capital initially, but the majority of the women realised during the course of their offending 'careers' that the capital gained from offending was short-lived and eventually created more hassle for them than going straight. What capital they gained from offending was often overshadowed by the loss of capital incurred through involvement in the criminal justice system. Thus there was a growing disillusionment with offending as a continuing viable option for integration and sociability. Sommers et al. (1994) found a similar disillusionment amongst women in their study:

> Over time, the women in the study became ... further alienated, both socially and psychologically, from conventional life. The women's lives became bereft of conventional involvements, obligations, and responsibilities. The excitement ... that may have characterised their early criminal career phase gave way to a much more grave daily existence (Sommers *et al.* 1994: 137).

Once offending became a routine, there was a marked change in attitude to offending between the men and women. The men seemed to think *less* about what they were actually doing by offending (and became increasingly opportunistic about it) whereas the women seemed to think *more* about their behaviour and its adverse consequences, but nevertheless often continued to offend out of necessity, having weighed up the consequences. The disadvantages of offending for these young women were thus almost twice as apparent as they were for the men, notably in relation to criminal justice system 'fatigue' (the constant cycle of offending, conviction, incarceration, liberty, poverty, offending and so on) and endangering one's relationships and reputation. It was these growing disadvantages over time, coupled with serious addictions, which resulted in many of these women deciding to stop offending.

Women's rationale for stopping offending

The women were more than twice as likely as the men to see the advantages of *starting* offending, in terms of monetary gain, either for consumables or drugs. Indeed, their calculation of the monetary gain in starting offending makes the fact that they eventually stop offending all the more incongruent, given that they seemingly stopped more easily than the men. Likewise, given that the men could see few advantages in starting offending, it is perhaps surprising that they carry on with such activity for so long. However, the disadvantages nevertheless outweighed the advantages over time and it was, in particular, the so-called 'criminal justice system fatigue' of being caught and convicted that was commonly stated by the women as a prime reason for wanting to stop offending, coupled with a realisation of what they increasingly had to lose by continuing to offend:

> I had just grown up, realised the serious trouble I had been in... and well, at twenty, I had my own house at this point... At the start, I had all nice stuff in it and then like with the heroin, I had sold it all for twenty pounds at a time. Everything, and then I just thought to myself 'what am I doing here? I've got nothing. I'm in my twenties'. Do you know what I mean? ... and I was 'right, that's enough, time to grow up here' ... the police knew ... it was this house I was dealing in, right, and they were sitting right outside ... the door was going constantly ... that was enough. That was enough after that (23-year-old female).

Whilst they may have drifted into offending, the majority made proactive decisions to stop, irrespective of the lack of positive incentives or sources of capital accumulation available to them. There were few perceived 'pull' factors involved in their decision to stop offending, with the criminal justice system, a drug addiction, loss of trust within the family and a deteriorating reputation being the main 'push' factors. At the time of stopping offending, the majority did not have employment or a stable relationship, often seen as the main catalysts to stopping offending (see, for example, Maruna 2001; Sampson and Laub 1993). However, many of the women were encouraged in their decision to stop by the support (the social and symbolic capital in particular) of friends, family, children and loving relationships with law-abiding partners:

My son was my staying power. He kept me going. I couldn't do any more to him (33-year-old woman).

[My fiancé] brought a really different side out on me. He makes me relaxed, more calmer, and it's like as if I found someone who really cares and actually is interested in me, for who I really was (25-year-old female).

Generally, it could be said that the process of stopping offending for the women resulted more from *actual* commitments (to children, partners or parents), whereas for the men stopping offending was more in preparation for *potential* commitments (aspirations for employment or raising a family). Having real rather than imaginary responsibilities was no doubt a factor which precipitated earlier desistance amongst the women:

I had to [stop offending] if I wanted to keep [my fiancé]. He wouldnae have stayed around … I don't want to lose him. He means too much … I miss seeing [my daughter] … I think she's gonna be my strongest part … I've got responsibilities to try and be a mum again (25-year-old female).

I'm sick of it. You do get sick of it … I've got to grow up and fucking have kids and, ken what I mean … I'm slowly but surely getting there, ken … I'll get my own flat (21-year-old male).

However, whilst commitments to one's self or family were instrumental in promoting a non-offending lifestyle, because of the drug addictions that the majority of the women in this sample had developed, stopping offending was only possible if and when their drug use reduced, stabilised or ceased altogether. If they did not need drugs, the majority said they would not need to offend, and this has been borne out in other studies of offending (Jamieson *et al.* 1999). So their main preoccupation in attempting to stop offending was to give up drugs. A high proportion of the women in this sample were prescribed methadone in the later stages of an addiction – eight women compared to one man were given methadone prescriptions. They suggested that this was a saving grace in their fight to stop drug taking and offending – although they recognised that methadone was also an addictive drug in its own right:

Methadone's harder to come off than heroin but rather than stealing, I'm getting it for free ... I don't have to steal to get money now ... Methadone calms you down and makes me go to sleep and relax, but it's sore to come off it but I want off it. I don't want to be on it. I want babies and a normal life. That's what I want. It's all I've ever wanted (23-year-old female).

This striving for normality and independence was much more noticeable amongst the women than the men, and the means of achieving it seemingly more readily available to them – such as through being able to give their love and attention to another person – whether that be a partner or their own children. Whereas offending had given them some semblance of control and capital in childhood and early youth, such capital was often eroded by a violent relationship or drug abuse. Once out of such relationships and once drug use had been stabilised or had ceased altogether, opportunities for 'normality' and 'adult' status seemed more achievable. The women in the sample were also more concerned than the men about their reputations within the wider community, their need to be good mothers and the possibility of incarceration and losing their children and family life if they continued to offend or take drugs. This new sense of responsibility and care in young adulthood – a chance to spend some of their accumulated capital – was a viable source of stability and conventionality to the women in the sample, and is described in greater detail in the following section.

Opportunities for capital expenditure

It has been demonstrated within this study that young people may use offending as a means of gaining recognition, attention, income or friends, not least at a time when other sources of capital accumulation are unattainable or restricted. For those who stopped offending in their twenties, many had found opportunities to accumulate capital through means other than offending, opportunities which did not result in criminal justice system involvement, a lack of control or wider social disapproval. Such opportunities for capital accumulation included improved family relationships, not being dependent on illegal drugs, having a job or their own tenancy and being a parent themselves. However, it is acknowledged that many who had *not* stopped offending also had access to such opportunities for accumulating capital but were unable or unwilling, for varying reasons, to desist from crime. This anomaly has been a major source of concern for criminologists and suggests that capital accumulation on its own cannot account for why people stop offending. It is therefore suggested here that capital *expenditure* is a missing link in the chain of events surrounding both youth transitions and youth offending.

Whilst capital accumulation is a crucial factor in aiding both a smoother transition to adulthood *and* to a non-offending lifestyle, the added factor of capital expenditure is required to ensure that young people have the opportunity and incentive to desist from crime as well as the longer-term opportunities afforded their counterparts in adulthood. My argument is that 'social recognition' – namely, *the attainment of a combination of accumulation and expenditure of social, economic, cultural and symbolic capital that is both durable and legitimated* – is a possible way forward in understanding the temporary nature of much youth crime. Social recognition may well be a helpful concept in understanding why young people stop offending in transition because it expresses the capacity and need that young people have for longer-term reciprocal relations of trust and responsibility within the wider society, epitomised by capital expenditure. Two particular opportunities for capital expenditure made stopping offending more likely for many of the respondents in this study. These two opportunities were 'generativity' and 'taking on responsibility':

- Generativity means the passing on of care, attention or support to future generations based on one's own experiences – a concern and commitment for others through parenting, teaching or counselling.

- Taking on responsibility means having the desire, opportunity, incentive and capacity to be trusted with a task of benefit to others.

Examples of generativity would be wanting to become a drugs counsellor or probation worker (because of one's own experiences of such workers in the past); wanting to ensure that their own children have a better life than they had; and wanting to make restitution to the local community for past offending. Obvious examples of responsibility-taking would be having employment, or having responsibility for one's own children or family. Both generativity and responsibility-taking are ways of spending the capital that one has already accumulated. The following quotations from respondents give an idea of what is meant by generativity and responsibility taking respectively:

[I want to] get a really good job in the social work or something like that ... I get on with the younger ones up here and I try and say to them: 'don't do what I done, stop taking [drugs] because it ruins everything' (23-year-old female).

I've got responsibility to myself, to keep myself out of trouble and off drugs and I've got my baby on its way. I've got a responsibility towards [my partner] as well ... Attend probation, hospital, lawyers (27-year-old female).

One obvious source of both generativity and responsibility taking for the women in the sample was having children. Sixteen of the women mentioned at interview that they had children. McRobbie (2000) suggests that young women, notably those with no immediate employment prospects or other sources of capital accumulation, may choose motherhood as a positive option:

For girls who had never been brought up to consider themselves as wage-earners, never mind career women, bringing forward motherhood by a few years was hardly a surprising step, indeed it was from their point of view a resourceful activity (McRobbie 2000: 206).

Cain (1996) equally acknowledges that motherhood may bring social and housing stability in the short term, thus easing at least one aspect of the transition to adulthood. Nevertheless, she argues that: 'early domestic careers of pregnancy, childrearing and home-caring served, typically, to locate young women in situations of economic and often domestic, subordination' (Cain 1996: 143). In addition, as highlighted by recent cultural criminological research, the attraction of motherhood as an alternative occupation for young women with few other legitimate opportunities in the transition to adulthood, has been vilified in the media as epitomising a rejection of family values, sexual promiscuity and a misuse of welfare benefits (McRobbie 2000; Rolfe 2005).

Nevertheless, many respondents in this sample, both male and female, saw parenthood as a positive choice for them. However, several commented on their concerns that they wished to be better parents than their own parents had been, thus ensuring that their own children were not compromised in the way that they themselves had been. This concern ironically was voiced more by the men than the women: 'My main goal is to watch my kids grow up healthy and keep them away from drugs' (26-year-old male); 'I'm teaching my kids to be nothing like this. My kids won't be like that' (23-year-old male). However, one of the young women feared for the safety of her own daughter, having been abused herself at a young age. Her need to protect her child illustrates a generative expenditure of social and cultural capital:

> cos she's a girl as well and I feel as if I've got to be there 24 hours a day to protect her but I know if she's with [my partner], I know she's alright when she's with him (21-year-old female).

Although this sample was relatively small, what was striking about the findings was that those who had desisted from crime were more likely to have had opportunities for responsibility and generativity than those who were still persistent offenders. However, these opportunities were not always durable or necessarily recognised by the wider society. Bourdieu, in his theory of social action (1986), suggests that capital needs to be 'durable' and 'legitimate' in order to be sustainable. Durability of capital means that it is generally unaffected by the structural constraints of the social world. Legitimacy means the tacit acceptance and recognition of one's actions or behaviour by the wider society. It could be argued that durability and legitimacy of capital are missing for young people in transition, especially disadvantaged young people. Youth is not a durable state and young people are greatly affected by structural constraints placed on them because of their age and status. Offending may be a viable means of gaining capital in the short term, but it is not a durable or legitimate source of capital in the longer term. These young people eventually realised that their offending was losing them the trust of significant others, was losing them their freedom and was resulting in more costs than benefits as they moved into adulthood.

What was particularly striking about the young women's narratives was that once they had got out of a cycle of offending, they stressed the importance of taking on responsibilities for others and wanting to give back to others for the damage or hurt they had caused them in the past, however indirectly. This suggested that the accumulation of capital is not enough to encourage stopping offending, but that young people need to have opportunities for the expenditure of capital also. A combination of expenditure and accumulation of capital is necessary not only in the transition to adulthood but also in the transition to a non-offending lifestyle. Young people are less likely to offend if they have durable and legitimate opportunities to take on responsibilities and to offer their skills and support to others, and it would seem that young women are more likely than young men to have such opportunities through caring for others. Social recognition suggests that young people recognise the needs of others (through generativity) and are concurrently recognised by others in addressing those needs (through being given responsibility). However, for varying reasons, such recognition is less likely to happen in the youth phase of transition, which is when the temporary accumulation and expenditure of capital through offending is most likely to occur.

Conclusion

Young people are in a 'liminal' state in the transition to adulthood and often lack not only sources of capital accumulation but also legitimate opportunities to spend it. Offending is one source of capital accumulation, pending wider opportunities within mainstream society. However, whilst they may offend during the transition to adulthood, this need not be a rebellion against mainstream norms, nor a permanent phenomenon, but could be seen as a short-term vehicle, however misguided, *towards* integration and conformity. The capital that the young people in this study gained from offending in youth was a viable, albeit short-term source of identity, status, recognition, reputation and power. Such 'informal' legitimation by their peers through offending could offer them some continuity and recognition in the absence of more conventional and formal legitimation and recognition by the wider society.

As they moved into adulthood, however, offending became less likely to give them longer-term social and symbolic capital, both of which were more likely to be gained from legitimate sources, although more often through opportunities to take on responsibilities for children or partners, rather than through employment; hence, the greater likelihood that the women would stop offending sooner than the men. When they had such opportunities, they tended, concurrently, to move away from offending peers and emphasised renewed contact with, and support from, family members or non-offending partners. Finally, those with no opportunities for capital accumulation or expenditure were more likely to continue to rely on offending to obtain the benefits of such capital. The key to stopping offending, therefore, may be in offering young people legitimate opportunities for generativity and responsibility-taking where they are recognised as valued members of society, thus placing more emphasis on sources of capital accumulation and expenditure than on age and status *per se*.

Notes

1 Although there are problems in gauging exactly when and to what extent people stop 'problematic' offending, the word 'desistance' is increasingly being used (notably in the UK) to denote the process or outcome of stopping offending.

References

Barry, M. (2006) *Youth Offending in Transition: The search for social recognition.* Abingdon: Routledge.

Bourdieu, P. (1977) *Outline of a Theory of Practice.* Cambridge: Cambridge University Press.

Bourdieu, P. (1986) 'The Forms of Capital', in J.G. Richardson (ed.), *Handbook of Theory and Research for the Sociology of Education.* Westport, CT: Greenwood Press.

Bourdieu, P. (1989) 'Social Space and Symbolic Power', *Sociological Theory*, 7: 14–25.

Bourdieu, P. (1990) *In Other Words: Essays towards a reflexive sociology*, translated by M. Adamson. Cambridge: Polity Press.

Brown, S. (2005) *Understanding Youth and Crime: Listening to youth?* Buckingham: Open University Press.

Burman, M. (2004) 'Breaking the Mould: Patterns of female offending', in G. McIvor (ed.) *Women Who Offend.* London: Jessica Kingsley.

Cain, M. (1996) 'Towards transgression: New directions in feminist criminology', in J. Muncie, E. McLaughlin and M. Langan (eds) *Criminological Perspectives: A reader.* London: Sage Publications.

Carrington, K. (2002) 'Feminism and critical criminology: Confronting genealogies', in K. Carrington and R. Hogg (eds) *Critical Criminology: Issues, debates, challenges.* Cullompton: Willan.

Cavadino, M. and Dignan, J. (1997) *The Penal System: An introduction*, (2nd edn) London: Sage.

Farrall, S. and Bowling, B. (1999) 'Structuration, Human Development and Desistance from Crime', *British Journal of Criminology*, 39 (2): 253–68.

Farrington, D. (1997) 'Human Development and Criminal Careers' in M. McGuire, R. Morgan and R. Reiner (eds) (2nd edn) *The Oxford Handbook of Criminology.* Oxford: Oxford University Press.

Flood-Page, C., Campbell, S., Harrington, V. and Miller, J. (2000) *Youth Crime: Findings from the 1998/99 Youth Lifestyles Survey.* Home Office Research Study 209. London: Home Office.

Graham, J. and Bowling, B. (1995) *Young People and Crime*. London: Home Office.

Hahn Rafter, N. and Heidensohn, F. (1995) 'Introduction: the development of feminist perspectives on crime', in N. Hahn Rafter and F. Heidensohn (eds) *International Feminist Perspectives in Criminology: Engendering a discipline*. Buckingham: Open University Press.

Heidensohn, F. (1994) 'Gender and Crime', in M. Maguire, M.R. Morgan and R. Reiner (eds) *The Oxford Handbook of Criminology*. Oxford: Oxford University Press.

Hirschi, T. and Gottfredson, M. (1983) 'Age and the explanation of crime', *American Journal of Sociology*, 89, 552–84.

Jamieson, J., McIvor, G. and Murray, C. (1999) *Understanding Offending Among Young People*. Edinburgh: The Stationery Office.

Katz, R. (2000) ' "Explaining girls" and women's crime and desistance in the context of their victimisation experiences', *Violence Against Women*, 6, 633–60.

Maruna, S. (2001) *Making Good: How ex-convicts reform and rebuild their lives*. Washington, DC: American Psychological Association.

MacDonald, R. and Marsh, J. (2005) *Disconnected Youth? Growing up in Britain's poor neighbourhoods*. Basingstoke: Palgrave Macmillan.

McRobbie, A. (2000) *Feminism and Youth Culture* (2nd edn), Basingstoke: Macmillan.

Morris, A. (1987) *Women, Crime and Criminal Justice*. Oxford: Basil Blackwell.

Muncie, J. (1999) *Youth and Crime: A critical introduction*. London: Sage.

Rolfe, A. (2005) ' "There's helping and there's hindering": Young mothers, support and control', in M. Barry (ed.) *Youth Policy and Social Inclusion: Critical debates with young people*. London: Routledge.

Rutherford, A. (1986) *Growing out of Crime: The new era*. Winchester: Waterside Press.

Sampson, R.J. and Laub, J.H. (1993) *Crime in the Making: Pathways and turning points through life*. Cambridge, MA: Harvard University Press.

Scraton, P. (1990) 'Scientific knowledge or masculine discourses?' in L. Gelsthorpe and A. Morris (eds), *Feminist Perspectives in Criminology*. Buckingham: Open University Press.

Shover, N. (1996) *Great Pretenders: Pursuits and careers of persistent thieves*. Boulder, CO: Westview Press.

Smart, C. (1976) *Women, Crime and Criminology*. London: Routledge.

Sommers, I., Baskin, D. and Fagan, J. (1994) 'Getting out of the life: crime desistance by female street offenders', *Deviant Behaviour: An interdisciplinary journal*, 15: 125–49.

Turner, V. (1967) *The Forest of Symbols: Aspects of Ndombu ritual*. Ithaca, NY: Cornell University Press.

Turner, V. (1969) *The Ritual Process: Structure and anti-structure*. Chicago: Aldine.

Uggen, C. and Kruttschnitt, C. (1998) 'Crime in the Breaking: Gender differences in desistance', *Law and Society Review*, 32 (2): 339–66.

Wyn, J. and White, R. (1997) *Rethinking Youth*. London: Sage.

Chapter 3

Sentencing and gender

Loraine Gelsthorpe

Introduction

Research on sentencing in England and Wales (and the UK more generally) quickly leads to the conclusion that there have been differences in the way in which men and women have been treated in the courts over the years. The disparities in treatment are all too evident. But whether or not such differences can be justified is an interesting question. On the one hand, women commit fewer and less serious offences than men. National figures in relation to crime suggest that four in every five offenders are male. Men outnumber women in all major crime categories. Indeed, between 85 and 95 per cent of offenders found guilty of burglary, robbery, drugs offences, criminal damage or violence against the person are male (Home Office 2006). Where women do offend, they are more likely to commit property related offences than anything else; there have been slight increases in lower-level violence (around pubs and clubs) in the last few years, and increases in drugs-related offences (as for males) (Home Office 2006) but neither of these things suggest seismic changes in patterns of crime. Broadly, women commit less serious crimes and they are less likely to persist in crime than males (McIvor 2004; Fawcett Society 2004).

It follows that we might easily expect sentencing patterns to reflect these differences. But analysis suggests that some women are as likely to be treated severely, if not more harshly than men. Close analysis of the treatment of women in the courts reveals that sentencers take into account a whole range of factors relating to gender differences, and that some of these are irrelevant to the task. Indeed, notwithstanding sociological analyses which suggest that the whole sentencing arena has changed to reflect a punitive turn in late modern society, it is arguable that a penal welfare complex which emphasises the dominance of a familial ideology has prevailed in relation to the treatment of women in some ways. At the same time, there are strong arguments to suggest that women *ought* to be treated differently from men, not just in terms of the lesser seriousness of their crimes and the risks that they pose to the community in terms of reoffending, but in terms of their criminogenic needs.

This chapter will thus review gender and sentencing issues in England and Wales,[1] but more particularly focus on the arguments and supporting evidence that women *ought* to be treated differently from men on grounds that they present different risks and have different needs. Such arguments have recently gained credibility in light of the 'gender duty' enshrined in the Equality Act 2006. This move highlights the need to give proper consideration to gender differences rather than relying on the myths, muddles and gender misconceptions which have configured in sentencing in the past.

Women and sentencing

Criminal cases are allocated for trial and sentencing to one or other of two courts in England and Wales: the magistrates' courts (where lay magistrates, or in the busiest areas of the country, district judges, deal with summary and lower-level offences and where sentencing powers are restricted) and the Crown Court (where judges sit to deal with the more serious cases). There are also Youth Courts (located in magistrates' courts) which deal with nearly all cases involving young people (Gelsthorpe and Sharpe 2006). Most offences have fixed maximum penalties assigned to them.[2] Below this, the sentencer is afforded considerable discretion in the type of sentence passed although sentencing is shaped by guidelines from the national Sentencing Guidelines Council (SGC), a body set up by the government in the Criminal Justice Act 2003 in order to enhance existing mechanisms for providing systematic guidance. The SGC is chaired by the Lord Chief Justice and has both judicial and lay members.

The most lenient disposals are the absolute or conditional discharge, and bind overs. These are followed by fines and compensation orders.

Next, there is a community order to which various conditions (twelve in total) can be attached by the courts (for example, an unpaid work condition or drug treatment and testing condition). There is then a suspended sentence of imprisonment. Finally, the most severe sentence is imprisonment (Easton and Piper 2005).

There have been some historical fluctuations in terms of the number of women in the courts, but for the most part, men have dominated and the appearance of women has been a rarity (Zedner 1991). Contemporary sentencing statistics in England and Wales seems at first glance to support a 'chivalry hypothesis' (Home Office 2007) since a far greater proportion of women than men are cautioned (formally warned by the police rather than prosecuted as such, although cautions can be cited in court if a person subsequently reoffends; cautions only apply to minor offences and there are strict conditions on when they might be used, and importantly, the offender has to admit the offence). This phenomenon applies across the different age groups. Moreover, discharges and the fine are popular dispositions for adult offenders, but a smaller proportion of women than men receive custodial penalties and a greater proportion of women than men receive probation supervision or discharges (Home Office 2007). Compared with men, women are also generally given shorter sentences of imprisonment for all offences (except drugs) although there have been some recent changes in this regard, a point addressed later (Home Office 2007).

However, these statistics do not necessarily show that women are dealt with *more leniently* than men; they show that women are dealt with *differently* from men, but they do not tell us why this occurs. A number of British researchers have thus attempted to unravel the complexities of sentencing. Farrington and Morris (1983), for instance, analysing court records and decisions in a magistrates' court, found that there were some similarities and differences in the relationship between different factors and the sentencing of males and females. For example, sentence severity was predicted by factors such as offence and plea for males, while it was predicted by factors such as marital status and the involvement of co-defendants for females. Moreover, women only received more lenient sentences because they committed less serious offences and were less likely to have been previously convicted.

Using a different methodology (involving a matching technique) and looking at two magistrates' courts, Mair and Brockington's findings (1988) suggested that when matched, women were more likely to be discharged and less likely to be fined than men, disparities in sentences of imprisonment however, were reduced by matching. Further research by Moxon (1988) in the Crown Court and by Wilczynski and Morris (1993) in regard to case records of men and women who had killed their children, signalled leniency towards women. Although Dominelli's (1984) research on community service orders (now known as an 'unpaid work' condition) pointed towards the possibility that women were given such an order (a relatively severe penalty on the sentencing tariff) rather sooner than their male counterparts. Hedderman and Hough (1994) reported that females were less likely than males to receive custodial sentences for virtually all indictable offences (except drugs which was equal), and that custodial sentences were shorter for females for several offence types (except for criminal damage and drugs offences which were longer). Previous convictions did not explain the leniency towards females. Finally, in a Home Office (government sponsored) study designed to settle the matter of harshness or leniency towards women once and for all (given public controversies relating to this issue) Dowds and Hedderman (1997) reported that female shoplifters were less likely to receive a custodial sentence than comparable males, and were more likely to be given a community sentence or to be discharged.

Although both men and women were equally likely to receive a custodial sentence for a violent offence, this was less likely for females with previous convictions than their male counterparts. For a drugs offence, female first offenders were less likely to be given a custodial sentence than comparable males, however, this difference disappeared for repeat offenders. Females were more likely to be discharged while males were more likely to be fined for violence and drugs offences. But as a consequence of magistrates' reluctance to fine women, some women were given higher sentences, and only a proportion of them lower level sentences. As part of the same research, Gelsthorpe and Loucks (1997) found that magistrates treated females more leniently than males by giving them sentences aimed to help them lead law-abiding lives rather than punishing them; they viewed females as 'troubled' rather than 'troublesome'. Magistrates stressed that they relied on legal factors such as the nature of offence rather than on the personal circumstances of the offender when sentencing males and females. However, fines were viewed as unsuitable for women with dependants especially where they did not have the independent means to pay them. Magistrates also considered family circumstances and responsibilities as more relevant in mitigation for females than males. Furthermore, magistrates mentioned using their 'common sense' or 'gut feelings' and commented on defendants' appearance and demeanour in court. But gender role stereotyping cut across these approaches to sentencing so that anyone stepping outside the traditional role and presentation might not receive sympathetic treatment.

In subsequent research, Flood-Page and Mackie (1998) found that in magistrates' courts, a greater proportion of women first time offenders received a community sentence and a discharge and a smaller proportion were given a fine compared to their male counterparts. In the Crown Court, a greater proportion of men first time offenders received a custodial sentence, a community sentence, or a fine compared to their female counterparts, who were more likely to receive a suspended sentence or a discharge. Men with previous convictions were more likely to receive custody or a community sentence than women repeat offenders in the magistrates' courts. These women were more likely to receive a fine or discharge. In the Crown Court, men with previous convictions were also more likely to receive custody and less likely to receive a suspended sentence or community sentence compared to their female counterparts. Overall, men were significantly more likely to receive a custodial sentence than women, even after controlling for legally relevant factors such as offence type and previous convictions. The general gender disparity in sentencing may be partly explained by other factors such as the fact that women are more likely to be dealt with in the magistrates' court, of course, although this cannot account for the apparent gender differences found within court type.

In more recent research still, Steward (2006) demonstrates that whilst remand decisions are based primarily on offence seriousness, without consideration of gender, in some cases which are on the borderline between conditional bail and custodial remand, gender becomes more significant, with defendants being morally (re)constructed as women who do or do not 'deserve' bail.

In the probation context (where there is responsibility for the preparation of pre-sentence reports as well as the supervision of offenders on various orders and conditions), there have been a number of concerns about report-writing practices and the way in which they may contribute to differential court outcomes for women and men. Eaton (1983) for example, in observing cases in the magistrates' court and examining what were then called social inquiry reports (now pre-sentence reports), concluded that women assessed negatively were likely to be dealt with more severely than other women. Ten years later Stephen (1993) wrote in similar vein, arguing that the differential treatment of men and women by the courts was likely to be influenced by the way in which they are represented in pre-sentence reports; probation officers frequently provided explanations which highlighted personal traits in the case of male offenders and underlying emotional problems in the case of women. Indeed, there is substantial evidence that both the types of problems experienced and the motivations for offending are perceived by probation officers as being different for women and men and that this is reflected in the way in which they are 'presented' to the courts (Gelsthorpe 1992; McIvor and Barry 1998; Horn and Evans 2000).

In terms of perceptions of behaviour, women's offending is frequently thought to be rooted in poverty and financial dependence (Cook 1997; Hedderman 2004a). Financial penalties are often, therefore, inappropriate sanctions for women who offend. As stated, one Home Office study indicated that courts in England and Wales were reluctant to impose fines upon female offenders (Hedderman and Gelsthorpe 1997) because of their child-care responsibilities. In some cases this appeared to result in a more lenient response, in comparison with male offenders, by way of a conditional or absolute discharge. In other cases it appeared that women may be escalated up the sentencing tariff through the imposition of a community sentence – probation or community service – in lieu of a fine.

Further, various studies in different parts of the UK (Hine 1993; McIvor 1998) have found women to be under-represented in community service (now called the unpaid work condition which is attached to the community order in England and Wales), though there is also some evidence that when age, current offence and criminal history are controlled for women are as likely to receive community service as men (Mair and Brockington 1988). There are, moreover, clear differences in the characteristics of men and women sentenced to community service. Women on community service are more likely than men to be first offenders and there is some evidence that there is less consistency (in terms of criminal history and current offence) in the use of community service with women (Hine 1993). Indeed, in a thematic review of provision for women in 1996, Her Majesty's Inspectorate of Probation found that probation officers preparing pre-sentence reports often rejected community service orders as a viable option for women with childcare responsibilities and were unaware of the funds available to provide childcare so as to facilitate women being given this sentence (HMIP 1996). Moreover, there was a perception that women pose a higher breach risk on such orders, due to family responsibilities (despite evidence to suggest that women have more successful completions (Home Office 2005; Scottish Executive 2006).

Ironically, too, in a more recent study of community service, women appear to gain rather more from the orders than men. In a study of some 1851 offenders on community service 148 of them being women, Gelsthorpe and Rex (2004) reported that from offenders' own assessment of what they gained, 49% of the women indicated that they had improved their skills either a lot or quite a lot – compared with 35% of the men. Further, over 50% of the women indicated that they were either very likely or quite likely to do more training as a result of the community service or that it had at least improved their chances of getting a job (compared with under 40% of the men).

Probation (now 'supervision as a requirement of a community order' under the Criminal Justice Act 2003 in England and Wales), on the other hand, has traditionally been used more with women than with men though there is evidence that women are given probation at a lower point on the sentencing tariff. McIvor and Barry (1998), for instance, found that women who were subject to probation supervision in Scotland had fewer previous convictions and were more likely to be first offenders than men. The fact that women tend to have less extensive criminal histories than men may account, at least partly, for the common finding that women probationers are more likely to succeed on probation than men (e.g. McIvor and Barry 1998).

Combined with observational research in the court room, accumulated research evidence suggests that sentencers treat women differently from men due to chivalry, paternalism, familial protection, or enforcement of gender appropriate behaviour. But what is also clear is that sentencers operate a bifurcated system of sentencing which distinguishes between those women who conform to gender stereotypes, and those who do not (Gelsthorpe 2001). In this sense, the sentencing picture in England and Wales broadly mirrors the picture found elsewhere (see, for example, Daly 1987; Steffensmeier et al. 1993).

The 'punitive turn'

At the same time, what is unmistakable is the fact that the sentencing of women, as with the sentencing of men, has taken an increasingly punitive turn over the past few years. David Garland (2001) has offered a detailed and insightful historical–cultural account of how the crime control developments witnessed in the late twentieth century have 'adapted' and 'responded' to the late modern world (with all its social transformations relating to globalisation, technological developments, the loss of traditional communities and so on), and to its political and cultural values. Garland's analysis revolves around the notion that we can understand the development of strategies of control by thinking about punishment and control as a cultural adaptation to 'late modernity' and the free market. In other words, he tells us that we need to understand the socially conservative politics that came to dominate the USA and the UK in the 1980s in order to understand the culture of control – what critics have previously described as 'prison-centricity' and what might be described as 'the carceral centrifuge'.

There are many positive features to *The Culture of Control* by David Garland (2001). They include the recognition of the interdependence of social, economic and political influences, his recognition of the links between crime and punishment and the emphasis he gives to the public in terms of their lived adaptations to the new crime control situations that face them (rather than seeing their views as mere reflections of 'elite spokespeople' within politics or the mass media).[3] The story line is simple: a penal welfare complex (by which he means rehabilitative interventions and individualised sentencing based on careful assessment of needs) has given way to a culture of control and we are currently witnessing ever increasing prison rates is a straightforward reflection of this.

But the omission of any major consideration of women in this important commentary on the growing culture of control in England and Wales epitomises one of the problems endemic in criminal justice policy itself – the continuing invisibility of women (Gelsthorpe 2005). Indeed, although Garland (2001) does not give recognition to this, the treatment of women illustrates the apparently dualistic and polarised penal policies that Garland describes so well.

We should note one or two things here: Firstly, that the feminist critique of criminology has identified that beliefs about female offenders which locate their offending behaviour in the discourse of the pathological have long since persisted, despite the introduction of more sociological and social constructionist ideas in relation to males' offending behaviour (see Smart 1976 and Gelsthorpe 2002, 2004, for example). The discourse of the pathological, of course, lends itself to penal-welfarism. Secondly, looking back in history we can see very clearly how penal welfarism developed for women. Calls for differentiation in the treatment of male and female offenders from the mid 1850s onwards led to a number of significant changes in the nineteenth century – ranging from the special provisions for the women's police service to take statements from women and children, to plans for the redevelopment of the women's prison system as a 'therapeutic community' (Holloway prison in particular; see Rock 1996) so as to accommodate their 'special needs'.

Institutional arrangements for women aside, the sentencing of women and the content of institutional regimes provided for women and girls within have long since reflected elements of the 'penal-welfarism' that Garland (2001) describes so well in *The Culture of Control*. Broadly speaking, a large body of research has identified three main themes that are particularly relevant to the treatment of women: pathology, domesticity and respectability. First, a woman who enters the criminal justice system has been described as 'incongruous' (Worrall 1990). Explanations for her presence are sought within the discourse of the 'pathological' and the 'irrational': menstruation, mental illness, poor socialisation, and the menopause have all featured in explanations here, and all have been subject to critique (see Smart 1976, and Morris 1987, for example). Men are not viewed as being so out of place in the court-room and so their offending is explained in different ways, within the discourse of 'normality' and 'rationality'. In addition, and as previously indicated, certain factors such as marital status, motherhood, social problems, and welfare needs seem to influence the sentencing of women but not that of men. Similar social, pathological and familial themes can be identified within prisons (Carlen 1983; Dobash *et al.* 1986). Pat Carlen has captured the nature of the penal-welfare direction of the treatment of women in British prisons in her memorable claim that women's prisons 'Discipline, Infantilise, Feminise, Medicalise and Domesticise' (1985: 182).

The 'punitive turn' towards women

Nevertheless, one of the most striking trends in sentencing across western jurisdictions – including England and Wales (and the UK more generally) in the last decade or so is the marked rise in the number of women in prison, which has far outstripped a smaller proportionate increase in the populations of imprisoned men. Receptions into women's prisons more than doubled between 1990 and 2000, for example. Higher female prison populations appear to reflect both increases in the numbers of women given custodial sentences and higher average sentence lengths, but there is no real indication of major changes in the seriousness of offences committed by women or changes in the type of women committed to prison that would help account for the punitive trend (Gelsthorpe and Morris 2002; Deakin and Spencer 2003; Hedderman 2004b). Nor can it be argued that sentencing has been made more equal between men and women resulting in women being treated more harshly; as indicated above, the picture of sentencing is far more complex. We know that gender-related factors do mediate sentencing, but not in a clear cut way.

Pat Carlen (1998) sees the increase in the prison population as primarily the result of an increased punitiveness towards women. The 'feminisation of poverty' which characterises the period may be relevant to an understanding of this perception (Glendinning and Millar 1992). Certainly, by the end of the 1990s there was much evidence to suggest that women offenders experienced a good number of social problems (poverty, debt, drug and alcohol abuse, lack of qualifications and work, histories of abuse). Thus there may be a two-fold effect of up-tariffing women because of a reluctance to fine them and a perception that a prison sentence creates a reasonable prospect of women's social needs being met: punitive and penal-welfare approaches combined. Carlen's (1998; 2002) claim regarding *gender-specific* punitiveness reflects her findings from a cross-national study of the penal treatment of women in the United States of America, Canada, England, Wales and Scotland. In exploring the differences she concludes that the language of reform and empowerment (promoted by liberal penal reformers, feminist reformers and criminal justice professionals alike) has been hijacked by the very people who promote the discourse of punishment – namely the state – in what she describes as 'carceral clawback'. In other words, the practical moves to improve prison regimes and conditions for women have possibly made prison sentences seem *more* suitable for women than hitherto.

Whatever the specific reasons for the increase, the trend is particularly concerning in view of the relatively minor offences in respect of which women are imprisoned and the vulnerability of many women who receive custodial sentences (Prison Reform Trust 2000; Fawcett Society 2004). Studies of imprisoned women in England and Wales (Morris *et al.* 1995; Caddle and Crisp 1997) and Scotland (Loucks 1998) lend support to a general conclusion that imprisoned women are usually 'marginalised women'. (As is the case with men we might add, although the view that the prison system has not accommodated women's particular needs and that their imprisonment may damage their children, adds potency and poignancy to concerns about the number of women imprisoned).

Gender sensitive responses to women

A major criticism of sentencing and the treatment of women in the criminal justice system in recent years has been that sentencing and criminal justice interventions have increasingly been driven by a concern with 'evidence-based practice' and the 'what works' agenda but that these practices are not necessarily responsive to women and their needs (McIvor 1999; Shaw and Hannah-Moffat 2000; Hollin and Palmer 2006). While Dowden and Andrews (1999) concluded from a meta-analysis of interventions with female offenders that interventions are more effective if they address women's criminogenic needs, they also acknowledged that further research is required to identify the relationship between particular problems (such as past victimisation and self-esteem) and offending by women (see Rumgay 2005).

Although women's offending tends to be under-explored and less well understood than offending by men, it is now recognised that they are likely to have different 'criminogenic needs' (Hedderman 2004a) because their routes into offending and reasons for offending are often different from those of men (Gelsthorpe 2004; Jamieson *et al*. 1999). Research evidence indicates that some needs may indeed be similar (for example, criminal history, unemployment, substance misuse), though how they have come about and how they contribute to offending may be different for men and women and there are others which appear to be more specific to women, such as physical and sexual abuse (Hollin and Palmer 2006). This clearly has implications for the focus and content of interventions which follow sentencing for both custodial and non-custodial interventions. As Hedderman concludes from her analysis of research on men's and women's criminogenic needs:

> ... overall the available evidence suggests that programmes which focus on male criminogenic factors are unlikely to be as effective in reducing reconviction among women offenders as they are for men. This is not only because they focus on factors which are less relevant to or operate differently for women, but also because they fail to address factors which are unique to, or more relevant for, women who offend. (2004a: 241)

A focus on criminogenic needs has been driven by, and, in turn, has driven, the use of structured assessment tools in probation practice, with tools such as OASys and LSI-R widely used across the UK. The use of structured assessment tools may be perceived as helpful, but equally, their focus on risk of reoffending and risk of harm may encourage assessments that are resource-led rather than needs-led (Maurutto and Hannah-Moffat 2006). It is arguable that risk and needs assessments are likely to be highly gendered because the factors that they incorporate are drawn predominantly from studies of men (Shaw and Hannah-Moffat 2000 2004). Practitioners have also expressed concern about the applicability of structured risk assessment tools with particular groups of offenders, such as women, Black and minority ethnic (BME) offenders, those with mental health problems or perpetrators of domestic abuse (McIvor and Kemshall 2002; Gelsthorpe and McIvor 2007).

Critics of 'evidence-led' policy and practice have also drawn attention to important differences in developmental processes between women and men (e.g. Gilligan 1982) which have implications for the type of interventions which are likely to engage women effectively in the process of change. Moreover, educationalists such as Belenky *et al.* (1986) have argued that women's learning differs from men's learning both in terms of its developmental sequence and in terms of its underlying theory (see also Covington 1998). The researchers argue that women view knowledge more as a set of connections than a set of distinctions, and that most women prefer to learn in collaborative, rather than competitive, settings. Further, women most often take a 'believing approach' in engaging and discussing new ideas, attempting to empathize with the speaker and co-operatively assimilating knowledge. Set alongside evidence which suggests that women-only environments facilitate growth and development (Zaplin 1998), these theoretical insights point to a need for work with women in non-authoritarian co-operative settings, where women are empowered to engage in social and personal change. A rigorous analysis of the 'responsivity' principle conducted by Blanchette and Brown (2006) concerning *how* treatment should be delivered in different criminal justice settings emphasises not only the importance of matching treatment style to offender learning styles, but that alongside structured behavioural interventions case specific factors should also be addressed. These include 'women-specific' factors such as health care, childcare and mental health (and factors relating to race and gender combined, Gelsthorpe 2006).

There have been various attempts to get policy makers to respond such to criticisms and claims from researchers. A succession of reports which have attracted media attention (for example, Prison Reform Trust 2000; Fawcett Society 2004, 2006; Howard League 2006) combined with damning Prison and Probation Inspectorate Reports have served to promote a response at governmental levels. The Government's 'Women's Offending Reduction Programme' (WORP) was launched in 2004 to help co-ordinate departments and sensitise them to women's needs. It also aims to improve community-based provision for women offenders (WORP 2004–5) so that prison might be used as a last resort. The approach has led to the setting up of multi-agency 'Women's Offending Action Teams' (WOATS), which can provide a floating service, or be placed in a 'one stop shop' type provision from a women's centre. Thus in March 2005, the Home Secretary announced the setting up of two pilot centres designed to address women's needs in sentencing. These centres (in two different regions in the country) are now being evaluated.

The recognition that women who offend often have different needs from men is not new of course, indeed, there have been a number of 'bottom-up' initiatives over the years. Some Probation Service practitioners in England and Wales developed specific groupwork programmes for women, for example (Mistry 1989; Jones *et al.* 1991). This was a small practical way of ensuring that the particular needs of women were addressed in a safe and non-threatening environment conducive to the development of 'reciprocal relationships' (Eaton 1993; Worrall 1995) which appeared to be central to women's growth and change. Durrance and Ablitt (2001) explored the use of the Women's Probation Centre in Camden, which runs a wide-ranging programme for women, and attributed the substantially lower reconviction rate among women (compared to predicted reconviction rates) to the creative and gender-specific programme. A similar rationale underpinned other innovative provision, such as the women's groupwork programme (now the Asha Centre) developed in Hereford and Worcester (now West Mercia); probationers indicated that it provided them with considerable support – especially since it involved multi-faceted, multi-agency provision and served to introduce women to other services and provision beyond the criminal justice system (Roberts 2002).[4]

In Scotland, policy concern about the potentially damaging consequences of imprisoning women was triggered to a large extent by a number of suicides at Cornton Vale – the only dedicated Scottish female prison. A review of the use of custody and community disposals for female offenders in Scotland, commissioned by the Chief Inspectors of Social Work and Prisons and entitled '*A Safer Way*', concluded that 'the backgrounds of women in prison are characterised by experiences of abuse, drug misuse, poor educational attainment, poverty, psychological distress and self-harm' (Scottish

Office 1998: 13). It made a number of recommendations including a review of the prison estate, the development of bail provision for women who have been accused of an offence, the increased use of supervised attendance orders for women who default on payment of their fines, and the development of an inter-agency forum aimed at developing services for female offenders in Glasgow. Subsequent developments have aimed to shift the penal culture away from punishment and towards rehabilitation and 'treatment'. The setting up of the '218 Time Out Centre' in Glasgow in December 2003 with funding from the Scottish Executive Justice Department which provides residential and non-residential services for women who are involved in the criminal justice system and which adopts a 'holistic', gender-appropriate approach to women's needs has proved to be a very positive development, with reported reductions in drug and alcohol use and offending, and improvements in health and well-being (Loucks *et al.* 2006). Costing no more than an alternative prison sentence 218 has developed a model of intervention based on a recognition of the distinctive needs of women.

Looking to the future

The Criminal Justice Act 2003 has introduced a new framework for sentencing in England and Wales. It re-emphasises a range of aims: formal equality and consistent sentencing (desert), punishment, the reduction of crime by deterrence, reform and rehabilitation, the protection of the public, and the making of reparation by offenders. Thus the way is made clear for needs and risks and individualised sentencing to come to the fore. Will this help women? Will it help keep more of them out of custody? Given what we know about the sentencing of women in the past, when concerns for proportionality have been both wittingly and unwittingly over-shadowed by traditional perceptions of 'women's needs' (reflecting stereotypical concerns and a familial ideology) there is some doubt. There have been concerns that the introduction of the new penal aims may well introduce new risks for women offenders. There have been worries about the introduction of intermittent custody[5] for instance, as it was thought that this might prove an attractive option for sentencers not wishing to completely disrupt women's child-care arrangements but nevertheless wishing to impose a custodial sentence. However, in practice, the sentence has not proved popular with sentencers. There were also worries that custody plus (imprisonment plus a follow up licence period involving a particular menu of supervision and support conditions) would also create difficulties for women (especially since the menu of conditions at this stage in sentencing omits mental health treatment, drug rehabilitation, and alcohol treatment, all of which women are shown to need), but a change in Home Secretary combined with a financial crisis because of the demand for more prisons to address overcrowding, means that custody plus will not at present be introduced.

Alongside legislative reforms, a National Offender Management System (NOMS) has been set up as a response to a government led review of the structures relating to probation and prisons. It is an overarching body designed to promote streamlined offender management throughout the system.[6] However, despite developments in largely practitioner-led gender appropriate programming in England and Wales and Scotland, provision for women under NOMS, is uncertain. As well as presenting different needs compared to male offenders, women generally present lower risk of harm and reconviction than men (see Farrington and Painter 2004; Fawcett Society 2004). The NOM model of provision, however, allocates resources according to risk of harm or reconviction based on four tiers of service delivery. There is concern that women will fall disproportionately into the first two tiers (made up of lower risk offenders, with fewer criminogenic needs) with the implication that women offenders may be more likely to be the subject of orders attracting fewer resources, supervised by less qualified and or experienced offender managers, whilst men (particularly high risk sexual and violent offenders) will receive much greater attention. Moreover, provision for women who fall into tier 3 of the new NOMS four-tier model (where interventions mostly consist of accredited programmes or drug rehabilitation requirements) is likely to be problematic, given that there is currently only one accredited programme for them at present. Further, accredited programmes have tended to be dominated by cognitive-behavioural approaches rather than adopting a holistic approach, which 'bottom-up' initiatives have suggested are more likely to work with women (Roberts 2002).

Thus despite some innovations on the ground, there are continuing concerns about the new legislation and structural developments and how they will impact on women. But there are perhaps two small sources of optimism. The first concerns the fact that national pressure groups such as the Fawcett Society, the Howard League for Penal Reform and the Prison Reform Trust all continue to draw attention to women's distinctive needs in criminal justice matters. Increasingly, such groups serve to lobby junior ministers in government and set in train further reviews and reports. Whilst such initiatives can lead to a kind of despair that no-one ever listens beyond suggesting further review and research, these efforts keep the issues in the public mind and there is hope that the 'drip drip' effect will ultimately have purchase in the political mind too so as to facilitate appropriate gender sensitive sentencing and treatment for women.

The second source of optimism relates to new legislation concerning equality. Public sector equality duties (regarding religion, race, disability and so on) are developing apace in the United Kingdom. A key part of the Equality Act 2006 is the 'gender duty' which brings equality issues concerning women in line with other public sector equality duties. In particular, the legislation promotes the introduction of Gender Impact Assessments (GIAs). This is a move which highlights the need to give further attention to what works for women in sentencing. Of course, *equality* of treatment need not be equated with the *same* treatment. In other words, whilst it is important that negative discrimination is avoided, it is equally important that dimensions of diversity are appropriately accommodated as a means of promoting both *procedural* justice and *social* justice (Gelsthorpe and McIvor 2007). As previous researchers have argued (e.g. Tyler 1990; Tyler and Huo 2002) fairness in procedures and responsiveness to particular needs (including gendered needs) may have impact on perceptions of the legitimacy of sentencing. In turn, this might enhance intrinsic motivation to change as opposed to any extrinsic motivation that derives from punishment and deterrence and which is bound to be short-lived.

Failure to acknowledge and accommodate gender differences in sentencing and interventions therefore may well undermine the perceived legitimacy of criminal justice agencies and the reasonableness of any expectation that offenders' behaviour will change. Attention to these differences is arguably an important prerequisite to promoting social justice, social inclusion and citizenship, and the responsibilities and relationships which flow from these things which may enhance offenders' reintegration and help promote their desistance from crime.

Notes

1 It should be noted that Scotland and Northern Ireland have different sentencing systems, but reference is made to research findings and developments in Scotland in particular because of their relevance to analyses of sentencing in England and Wales.

2 These maxima are either in the form of length of custody or amount of fine.

3 For detailed critical discussion of *The Culture of Control* see Matravers (2005) *Managing Modernity. Politics and the Culture of Control.*

4 These practices have drawn on gender specific programming in North America where an array of programmes have emerged – united by a common emphasis upon addressing female offenders' needs, using methods with are deemed appropriate for engaging effectively with damaged and vulnerable women (Covington and Bloom, 1999).

5 Intermittent custody involves part week in prison, part week out of prison under the supervision of probation.

6 The introduction of NOMS is not without controversy since it also opens up the traditional probation functions to providers beyond the probation service (on the basis of competition) and there are fears that this will result in a loss of appropriate provision for offenders as much as potential gain. For a detailed discussion see the Introduction in Gelsthorpe and Morgan (2007) (eds) *Handbook of Probation.*

References

Belenky, M., Clinchy, B., Goldberger, N. and Tarule, J. (1986) *Women's Ways of Knowing.* New York: Basic Books.

Bloom, B. and Covington, S. (1998) *Gender-Specific Programming for Female Offenders: What is it and why is it important?*, Paper presented at the Annual Meeting of the American Society of Criminology, Washington, DC.

Blanchette, K. and Bloom, S. (2006) *The Assessment and Treatment of Women Offenders: An integrated perspective.* Chichester: John Wiley.

Caddle, D. and Crisp, D. (1997) *Imprisoned Women and Mothers.* Home Office Research Study 162. London: Home Office.

Carlen, P. (1983) *Women's Imprisonment: A study in social control.* London: Routledge and Kegan Paul.

Carlen, P. (1985) 'Law, Psychiatry and Women's Imprisonment: A sociological view', *British Journal of Psychiatry*, 146 (June), 618–21.

Carlen, P. (1998) *Sledgehammer: Women's imprisonment at the millenium.* Basingstoke: Macmillan Press.

Carlen, P. (2002) (ed.) *Women and Imprisonment: The struggle for justice.* Cullompton: Willan Publishing.

Cook, D. (1997) *Poverty, Crime and Punishment.* London: Child Poverty Action Group.

Covington, S. (1998) 'The relational Theory of Women's Psychological Development: Implications for the criminal justice system', in R. Zaplin, (ed.) *Female Offenders: Critical perspectives and effective interventions.* Gaithersburg, Maryland: Aspen Publishers.

Covington, S. and Bloom, B. (1999) *Gender-responsive Programming and Evaluation for Women in the Criminal Justice System: A shift from what works? to what is the work?,* Paper presented at the Annual Meeting of the American Society of Criminology, Toronto.

Daly, K. (1987) 'Structure and practice of familial-based justice in a criminal court', *Law and Society Review,* 21: 267–90.

Deakin, J. and Spencer, J. (2003) 'Women behind bars: explanations and implications', *Howard Journal,* 42: 123–6.

Dobash, R., Emerson Dobash, R. and Gutteridge, S. (1986) *The Imprisonment of Women.* Oxford: Basil Blackwell.

Dominelli, L. (1984) 'Differential justice: domestic labour, community service and female offenders', *Probation Journal,* 31: 100–3.

Dowden, C. and Andrews, D.A. (1999) 'What works for female offenders: A meta-analytic review', *Crime and Delinquency,* 45 (4): 438–52.

Dowds, L. and Hedderman, C. (1997) 'The sentencing of men and women', in C. Hedderman and L. Gelsthorpe (eds) *Understanding the Sentencing of Women,* Home Office Research Study 170. London: Home Office, 9–22.

Durrance, P. and Ablitt, F. (2001) "Creative solutions" to women's offending: an evaluation of the Women's Probation Centre', *Probation Journal,* 28 (4): 247–59.

Eaton, M. (1993) *Women After Prison.* Buckingham: Open University Press.

Easton, S. and Piper, C. (2005) *Sentencing and Punishment: The quest for justice,* Oxford: Oxford University Press.

Farrington, D. and Morris, A. (1983) 'Sex, sentencing and reconviction', *British Journal of Criminology,* 23 (3): 229–48.

Farrington, D. and Painter, K. (2004) *Gender differences in risk factors for offending,* Findings 196. London: Home Office.

Fawcett Society (2004) *Women and the Criminal Justice System. A report of the Fawcett Society's commission on women and the criminal justice system.* London: Fawcett Society.

Flood-Page, C. and Mackie, A. (1998) *Sentencing practice: an examination of decisions made in magistrates' courts and the Crown Court in the mid-1990s,* Home Office Research Study 180. London: Home Office.

Garland, D (2001) *The Culture of Control.* Oxford: Oxford University Press.

Gelsthorpe, L. (1992) *Social inquiry reports: race and gender consideration,* Home Office Research Bulletin 32. London: HMSO.

Gelsthorpe, L. (2001) 'Critical decisions and processes in the criminal courts', in E. McLaughlin, and J. Muncie (eds) *Controlling Crime.* London: Sage/ Open University.

Gelsthorpe, L. (2002) 'Feminism and Criminology', in M. Maguire, R. Morgan, and R. Reiner (eds) *The Oxford Handbook of Criminology* (3rd edn). Oxford: Oxford University Press.

Gelsthorpe, L. (2004) 'Female offending; A theoretical overview', in G. McIvor, (ed.) *Women Who Offend.* London: Jessica Kingsley.

Gelsthorpe, L. (2005) 'Back to basics in Crime Control: Weaving in women', in M. Matravers (ed.) *Managing Modernity: politics and the culture of control.* London: Routledge.

Gelsthorpe, L. (2006) 'The experiences of female ethnic minority offenders: the other "other"', in S. Lewis, P. Raynor, D. Smith and A. Wardak (eds) *Race and Probation.* Cullompton: Willan Publishing.

Gelsthorpe, L. and Morris, A. (2002) 'Women's imprisonment in England and Wales: a penal paradox', *Criminal Justice*, 2 (3): 277–301.

Gelsthorpe, L. and Rex, S. (2004) 'Community Service as reintegration: exploring the potential', in G. Mair (ed.) *What Matters in Probation.* Cullompton: Willan Publishing.

Gelsthorpe, L. and Sharpe, G. (2006) 'Gender, Youth Crime and Justice', in B. Goldson and J. Muncie (eds) *Youth Crime and Justice.* London: Sage.

Gelsthorpe, L. and McIvor, G. (2007) 'Difference and diversity in Probation', in L. Gelsthorpe and R. Morgan (eds) *Handbook of Probation.* Cullompton: Willan Publishing.

Gelsthorpe, L. and Morgan, R. (2007) *Handbook of Probation.* Cullompton: Willan Publishing.

Gilligan, C. (1982) *In a Different Voice.* Cambridge MA: Harvard University Press.

Glendinning, C. and Millar, J. (1992) *Women and Poverty in Britain: The 1990s.* London: Harvester Wheatsheaf.

Hedderman, C. (2004a) 'The "criminogenic" needs of women offenders', in G. McIvor (ed.) *Women Who Offend.* London: Jessica Kingsley.

Hedderman, C. (2004b) 'Why are more women being sentenced to custody?', in G. McIvor (ed.) *Women Who Offend.* London: Jessica Kingsley.

Hedderman, C. and Gelsthorpe, L. (1997) *Understanding the Sentencing of Women,* Home Office Research Study 170. London: Home Office.

HMIP (1996) (Her Majesty's Inspectorate of Probation) *Report on Women Offenders and Probation Service Provision for Women Offenders.* London: Home Office.

Hine, J. (1993) 'Access for women: Flexible and friendly?', in D. Whitfield and D. Scott (eds) *Paying Back: Twenty years of community service.* Winchester: Waterside Press, 59–87.

Hollin, C. and Palmer, E. (2006) 'Criminogenic need and women offenders: A critique of the literature', *Legal and Criminological Psychology*, 11 (2): 179–95.

Home Office (2005) *Offender Management Caseload Statistics 2004: England and Wales.* Home Office Statistical Bulletin 15/05, London: RDS, NOMS.

Home Office (2006) *Criminal Statistics 2005 England and Wales,* Home Office Statistical Bulletin 19/06, London: Home Office,
http://www.homeoffice.gov.uk/rds/pdfs06/hosb1906.pdf

Home Office (2007) *Sentencing Statistics 2005, England and Wales.* London: HMSO.

Horn, R. and Evans, M. (2000) 'The Effect of Gender on Pre-Sentence Reports', *Howard Journal*, 39 (2): 184–197.

Howard League for Penal Reform (2006) *Women and girls in the penal system*, Prison Information Bulletin 2, London: The Howard League.

Jamieson, J., McIvor, G. and Murray, C. (1999) *Understanding Offending Among Young People*. Edinburgh: The Stationery Office.

Jones, M., Mordecai, M., Rutter, F. and Thomas, L. (1991) 'The Miskin Model of groupwork with women offenders', *Groupwork*, 4: 215–30.

Loucks, N. (1998) *HMPI Cornton Vale: Research into Drugs and Alcohol, Violence and Bullying, Suicides and Self-Injury, and Backgrounds of Abuse*, SPS Occasional Paper 1/98, Edinburgh: Scottish Prison Service.

Loucks, N., Malloch, M., McIvor, G. and Gelsthorpe, L. (2006) *Evaluation of the 218 Centre*. Edinburgh: Scottish Executive Social Research.

Mair, G. and Brockington, N. (1988) 'Female offenders and the Probation Service', *Howard Journal*, 27 (2): 117–26.

Matravers, M. (ed.) *Managing Modernity. Politics and the culture of control*. London: Routledge.

Maurutto, P. and Hannah-Moffat, K. (2006) 'Assembling risk and the restructuring of penal control', *British Journal of Criminology*, 46 (3): 438–54.

McIvor, G. (1998) 'Jobs for the boys?: Gender differences in referral for community service', *Howard Journal of Criminal Justice*, 37, 280–90.

McIvor, G. (1999) 'Women, crime and criminal justice in Scotland', *Scottish Journal of Criminal Justice Studies*, 5 (1): 67–4.

McIvor, G. (2004) (ed.) *Women Who Offend: Research highlights in social work*, 44: London: Jessica Kingsley.

McIvor, G. and Barry, M. (1998) *Social Work and Criminal Justice Volume 6: Probation*. Edinburgh: The Stationery Office.

McIvor, G. and Kemshall, H. (2002) *Serious Violent and Sexual Offenders: The use of risk assessment tools in Scotland*. Edinburgh: Scottish Executive Social Research.

Mistry, T. (1989) 'Establishing a Feminist Model of Groupwork in the Probation Service', *Groupwork*, 2: 145–8.

Morris, A., Wilkinson, C., Tisi, A., Woodrow, J. and Rockley, A. (1995) *Managing the Needs of Female Prisoners*. London: The Home Office.

Moxon, D. (1988) *Sentencing Practice in the Crown Court*, Home Office Research Study 103, London: HMSO.

National Offender Management Service (2005) *Offender Management Caseload Statistics, England and Wales*. London: NOMS.

Prison Reform Trust (2000) *Justice For Women: The need for reform*, The Report of the Committee on Women's Imprisonment, Chaired by Professor Dorothy Wedderburn, London: Prison Reform Trust.

Roberts, J. (2002) 'Women-centred: the West Mercia community-based programme for women offenders', in P. Carlen (ed.) *Women and Punishment: The struggle for justice*. Cullompton: Willan Publishing, 110–24.

Rock, P. (1996) *Reconstructing a Women's Prison*. Oxford: Clarendon Press.

Rumgay, J. (1996) 'Towards a needs-based theory', *VISTA*, September 104–15.

Rumgay, J. (2005) *When Victims Become Offenders: In search of coherence in policy and practice.* Occasional Paper, London: Fawcett Society.

Scottish Executive (2002) *A Better Way: The report of the ministerial group on women's offending.* Edinburgh: Scottish Executive.

Scottish Office (1998) *Women Offenders – A safer way: A review of community disposals and the use of custody for women in Scotland.* Edinburgh: The Scottish Office.

Scottish Executive (2006) *Criminal Justice Social Work Statistics 2004–5.* Edinburgh: Scottish Executive.

Shaw, M. and Hannah-Moffatt, K. (2000) 'Gender, diversity and risk assessment in Canadian corrections', *Probation Journal,* 47 (3): 163–72.

Shaw, M. and Hannah-Moffatt, K. (2004) 'How cognitive skills forgot about gender and diversity', in G. Mair (ed.) *What Matters in Probation.* Cullompton: Willan Publishing.

Smart, C. (1976) *Women, Crime and Criminology.* London: Routledge.

Steffensmeier, D., Kramer, J. and Striefel, C. (1993) 'Gender and imprisonment decisions', *Criminology,* 31: 411–46.

Stephen, J. (1993) *The Misrepresentation of Women Offenders,* Social Work Monographs 118. Norwich: University of East Anglia.

Steward, K. (2006) 'Gender considerations in remand decision-making' in F. Heidensohn (ed.) *Gender and Justice. New concepts and approaches.* Cullompton: Willan Publishing.

Tyler, T. (1990) *Why People Obey the Law.* New Haven CT: Yale University Press.

Tyler, T. and Huo, Y.T. (2002) *Trust in the Law: Encouraging public co-operation with the police and courts.* New York: Russell Sage Foundation.

Wilczynski, A. and Morris, A. (1993) 'Parents who kill their children', *Criminal Law Review,* 31–6.

Women's Offending Reduction Programme (WORP) 2004–5 Annual Review http://www.homeoffice.gov.uk/documents/worp-annual-review-0405?view=Binary.

Worrall, A. (1990) *Offending Women: Female lawbreakers and the criminal justice system.* London: Routledge.

Worrall, A. (1995) 'Gender, criminal justice and probation', in G. McIvor (ed.) *Working With Offenders: Research highlights in social work,* 26: London: Jessica Kingsley.

Zaplin, R. (1998) *Female Offenders: Critical Perspectives and Effective Interventions,* Maryland, Gaithersberg: Aspen Publishers, Inc.

Chapter 4

Risks and needs: factors that predict women's incarceration and inform service planning

Margaret Severson, Marianne Berry and Judy L. Postmus

Introduction

Over the last two decades, research has shed some light on the common and tragic histories of abuse reported by incarcerated women. These women frequently tell of histories of physical and/or sexual victimisation and when compared to incarcerated men, they are more than three times as likely to report having experienced physical or sexual abuse prior to their incarcerations (ACA 1990; Greene 2000; Greenfeld and Snell 1999; Harlow 1998; Snell and Morton 1994; Veysey 1998). Many incarcerated women also report being victims of youth maltreatment, having injuries caused by chronic neglect, physical abuse and assault, and sexual abuse (Cicchetti and Carlson 1989; Wolfe 1999). Children who have been maltreated suffer emotional and social injuries, accompanied by a loss of trust in others and a diminished desire to ask for help or to disclose one's problems or vulnerabilities (Bellis *et al.* 2001; Berry 2001; Besharov and Laumann 1997; Briere 1992; Cowen 1999; Dore 1999; Hampton 1995; Kirby and Fraser 1997; Kurtz *et al.* 1993).

There is ongoing debate in the literature about 'whether women's needs should be incorporated into risk assessments' (Blanchette and Brown 2006: 53). Some authors suggest that (re)characterizing unmet needs as risks for criminal behaviour (i.e. criminogenic risks) and incarceration obscures the basic fact that women still lack significant protection from physical and sexual abuse as children, youths and adults and is inconsistent with a feminist perspective which embraces principles of empowerment rather than blame (see, e.g. Hannah-Moffat 2004; Shaw and Hannah-Moffat 2006). Indeed, little has been written which identifies women's opportunities to access various types of social services and social supports after their victimisation experiences, and then details the perceived helpfulness of those services. Such information is important to record for its potential use as a foundation for intervention programs and for developing preventive strategies that might interrupt the movement into criminal behaviours that ultimately lead some of these women to prison (Severson 2001).

What is reported here is part of a larger research study that explored the differential risk, need and mitigating protective factors related to histories of physical and sexual victimisation reported by incarcerated and non-incarcerated women. The chapter examines the findings of this study with regard to the sample of incarcerated women and the sample of 'free' women living in four different communities, the latter of whom had not received domestic violence and/or sexual assault services for the 12 months prior to their completing the research interview. We report on the prevalence rates of youth maltreatment and adult physical and sexual victimisation and on women's post-victimisation service utilisation and appraisal, including the impact of service usage and non-usage on adult outcomes of health, mental health, substance use, and incarceration. Our definitions of risk and need are not situated in a criminogenic context as dynamic and alterable factors; instead, they should be viewed as the markers for intervention prior to whatever negative sequelae are set in motion.

Incarcerated women: a growing population with histories of risk, need and victimisation

In the United States, the rate of incarceration for women is rising considerably faster than that for men. Between 1995 and 2003, the imprisoned female population increased 48% compared to a 29% increase for males (Harrison and Beck 2004). Women were more likely than men to have been sentenced on drug and property crimes (Harrison and Beck 2004). The trend continues as well, evidenced by the most recent data indicating that women comprised seven per cent of the incarcerated population at midyear 2005, up nearly one per centage point within a six month period of record-keeping (Harrison and Beck 2006).

A variety of risk factors has been identified in incarcerated populations in general. These are often intransigent or immutable factors and include social class, race, education, substance use and age. When looking at incarcerated populations by gender, it can be said that most incarcerated women are young and poor; and many have children under the age of eighteen (over 70%) for whom they are solely responsible (Richie 2001; U.S. Department of Justice 1998). Greenfeld and Snell, (1999) indicate that two out of three incarcerated women are African American and others suggest that the increased incarceration of this group of women is part of a larger cultural phenomenon that reflects their social exclusion in society (Henriques and Manatu-Rupert 2001).

Significant levels of alcohol and drug use and abuse are found among incarcerated women with 60% of women reporting having used drugs one month prior to their arrests and 50% reporting daily drug usage. Forty per cent of women report being under the influence of drugs at the time of their offenses; 33% committed the offence to obtain money for their habits (Greenfeld and Snell 1999).

Finally, most women offenders report histories of physical and sexual victimisation. The Bureau of Justice Statistics reports 44% of women living under any type of correctional authority were physically or sexually assaulted and injured at some time during their lives (Greenfeld and Snell 1999). Other studies reveal similar findings. Harlow (1999) reported a significant per centage (23%–37%) of female inmates described having been physically and sexually abused and injured as children compared to twelve to seventeen per cent of the general adult population. Browne *et al.* (1999) found experiences of sexual abuse as children reported in as little as 18% and as high as 59% of the women's prison population.

High rates of adult victimisation have also been reported, with 23 to 68 per cent of incarcerated women reporting sexual assault and 25 to 80 per cent reporting intimate partner violence (Browne *et al.* 1999). The substantial variance in percentages in these reports may be explained by the wording of the questions asked about victimisation (Browne *et al.* 1999); the more detailed the questions, the more likely that victimisation will be disclosed. Zweig *et al.* (2002) studied women victims who faced multiple risks such as substance abuse, mental illness and incarceration. They found that problems encountered by such women included a lack of services, multiple barriers to service usage, uneducated service providers, and batterers using women's perceived lack of options to further control or victimise them.

'Free Women': histories of risk, need and victimisation

Each year in the United States, 1.4 million women are victimised at the hands of an intimate partner, defined as a current or former husband, cohabiting partner or dating partner (Tjaden and Thoennes 1998). Appropriately characterised as a public health problem (Arias 2004), the consequences of abuse have varying degrees of impact on the functioning and well-being of victims, depending on the type, severity, and duration of the abuse. Physical injuries leave temporary and permanent scars on victims (Browne 1993) and victims may also experience non-specific health symptoms that affect their functioning such as chronic fatigue, disturbed eating and sleeping patterns, headaches, and gastrointestinal disorders (Eby *et al.* 1995; McNutt *et al.* 2002). The more severe, frequent, and long-lasting the abuse, the more likely there will be deterioration of both the physical and emotional health of victims (Follingstad *et al.* 1991; McCauley *et al.* 1998). Emotional reactions vary as well as physical, and include fear, anger, guilt, frustration, depression, anxiety, paranoia, worthlessness, and shame (Browne 1993; Carlson 1990). Physical abuse is associated with the experience of depression and anxiety (Plichta 1996), post-traumatic stress disorder (O'Leary 1993; Saunders 1994; Walker 1993), and suicidal ideation or attempts (Gelles and Straus 1990; Plichta 1996). Victims may turn to alcohol or other mind-altering substances in the wake of the violence (Miller and Downs 1993; Plichta 1996).

As to the experiences of rape and sexual assault, for all women these experiences are associated with several physical consequences, including injury, stress-related problems, and chronic health problems (see review of research by Koss and Heslet 1992). The psychological and emotional effects of sexual assault most commonly include fear, post-traumatic stress disorder, depression, suicide attempts, reduced self-esteem, and substance abuse (Goodman *et al.* 1993). Child maltreatment includes many types of violence and abuse such as physical, sexual, and emotional abuse or neglect. Abused children experience emotional and social problems which may lead to poor relationships with parents and/or siblings, self-medication with drugs and/or alcohol, high levels of traumatic stress including post-traumatic stress disorder, major depression, and other negative consequences experienced across a woman's lifespan (Banyard 1999; Peleikis, Mykletun, and Dahl 2004).

Methodology

As part of a larger study funded by the United States National Institute of Justice (Postmus and Severson 2005), the research reported here is concerned with several primary areas of inquiry: what are differentially situated women's histories of victimisation; what were their opportunities and access to social services in the aftermath of the victimisation; and what were their appraisals of the helpfulness of those services?

We sought to determine whether incarcerated women differed from non-incarcerated women: (a) in their histories of deprivation, violence and victimisation, (b) in their coping strategies and the social support resources available to them and (c) in their use and appraisal of formal supports and services. The answers to these queries can inform the development of relevant and predictive risk and need assessment tools to prevent incarceration.

Corrections and community samples

Convenience and snowball sampling procedures were used to recruit women to self-select for participation in the study. Sampling occurred in five distinct communities in one Midwestern state, three urban, one rural, and the fifth in the Correctional Facility for Women (CFW), the only women's correctional facility in this Midwestern U.S. state. Here we report on 266 of the 423 interviews completed – 157 women from the prison and 109 women from the four urban and rural communities who had not received domestic violence and/or sexual assault services in the prior 12 months. There were an additional 157 women in the sample who had received domestic violence services – they were excluded for the purposes of this analysis, but their experiences are detailed elsewhere (Postmus and Severson 2005).

Regardless of their security classifications and housing assignments, all incarcerated women age eighteen and older who had been incarcerated in the CFW for at least one month were eligible to participate in this study. The one month incarceration requirement assured a certain basic adjustment to prison given the chaotic and sometime intimidating experiences inmates endure during the first few weeks of their incarceration (Browne *et al.* 1999).Women were recruited by informational flyers and through referrals from the health, mental health and classification personnel at the CFW. Because the researchers were not allowed to pay a cash incentive to the 157 incarcerated participants, at the end of the data collection process a mental health professional was hired to facilitate a series of voluntary psycho-educational groups for the women participants and for other incarcerated survivors of sexual and/or physical violence.

Similar recruitment strategies were used to assemble the sample of community women. Flyers posted in common public areas like grocery stores and word-of-mouth generated a total community sample of 109 women, who were each paid a cash incentive of US$25. Recruitment materials were written in both Spanish and English.

Over a twelve-month period structured interviews of the incarcerated women were conducted at the prison and, for the community women, in a mutually agreed-upon safe and private place. Interview topics included the types of victimisation experiences, use of post-victimisation services, perceptions of the helpfulness of those services, the barriers, if any, which impeded their service usage, current physical and emotional health, and alcohol and substance use. The average time to complete an interview was one hour.

Survey and interview measures

The survey included a combination of existing and modified standardised instruments. Women in the prison were asked to respond to certain questions by referencing the 12 month period prior to their incarceration. The Childhood Maltreatment Interview Schedule (Briere 1992) was used to measure sexual, physical, and emotional abuse during childhood and adolescence. Interpersonal violence was measured using the Abusive Behaviour Inventory (ABI) (Shepard and Campbell 1992). Sexual assault in adulthood was measured using the Sexual Experiences Survey (SES) (Koss and Oros 1982).

Coping strategies were measured using the Brief-COPE scale, a 28-item instrument designed to assess a variety of coping reactions/strategies in response to stress. Alpha reliabilities range from 0.50 to 0.90 (Carver 1997). It is important to caution that this scale was developed and refined with persons living freely, not incarcerated, and has seldom been used in studies of incarcerated women. As a result, behaviours that may be considered maladaptive when one freely can make choices, may actually be adaptive in a prison setting.

For each item on the Brief-Cope Scale, the participant rates how often she uses a particular coping strategy on a four-point scale (1 = I haven't been doing this at all; 2 = I've been doing this a little bit; 3 = I've been doing this a medium amount; 4 = I've been doing this a lot). The 28 items were divided into two groups; adaptive coping behaviours and maladaptive coping behaviours. For the Adaptive Coping score, the participant's responses to sixteen items were summed and calibrated, with a final adaptive coping score of between zero and 100. The higher the score, the higher the adaptive coping. Similarly, for the Maladaptive Coping score, the participant's answers to twelve items were summed and calibrated, with a final maladaptive coping score of between zero and 100. The higher the score, the higher is the maladaptive coping. The alpha coefficients in this study are 0.81 for adaptive coping and 0.68 for maladaptive coping.

Perceived social support from family and friends was measured with the Social Support Appraisal Scale developed by Vaux and colleagues (1986). This scale has good internal consistency with alpha ranges from 0.81 to 0.90. It also has good concurrent, predictive, known-groups, and construct validity; it also correlates in predicted ways with several other measures of social support (Vaux et al. 1986). For each item on the Social Support Appraisal Scale, the participant indicates on a four-point scale whether she strongly agrees, agrees, disagrees, or strongly disagrees with each relational statement about herself. All items on the Social Support Appraisals Scale were scored or reverse-scored into negative numbers, so that the more negative the number, the less support on each of 23 items. These 23 items were then summed and calibrated to produce a Social Support score that ranged from minus 100 to zero, with a higher score indicating a greater level of social support. The alpha coefficient for this study sample is 0.93.

Support from agencies included any support received from health, mental health, or community agencies and was measured using revised questions from the National Co-morbidity Survey of 1992 (NCS 1992). These 24 services were sorted into three categories of support: *therapeutic* (six services), *crisis intervention* (six services), and *long-term tangible support* (twelve services). To the question 'Which services did you receive for the abuse experiences you had as an adult or child?' women answered 'yes' or 'no' to each service choice.

Participants were also asked to choose from a list of fifteen possible barriers to seeking services or support following victimisation and to indicate for each item whether it was true for her. The Short-Form-36 Health Survey, an abbreviated version of the Rand Medical Outcomes Study (Stewart et al. 1988), was used and divided into two subscales: Physical Health and Mental Health. Finally, the National Co-morbidity Survey (NCS 1992) produced information on whether the participant believed she had a drug and/or alcohol problem.

Results

Socio-economic conditions of women

Table 4.1 below shows the demographic characteristics of this sample population. As expected, there are some demographic differences between the sample of incarcerated and non-incarcerated women, but not many. There is no difference in the mean ages of the women; women in prison average 35 years old while community women average 38 years old. The vast majority of women in both samples have children, and many of these children are very young. Women in the prison population, although not different in age from the community sample, are significantly more likely to be a parent to older children, particularly teenagers. Therefore, incarcerated women began childbearing at an earlier age.

There is a difference in education level, with 51% of the community sample completing some or all of college, compared to only 27% of the incarcerated women. Significantly more incarcerated women (80%) than community women (56%) have ever received welfare benefits.

Women in the prison sample are much more likely than community women to report that, in the twelve months prior to the study (prior to their incarceration, for the incarcerated sample), they lived with a male partner. There is no difference between samples in the per centages of married women. Women in prison are significantly more likely to have lived with their parents just prior to incarceration.

The participants reflect a range of cultural, ethnic and racial diversity. Overall, 58% of the prison sample is European-American; the remaining 42% are of another ethnic type. Not unlike prison populations around the United States, racial minorities, particularly African American/Black women are over-represented in this sample. However, the community sample in this Midwestern state is notable in its racial makeup; only 39.4% were European-American with almost a third of this sample reporting Hispanic/Latina ethnicity.

Violence and victimisation

Descriptive statistics were generated to determine the extent to which the two groups of women were victims of interpersonal violence, sexual violence and child maltreatment (see Table 4.2). This study

Table 4.1 Demographic characteristics of sample

	Total % (n=266)	Prison % (n=157)	Communities % (n=109)
Mean age of participant	36.3	35.1	38.1
Highest grade completed**			
Grade School 1–8	6.4	6.4	6.4
High School 9–12	55.1	66.6	38.7
College 13–16	36.9	27.0	51.3
Graduate School	1.6	0	3.6
Ever received welfare benefits	70.2	80.1	56.0
In the prior 12 months, (a) aside from yourself, who else was living in your home? (multiple responses)			
Male partner**	22.6	29.9	11.9
Husband	30.1	30.6	29.4
Own children	51.5	45.9	59.6
Partner's children	3.4	3.8	2.8
Female partner	4.5	5.7	2.8
One or more roommates	9.8	12.7	5.5
Parents*	13.5	17.0	7.3
Relatives	11.7	8.3	16.5
I lived alone	8.6	6.4	11.9
Do you have any children?			
Yes	84.2	87.9	78.9
No	15.8	12.1	21.1
Have children:			
Less than 5 yrs. old	23.7	19.7	29.4
Between 5 and 12 yrs. old	45.1	51.6	35.8
Between 13–17 yrs. old**	36.8	45.2	24.8
18 years of age and older	33.8	35.0	32.1
Ethnicity**			
White	50.4	58.0	39.4
Black/African American	26.3	27.4	24.8
Hispanic/Latina	16.2	5.7	31.2
American Indian	3.8	4.5	2.8
Other	2.3	2.5	1.8
Asian/Pacific Islander	1.1	1.9	0

(a) For prison population, for the 12 months prior to incarceration
 * Difference between the three groups significant at .01 level
** Difference between the three groups significant at .001 level

Table 4.2 Prevalence of Victimization

	Total % (n=266)	Prison % (n=157)	Communities % (n=109)
Total sexual assault*	83.7	89.2	75.7
Sexual coercion	76.5	80.9	70.1
Attempted rape	48.9	53.5	42.1
Rape *	65.5	72.6	55.1
Total intimate partner violence**	96.6	100	91.7
Psychological intimate partner violence**	96.6	100	91.7
Physical intimate partner violence**	88.3	95.5	78.0
Sexually abused as a child **	59.6	68.2	47.2
Physically abused as a child	48.8	53.9	41.5

* Difference between the three groups significant at .01 level
** Difference between the three groups significant at .001 level

finds high levels of self-reported victimisation, both in childhood and adulthood, with over half of the study sample reporting the experience of almost every separate type of violence about which they were queried (attempted rape and childhood physical abuse, least common, are still reported by 49% of the sample). Victimisation is common for both groups of women. Beyond this high prevalence of violence for all women in the study, women in prison have a significantly higher prevalence of sexual assault, particularly for the experience of rape. The women in prison also have a significantly higher prevalence of violence with intimate partners, both physical and psychological. One hundred per cent of the prison sample report experiencing some form of psychological victimisation, compared to 91% of women in the community. Finally, a significantly higher proportion of women in prison report experiencing sexual abuse as a child.

Given the high prevalence of all types of violence in this sample, co-occurrence of types of victimisation is also common for these women (see Table 4.3). Significance tests are not run for co-occurrence rates, given that there could be multiple responses. When examining the experience of childhood victimisation, about one-third of this sample did not experience either physical or sexual abuse as a child, while 41% experienced both. When only one type of childhood maltreatment is reported, it is most likely to be sexual abuse. Non-

Table 4.3 Co-occurrence of types of victimization

	Total % (n=266)	Prison % (n=157)	Communities % (n=109)
Child Abuse			
No child abuse experienced	32.7	26.0	42.5
Physical abuse only	7.7	5.8	10.4
Sexual abuse only	18.5	20.1	16.0
Both physical and sexual abuse	41.1	48.1	31.0
Physical IPV and rape			
None	7.6	2.5	15.0
Physical IPV only	26.9	24.8	29.9
Rape only	3.8	1.9	6.5
Both physical IPV and rape	61.7	70.7	48.6
Child and adult victimization			
(multiple response)			
Child sex abuse/phys. IPV	55.0	65.6	39.6
Child sex abuse/rape	50.0	57.8	38.5
Child phys. abuse/phys. IPV	47.3	52.6	39.6
Child phys. abuse/rape	41.1	46.8	33.7

incarcerated women are less likely to report childhood victimisation, and when they do, physical abuse is more likely for this population than for incarcerated women.

In adulthood, over half of the study sample has experienced both rape and physical violence with an intimate. This is the most common combination of victimisation for all women. This combination is especially likely for incarcerated women.

Finally, examining the co-occurrence of childhood and adult victimisation, between 40 and 55 per cent of all women report experiencing violence in both childhood and adulthood. Women in the prison sample are more likely to experience childhood/adult victimisation combinations than are non-incarcerated women. The most common co-occurring victimisations experienced for the entire sample are childhood sexual abuse and adult violence between intimates, with 55% of the study sample and 66% of the prison sample reporting this combination.

Well-being in Adulthood

Table 4.4 details the adult outcomes for this sample. It needs to be noted that higher scores on the Rand Health Survey indicate better

Table 4.4 Current outcomes in adulthood

Adult outcome	Instrument	Total (n=266)	Prison (n=157)	Community (n=109)
Health	Mean physical health score (a)	68.9	70.7	66.4
Mental health	Mean mental health score (a)	60.4	62.2	57.9
Alcohol	Alcohol problems? *Yes***	19.2%	26.1%	9.3%
Drug	Drug problems? *Yes***	34.7%	55.4%	4.6%

(a) Score of 0–100

physical and mental health. There are no significant differences between the two samples in their degree of physical or mental health. On average, women report better physical health than mental health in each sample. Physical health scores average 69 points on a 100-point scale, and mental health scores average 60 points.

When asked if she currently has an alcohol and/or drug problem, women in the prison sample are significantly more likely to report either an alcohol problem or a drug problem. Self-reported drug problems (55% of prison sample) are reported at rates more than double that of alcohol problems (26%) for women in prison. Rates of substance use are very low in the community sample, however, and are higher for alcohol (9%) than for drug use (5%).

Coping strategies and social support

The two coping scales, adaptive and maladaptive coping, were scored on a 100-point scale; the higher the score, the more the adaptive or maladaptive coping skills were reportedly used. Social support was measured as a negative number; the lower the negative number, the lower the perceived support. There are significant differences between the two groups in their use of adaptive coping strategies and in their perceived social support (see Table 4.5). Incarcerated women reported greater use of adaptive coping strategies than did women recruited from the community. Conversely, incarcerated women reported poorer social support than women in the community.

A woman's victimisation experiences are highly correlated with her use of coping strategies and social support (see Table 4.6 below.) Women who report experiencing physical or sexual abuse in childhood

Table 4.5 Coping strategies and social support

	Total (n=266)	Communities (n=109)	Prison (n=157)
Adaptive coping score (a)*	69.3	66.7	71.0
Maladaptive coping score (a)	50.4	50.7	50.2
Social support score (b)**	−50.2	−47.5	−52.1

(a) 0 to 100 point scale; mean score.
(b) −100 to 0 point scale; mean score
 * Difference between groups significant at .01 level
** Difference between groups significant at .001 level

Table 4.6 Correlation of victimization experiences and mediating factors (controlling for incarceration)

	Adaptive Coping	Maladaptive Coping	Social Support
Any child physical abuse		.24**	−.27**
Any child sexual abuse		.14*	−.19**
Any physical IPV	.16*		
Any rape		.21**	−.16**

 * Correlation is significant at .01 level.
** Correlation is significant at .001 level.

also report using more maladaptive coping skills and having lower social support, whether they are incarcerated or not. The experience of adult physical interpersonal violence is correlated with lower social support. Women who experienced rape are more likely to use maladaptive coping skills and have fewer social supports, whether incarcerated or not.

Use of social Services and Supports

Cross-tabulations were used to compare the two samples of women regarding the social services and supports they utilised as a result of their victimisation (see Table 4.7), the helpfulness of these services (see Table 4.8), and any barriers they encountered to using these services (see Table 4.9). Services were categorised post-hoc as either therapeutic in nature (noted in the tables with a 't'), crisis intervention

Table 4.7 Social services and supports used after victimisation

	Total % (n=266)	Prison % (n=157)	Communities % (n=109)
Service/support used			
Emotional support (t)	72.8	76.9	67.0
Professional counseling (t)	57.4	61.1	51.9
Medication (l)	53.6	59.2	45.4
Welfare (l)	46.4	51.6	38.9
Medical provider for emotional help (t)	45.7	51.6	37.0
Psychotropic medication (l)**	44.9	52.9	32.4
Legal services (l)	40.4	45.9	32.4
Support group (t)	40.2	43.9	34.9
Food bank (c) *	39.0	45.2	29.9
Religious counseling (t)	35.1	37.6	31.5
Educational (l)	27.9	32.5	21.3
Hospital stay for emotional prob. (t)	27.2	31.2	21.3
Domestic violence shelter (c)*	23.8	29.3	15.7
Job training (l)	20.8	21.7	19.4
Subsidized housing (l)	15.5	14.6	16.7
Rape crisis (c)	14.7	15.9	13.0
Homeless shelter (c)	14.3	15.9	12.0
Unemployment (l)	14.0	12.1	16.7
Child protection (c)**	13.6	19.1	5.6
Daycare (l)	12.8	12.1	13.9
Reproductive services (l)	7.5	7.6	7.4
Vocational rehabilitation (l)	7.2	8.3	5.6
Worker's compensation (l)	6.8	6.4	7.4
Internet support (t)	2.6	2.5	2.6
Mean number of service/supports used	6.7	6.8	6.5
Mean # of therapeutic services (t)	2.3	2.5	2.1
Mean # of crisis interventions (c)**	1.4	1.1	1.8
Mean # of long-term services (l)	3.0	3.2	2.6

* Difference between the three groups significant at .01 level
** Difference between the three groups significant at .001 level

Table 4.8 Helpfulness of social services and supports after victimisation (a)

Mean	Total (n=266)	Prison (n=157)	Communities (n=109)
How helpful was this service? (b)			
Child day-care (l)	4.50	4.42	4.60
Religious counselling (t)	4.30	4.36	4.21
Subsidised Housing (l)	4.34	4.39	4.28
Welfare (l)	4.33	4.35	4.29
Educational (l)	4.30	4.38	4.13
Food bank (c)	4.16	4.16	4.16
Job training (l)	4.22	4.32	4.05
Unemployment (l)	3.84	3.89	3.78
Rape crisis (c)	3.66	3.67	3.62
Domestic violence shelter (c)	3.25	3.07	3.76
Reproductive services (l)	3.95	4.25	3.50
Emotional support (t)	3.74	3.57	4.01
Professional counselling (t)	3.53	3.47	3.64
Vocational rehabilitation (l)	3.42	3.54	3.17
Medication (l)	3.61	3.58	3.67
Support group (t)	3.48	3.39	3.65
Medical provider (t)	3.49	3.51	3.45
Psychotropic medication (l)	3.50	3.48	3.54
Worker's compensation (l)	3.67	3.60	3.75
Homeless shelter (c)	3.49	3.50	3.46
Hospital stay (t)	3.00	2.94	3.13
Legal services (l)	3.16	3.18	3.12
Internet support (t)	3.00	3.25	2.67
Child protection (c)	2.97	2.90	3.33

(a) Ratings among those using each service.
(b) Scale from 1 (not helpful) to 5 (very helpful).

services ('c'), and long-term tangible supports ('l'). Women were asked to indicate which services they received at any time in the past for any of their abuse experiences, and to give an indication of the helpfulness of the services received. Because all of the women in the two samples experienced some form of victimisation, the entire sample reported using some form of post-victimisation intervention.

As indicated in Table 4.7, there were 24 different types of services or supports listed in the study interview that women could have

Table 4.9 Barriers to using services and supports

Barrier (a)	Total % (n=266)	Prison % (n=157)	Communities % (n=109)
I wanted to handle the problem on my own	81.4	86.5	73.8
I thought problem would get better by itself	68.8	74.4	60.7
I didn't think treatment would work	55.1	60.3	47.7
I was unsure about where to go or who to see	52.9	55.8	48.6
The problem didn't bother me very much at first	43.0	44.9	40.2
I was concerned about how much money it would cost	41.4	38.5	45.8
I was concerned about what people would think if they found out I was in treatment	40.7	41.7	39.3
I had problems with things like transportation or scheduling that made it hard to get to the services*	39.5	46.2	29.9
I thought it would take too much time or would be inconvenient*	36.6	42.9	27.4
I was scared about being put in hospital against my will	34.4	37.21	30.2
I received services before and it didn't work	31.9	35.9	26.2
My health insurance would not cover services	28.1	30.8	24.3
I was not satisfied with available services	21.0	21.8	19.8
My parents did not take me to get help	19.8	23.7	14.2
I could not get an appointment	6.1	7.1	4.7
Mean number of barriers named	5.8	6.2	5.3

(a) Percent answering yes, it was a barrier.
 * Difference between the three groups significant at .01 level
** Difference between the three groups significant at .001 level

sought after their victimisation. In general, the most commonly utilised post-victimisation services among those listed are those in the emotional support (73%) and counselling (57%) areas, followed by medication (54%), welfare benefits (46%), visits to medical providers (46%), and psychotropic medication (45%). Rates of service and support utilisation are somewhat higher for women in prison than for women in the community for almost every individual service, but most differences are not significant. Significantly more incarcerated women than community women used psychotropic medications, food banks, domestic violence shelters, and child protective services as a result of their victimisation.

The least commonly received services were often the more concrete and long-term tangible supports ('1'), including worker's compensation funds (7%), vocational rehabilitation (7%), reproductive services (8%), and child day-care (13%).

Women were asked to rate the helpfulness of each service or support received on a scale of one (not helpful) to five (extremely helpful). Only those women receiving the service rated its helpfulness. The mean helpfulness ratings were then compared between the two samples (see Table 4.8).

The top quarter of services perceived as being the most helpful include many services that are primarily long-term tangible supports. Child day-care, religious counselling, subsidised housing, welfare, educational services, and food banks are the top six services most highly rated as helpful to the participants. When compared to the top quarter of services received, only welfare benefits stand out as being both utilised by many women *and* considered helpful; the other services most utilised by women (emotional support, professional counselling, medication, medical providers, and psychotropic medication) are ranked in the bottom half of services listed in the order of their perceived helpfulness. The two samples of women (incarcerated and non-incarcerated) do not significantly differ in their views of any particular service as being helpful.

Women in this study were also asked whether or not a number of barriers or challenges prevented them from seeking or getting help after their experiences of victimisation. The barriers indicated by the two samples are listed below (see Table 4.9). Of the fifteen possible barriers listed, two barriers stand out as common to both groups of women. The first is the desire of the women to handle the problem on their own, reported by 81% of the total sample. The incarcerated women are particularly likely to cite this as a barrier to seeking services. The second barrier, thinking that the problem would get better by itself, is reported by 69% of the overall sample.

When cross-tabulations and phi coefficients are calculated comparing the two sample groups, two additional barriers emerge as being differently experienced by the two samples of women. Incarcerated women are statistically more likely to say that problems like transportation or scheduling make it harder to get services post-victimisation, and they also thought the service would take too much time or be inconvenient.

This study also sought to examine the association between the specific services a woman used post-victimization and her outcomes in adulthood. Table 4.10 provides a view of the correlations between a woman's usage of each of the 24 post-victimisation services and her adult well-being, in terms of physical health, mental health, current incarceration, current alcohol problem or current drug problem. There are a small number of associations between a particular service used and a woman's level of well-being in adulthood.

Of the long-term tangible supports used post-victimisation, the ones that appear to be associated with adult incarceration are use of psychotropic medication, participation in child protective services, and the non-use of domestic violence services. Use of several of the specific crisis intervention services post-victimisation is associated with other indicators of well being in adulthood, particularly mental health. Use of the following services is significantly associated with poorer mental health: psychotropic medications, medications for emotional reasons, receipt of welfare benefits, use of subsidised housing, use of a food bank, use of a domestic violence shelter, use of rape crisis services, a hospital stay, and use of a medical provider for post-victimisation services.

Of the therapeutic services used post-victimisation, several have strong associations with adult substance use. Women using psychotropic medications or medications for emotional reasons were also likely to report problems with drugs or alcohol. Substance use problems were also reported by more women who had received welfare benefits or food bank goods, Religious counselling, although used by many women, was not associated with adult well-being, including prevention of incarceration.

Finally, women who identify particular barriers when seeking services have poorer adult outcomes. When correlation coefficients were calculated between the barriers to service usage identified and a woman's well-being as an adult, several relationships emerge (see Table 4.11). Women who were incarcerated are more likely to

Table 4.10   Correlations of services used and adult outcomes

	Physical health	Mental health	Incar-ceration	Alcohol problem	Drug problem
Long-term tangible supports					
Psychotropic medication	−.185*	.202**	.178*	.254**	
Medication	−.209**	−.307**		.242**	.184*
Welfare		−.160*		.178*	.257**
Subsidised housing		−.170*			
Job training					
Education support					
Unemployment					
Workers comp.					
Vocational rehab					
Child day-care support					
Reproductive services					
Legal services					
Crisis intervention services					
Food bank	−.192*	−.176*		.178*	.294**
DV shelter		−.167*	−.157*		
Rape crisis services		−.180*			
Child protective services			.194**		
Homeless shelter					
Therapeutic services					
Support group				.205**	
Professional counselling				.187**	
Hospital stay	−.210**	−.216**			
Medical provider	−.177*	−.167*			
Emotional support					
Religious counselling					
Internet support group					

* Correlation is significant at the 0.01 level
** Correlation is significant at the 0.001 level

name the following as barriers to seeking services post-victimisation: wanting to handle the problem on her own, having problems with transportation or scheduling, and thinking services would take too much time or be inconvenient. Having problems with transportation or scheduling was associated with all poor adult outcomes, including incarceration, poor physical health, poor mental health, and alcohol and/or drug problems.

Table 4.11 Correlations of barriers to seeking services and adult outcomes

Barrier	Physical health	Mental health	Incar-ceration	Alcohol problem	Drug problem
I wanted to handle the problem on my own			.160*		
I thought problem would get better by itself					
I was unsure about where to go or who to see	−.239**	−.283**			
I didn't think treatment would work					
I was concerned about how much money it would cost		−.213**			
I had problems with things like transportation or scheduling that made it hard to get to the services	−.254**	−.298**	.163*	.173*	.220**
The problem didn't bother me very much at first					
I was concerned about what people would think if they found out I was in treatment					
I thought it would take too much time or would be inconvenient		−.163*	.159*		
I was scared about being put in hospital against my will	−.182*	−.316**			
My health insurance would not cover services		−.220**			
I received services before and it didn't work		−.181*			
I was not satisfied with available services		−.217**			
I could not get an appointment					

*Correlation is significant at .01 level.
**Correlation is significant at .001 level.

Discussion

This study pursued several areas of inquiry relevant to risk and need assessment and consequent service planning. Namely, what are differentially situated women's histories of victimisation; what were their opportunities and access to social services in the aftermath of the victimisation; and what were their appraisals of the helpfulness of those services?

Though supported in the existing literature, the extent to which women from both the prison and the community samples have experienced violence is startling. Though our sampling strategies may have resulted in some bias, the extent of reports of multiple victimisations in the study sample cannot be under estimated. About 66% of the women in the incarcerated sample reported having experienced both child and adult victimisations; and nearly 40% of the community women did the same. These results suggest that new investigations must be pursued with regard to value of the services used and the perceived helpfulness of them by women who have experienced cumulative risks or what has been referred to as 'enduring trauma', and also of their ultimate adult outcomes (Johnston 1995).

Methodological Limitations

This exploratory study is the first known study to identify differences in service usage between women living in various geographical areas and under two types of circumstances – one imprisoned, the other free, in one Midwestern state. While there is no reason to believe that life in the particular state would itself have an effect on these findings, undertaking similar inquiries in other states and in other prison systems across the country and around the world will lend support for the findings presented here. However, all of these findings should be narrowly interpreted as applying only to the women in this sample.

The convenience sampling used to generate the sample also limits the interpretation of these results. The wording of the flyers used to recruit the women from the correctional institution resulted in a sample of women who were more likely than not to have had histories of victimisation. While the flyer that was posted in the various locations in the communities (e.g. grocery stores) was not as explicit in detailing the purpose of the study as those posted in the prison, a similar sampling bias may have occurred.

The use of convenience sampling is certainly one of the challenges associated with sampling strategies when undertaking victimisation research. We were mindful of the extent of disclosure asked of women and worked to avoid any interviewing procedures that could be perceived as being coercive and harmful. The community women were paid US$25 compensation at the start of the interview and told the interview would end if they wished it to end with no questions asked. Very few women withdrew from the interview once it began.

The disparity in opportunity to provide remuneration between the 'free' women and the women in the prison is of concern. The commitment to in some way honour these women participants by providing them payment for their time and effort was unable to be fulfilled equally between the sample groups. A more equitable form of remuneration of the prisoner population must be found at the outset of future research.

Finally, there were also inherent limitations in the survey instrument. While overall we believe the survey instrument to be adequate in terms of the specificity of questions posed, that specificity probably also had something to do with the high prevalence rate of victimisation reported, a research challenge identified by other scholars (Browne *et al.* 1999). Still, with these limitations in mind, there is no doubt that the findings reported here and elsewhere are important from both the policy and practice perspectives.

Implications for the assessment of risk and need

The responses of these two groups of women, those incarcerated and those not, found similarities and differences in the experiences of these women; exploring those differences can illuminate the trajectories of women who are ultimately incarcerated. First, as corroborated by other research (see, for example, Bloom, Owen and Covington 2005) the incarcerated women had histories of greater material and social deprivation. Incarcerated women had received less formal education, had begun childbearing at earlier ages, and were more likely to receive welfare benefits. These three areas of need and risk are highly correlated, but it appears that the receipt of welfare benefits by women with lower education and earlier children is not offsetting these risks.

The incarcerated women in this sample were more likely than free women to be living with either a male partner or their parents (in the twelve months prior to their incarceration). This might be an indicator of the continuing economic need of this population, which can lead to participation in criminal activity. It may also be an indicator of the peculiar virulence of intimate partner violence – that for these women, the end of the violence, however long it lasts, results from their unmet needs for early intervention being transmuted into risks that end in their incarceration. In turn, incarceration provides them with sure protection against further violence at least for the period of their imprisonment.

While violence and victimisation were common to all women in this study (a likely artefact of the sampling strategy employed), incarcerated women had experienced more severe forms of violence. Incarcerated women were more likely than free women to have been raped in childhood or adulthood, and to have experienced both psychological and physical violence with an intimate partner in adulthood. In this specific Midwestern U.S. state, not unlike many other jurisdictions with mandatory arrest legislation, officers are required to make an arrest when evidence of the commission of a crime is apparent. An unintended and highly controversial consequence of this mandatory arrest policy is that the victim may be arrested along with the perpetrator or alone, depending on what is apparent to the officer at the time. Some states have now amended their mandatory arrest statutes to allow for officers to arrest what is called the 'predominant aggressor', that person whom police believe to be the most significant aggressor in the domestic violence incident (see, for example, 2005 *Wisconsin Act 104*).

Finally, in terms of the basic risks and needs experienced by incarcerated women, this population reported a much higher incidence of drug and/or alcohol problems, and lower levels of social support. Curiously, incarcerated women reported higher usage of adaptive coping strategies, but it may indeed be adaptive in the prison setting to be a model adaptive prisoner. There were no differences in the two samples in their physical or mental health, which again, may be an artefact of the physical and mental health services available to a woman once incarcerated.

Services and supports can mediate these risks and needs. Research indicates that most abused women seek help, usually first from family and friends and then from formal services (Davis and Srinivasan 1995; Horton and Johnson 1993). In this study, an attempt was made to determine which services women received post-victimisation. Additionally, when a woman participant reported having used a particular social service ('service usage'), she was also asked to rate how helpful the service was to her ('service appraisal'). In general terms, the most commonly used services in response to being victimised were: emotional support, professional counselling, medication for emotional problems, welfare, and visits to medical providers. However, the words 'used' and 'received' in the study are somewhat inaccurate as they imply the availability of the support. In fact, some of the supports – child day-care, subsidised housing, food, job training and educational supports – were probably not offered or known to some women, and not accessible by others. In other words, it is likely that structural barriers such as incarceration and transportation difficulties prevented some women from receiving a particular type of support; in other cases it is likely that women did not meet the eligibility criteria (e.g. job training and subsidised housing) for the support sought.

Women participants' appraisals of the helpfulness of services indicate that the most useful services were those that were more concrete or tangible in nature, including child day-care, religious counselling, subsidised housing, welfare, educational services, food bank, and job training. However, there were no differences between samples on how helpful women found any particular service.

Our findings indicate that, with the exception of welfare, the supports perceived as being most helpful were those that were the least received. So, emotional support, professional counselling, medication, support groups, and medical providers were perceived as being less helpful but were received more often than the supports which were more frequently reported to be more helpful but received less often. This is not dissimilar to the research reported on by Gordon (1996). His review of the research on women victims' use of services suggested that the most commonly used social service systems were, in order, the criminal justice, social service agencies, medical services, crisis counselling, mental health services, clergy, and women's groups. However, Gordon also found that the abused women did not necessarily view the services they received as helpful (Gordon 1996). Humphreys and Thiara (2003) studied the experiences of women victims of domestic violence who sought mental health services. Many of the women in this study reported experiencing negative or unhelpful experiences including the lack of attention paid to the experience of trauma, not providing trauma services; reifying the woman's experiences of abuse by focusing on her mental health; blaming the victim; and offering medication rather than counselling support.

As to the barriers to service receipt, significant differences were found between the incarcerated and 'free' groups in three categories: incarcerated women wanted to handle the problem (the victimisation and its after-effects) themselves; had problems with scheduling and transportation; and thought help would take too much time or be inconvenient. Women in communities experienced fewer barriers to seeking services, although more than half reported wanting to take care of the problem themselves and believing that the problem would resolve itself without intervention. These barriers may be related to the emotional difficulty of disclosing one's experience of victimisation and the stigma associated with receiving support services in the aftermath of that victimisation.

What is helpful to women offenders and free women who have histories of victimisation?

By any measure, histories of victimisation among the incarcerated population are common. Surprisingly, however, these histories are also common within the general population of women sampled here. These findings suggest that providing the 'right' kinds of risk and need assessments and then the services that will address the emotional, physical, mental, social, and economic effects of victimisation is critical. Judging from the histories of victimisation and deprivation experienced by incarcerated women, assessments of a woman's risk and need will necessarily include a history of economic deprivation and supports, education level achieved, family composition, including the number and ages of children for whom she is responsible, and social supports. All of these are key predictors of incarceration. Clearly, economic stress and material deprivation must be understood in all its contributions to a woman's likelihood of moving towards criminality and/or incarceration.

Once one's history is assessed, one method of determining what the 'right' services are is to listen to the important feedback victims provide. Recalling that for both groups of women in this sample, the services and supports received that were appraised and rated as being most helpful to them were those more tangible in nature – child day-care, housing, education, job training. Significantly, these were also the services that were received the least frequently. Instead, these women reported that the services they found least helpful – services more traditionally therapeutic in nature such as emotional support, counselling, medications, legal services, and support groups – were the services most frequently offered and received.

Consequently, policy makers and practitioners, including those who practice in the prison system, must focus on making available to women victims the services that are likely to help them move into their futures in physically, emotionally, socially and economically healthy ways. This is not to diminish the importance of therapeutic services; rather, we wish to highlight the importance of the tangible and crisis intervention services. It is quite possible that these women victims prioritised their service needs. We were unable to determine if the value of such services would be perceived to be more helpful if the women's needs for concrete assistance had been met. Thus, if her children are adequately cared for while she does her time or when she leaves for her job, she may be emotionally freed up to think about her psychological needs which can then be addressed in counselling. So, one service type does not necessarily trump the other; but instead, one may clear the way for the helpfulness of the other.

And of course, this idea begs yet another idea. It is quite likely that women victims know better than anyone else the range and detail of their needs and they understand what services will be helpful to them and of those services, those likely to be the most helpful. While it may make intuitive sense to use a therapeutic intervention with a women who has been physically and/or sexually abused in her life, these women victims have indicated that tangible services were more helpful to them in the aftermath of the victimisation. The barriers that prevent women from accessing these types of services, whether rooted in fiscal, temporal, social or personal beliefs, should be made the target of a concerted elimination effort. This research suggests that offering an array of tangible and crisis intervention services to women victims will be welcomed by this population. Perhaps in doing so, incarceration itself will be less utilised as a service intervention for victimised women.

References

American Correctional Association (1990) *What Does the Future Hold? Task force on the female offender.* Alexandria, VA: American Correctional Association.

Arias, I. (2004) 'The legacy of child maltreatment: Long-term health consequences for women', *Journal of Women's Health*, 13 (5): 468–73.

Banyard, V. (1999) 'Childhood maltreatment and the mental health of low-income women', *American Journal of Orthopsychiatry*, 69 (2): 161–171.

Bellis, M.D.D., Broussard, E.R., Herring, S.W., Moritz, G. and Benitez, J.G. (2001) 'Psychiatric co-morbidity in caregivers and children involved in maltreatment: A pilot research study with policy implications', *Child Abuse and Neglect*, 25: 923–44.

Berry, M. (2001) *The Family at Risk: Issues and trends in family preservation services*. Columbia, SC: University of South Carolina Press.

Besharov, D.J. and Laumann, L.A. (1997) 'Don't call it child abuse if it's really poverty', *Journal of Children and Poverty*, 3 (1): 5–36.

Blanchette, K. and Brown, S.L. (2006) *The Assessment and Treatment of Women Offenders. An Integrative Perspective*. Chichester: John Wiley.

Bloom, B., Owen, B. and Covington, S. (2005) *Gender Responsive Strategies for Women Offenders. A Summary of Research, Practice, and Guiding Principles for Women Offenders*. Retrieved on 30 August 2006 from http://nicic.org/pubs/2005/020418.pdf.

Briere, J. (1992) *Child Abuse Trauma: Theory and treatment of the lasting effects*. Newbury Park, CA: Sage Publications.

Browne, A. (1993) 'Violence against women by male partners: Prevalence, outcomes, and policy implications', *American Psychologist*, 48 (10), 1077–1087.

Browne, A., Miller, B. and Maguin, E. (1999) 'Prevalence and severity of lifetime physical and sexual victimization among incarcerated women', *International Journal of Law and Psychiatry*, 22 (3–4): 301–22.

Carlson, B.E. (1990) 'Domestic violence', in A. Gitterman (ed.) *Handbook of Social Work Practice with Vulnerable Populations* (pp. 471–502). New York: Columbia University Press.

Carver, C.S. (1997) 'You want to measure coping but your protocol's too long: Consider the brief cope', *International Journal of Behavioral Medicine*, 4 (1): 92–100.

Cicchetti, D. and Carlson, W. (1989) *Child Maltreatment: Theory and research on the causes and consequences of child abuse and neglect*. Cambridge: Cambridge University Press.

Cowen, P.S. (1999) 'Child neglect: Injuries of omission', *Pediatric Nursing*, 25 (4): 401–36.

Davis, L.V. and Srinivasan, M. (1995) 'Listening to the voices of battered women: What helps them escape violence', *Affilia*, 10 (1): 49–69.

Dore, M.M. (1999) 'Emotionally and behaviourally disturbed children in the child welfare system: Points of preventive intervention', *Children and Youth Services Review*, 21 (1): 7–20.

Eby, K.K., Campbell, J.C., Sullivan, C.M. and Davidson, W.S., 2nd. (1995) 'Health effects of experiences of sexual violence for women with abusive partners', *Health Care Women Int*, 16 (6): 563–76.

Follingstad, D.R., Brennan, A.F., Hause, E.S., Polek, D.S. and Rutledge, L.L. (1991) 'Factors moderating physical and psychological symptoms of battered women', *Journal of Family Violence*, 6 (1): 81–95.

Gelles, R.J. and Straus, M.A. (1990) 'The medical and psychological costs of family violence', in R.J. Gelles and M.A. Straus (eds) *Physical Violence in American Families: Risk Factors and Adaptations to Violence in 8,145 Families* (pp. 425–430). New Brunswick, NJ: Transaction Publishers.

Goodman, L.A., Koss, M.P. and Russon, N.F. (1993) 'Violence against women: Physical and mental health effects. Part I: Research findings', *Applied and Preventive Psychology*, 2: 79–89.

Gordon, J.S. (1996) ' Community services for abused women: A review of perceived usefulness and efficacy', *Journal of Family Violence*, 11 (4), 315–29.

Greene, J.C. (2000) 'Understanding social programs through evaluation', in N.K. Denzin and Y.S. Lincoln (eds) *Handbook of Qualitative Research* (2nd edn, pp. 981–1000). Thousand Oaks, CA: Sage.

Greenfeld, L.A. and Snell, T.L. (1999) *Women Offenders* (No. NCJ 175688). Washington, DC.: Bureau of Justice Statistics.

Hampton, R.L. (1995) 'Race, ethnicity, and child maltreatment: An analysis of cases recognized and reported by hospitals', in A. Aguirre and D.V. Baker (eds) *Sources: Notable Selections in Race and Ethnicity* (pp. 287–296). Guildford, CT: Dushkin Publishing Group.

Hannah-Moffat, K. (2004) 'Losing ground: Gendered knowledges, parole risk, and responsibility', *Social Politics*, 11 (3), 363–85.

Harlow, C.W. (1998) *Profile of Jail Inmates* (No. NCJ 164620). Washington, DC: Bureau of Justice Statistics, US Department of Justice.

Harlow, C.W. (1999) *Prior Abuse Reported by Inmates and Probationers* (No. NCJ 172879). Washington, DC: Bureau of Justice Statistics.

Harrison, P.M. and Beck, A.J. (2004) *Prisoners in 2003*. Department of Justice Office of Justice Programs Bureau of Justice Statistics Bulletin.

Harrison, P.M. and Beck, A.J. (2006) *Prison and Jail Inmates at Midyear 2005*. US Department of Justice, Office of Justice Programs, Bureau of Justice Statistics Bulletin.

Henriques, Z.W. and Manatu-Rupert, N. (2001) 'Living on the outside: African American women before, during, and after imprisonment', *Prison Journal*, 81: 6–19.

Horton, A.L. and Johnson, B.L. (1993) 'Profile and strategies of women who have ended abuse', *Families in Society*, 74 (8): 481–92.

Humphreys, C. and Thiara, R. (2003) 'Mental health and domestic violence: "I call it symptoms of abuse"', *British Journal of Social Work*, 33: 209–26.

Johnston, D. (1995) 'Effects of parental incarceration', in K. Gabel and D. Johnston (eds) *Children of Incarcerated Parents* (pp. 59–88). New York: Lexington Books.

Kirby, L.D. and Fraser, M.W. (1997) 'Risk and resilience in childhood', in M.W. Fraser (ed.) *Risk and Resilience in Childhood: An ecological perspective* (pp. 10–33). Washington, DC: NASW Press.

Koss, M.P. and Heslet, L. (1992) 'Somatic consequences of violence against women', *Archives of Family Medicine*, 1: 53–9.

Koss, M.P. and Oros, C.J. (1982) 'Sexual experiences survey: A research instrument investigating sexual aggression and victimization', *Journal of Counseling and Clinical Psychology*, 50 (3): 455–57.

Kurtz, P.D., Gaudin. J.M., Howing, P.T. and Wodarski, J.S. (1993) 'The consequences of physical abuse and neglect on the school age child: Mediating factors', *Children and Youth Services Review, 15*, 85–104.

McCauley, J.D., Kern, D.E., Kolodner, K., Derogatis, L.R. and Bass, E.B. (1998) 'Relation of low-severity violence to women's health', *Journal of General Internal Medicine*, 13: 687–91.

McNutt, L.-A., Carlson, B.E., Persaud, M. and Postmus, J.L. (2002) 'Cumulative abuse experiences, physical health and health practices', *Annals of Epidemiology*, 12 (2): 123–30.

Miller, B.A. and Downs, W.R. (1993) 'The impact of family violence on the use of alcohol by women', *Alcohol Health and Research World*, 17, 137–43.

NCS (1992) National comorbidity survey, Retrieved February 16, 2003, from www.hcp.med.harvard.edu/ncs

O'Leary, K.D. (1993) 'Through a psychological lens: Personality traits, personality disorders, and levels of violence', in R.J. Gelles and D.R. Loseke (eds) *Current Controversies on Family Violence* (pp. 7–30). Newbury Park, CA: Sage.

Peleikis, Mykletun and Dahl, (2004) 'The relative influence of childhood sexual abuse and other family background risk factors on adult adversities in female outpatients treated for anxiety disorders and depression', *Child Abuse and Neglect*, 28 (1): 61–76.

Plichta, S.B. (1996) 'Violence and abuse: Implications for women's health', in M.M. Falik and K.S. Collins (eds) *Women's Health: The Commonwealth Fund Study* (pp. 237–272). Baltimore, MD: Johns Hopkins University Press.

Postmus, J. and Severson, M.E. (2005) *Violence and Victimization: Exploring women's histories of survival.* Final Report, NIJ 2003-IJ-CX-1037.

Richie, B.E. (2001) 'Challenges incarcerated women face as they return to their communities: Findings from life history interviews', *Crime and Delinquency*, 47 (3): 368–89.

Saunders, D.G. (1994) 'Posttraumatic stress symptom profiles of battered women: A comparison of survivors in two settings', *Violence and Victims*, 9 (1): 31–44.

Severson, M.E. (2001) 'Women's mental health issues: Twentieth-century realities; twenty-first century challenges', in K.J. Peterson and A.A. Lieberman (eds) *Building On Women's Strengths: A Social Work Agenda For The Twenty-First Century* (2nd edn, pp. 95–118). New York: Haworth Press.

Shaw, M. and Hannah-Moffat, K. (2006) 'Risk assessment in Canadian corrections: Some diverse and gendered issues', in R. Immarigeon (ed.) *Women and Girls in the Criminal Justice System* (pp. 31–8 – 31–11). Kingston, NJ: Civic Research Institute.

Shepard, M.F. and Campbell, J.A. (1992) 'The abusive behaviour inventory: A measure of psychological and physical abuse', *Journal of Interpersonal Violence*, 7 (3): 291–305.

Snell, T.L. and Morton, D.C. (1994) *Women in Prison: Survey of State Prison Inmates, 1991.* Washington, DC: US Deptment of Justice.

Stewart, A.L., Hays, R.D. and Wate, J.E., Jr. (1988) 'The MOS short-form general health survey: Reliability and validity in a patient population', *Medical Care*, 26: 733–35.

Tjaden, P. and Thoennes, N. (1998) *Prevalence, Incidence, and Consequences of Violence against Women: Findings from the national violence against women survey*. Washington: National Institute of Justice.

US Department of Justice (1998) *Women in Criminal Justice: A Twenty Year Update: Special report*. Washington, DC: Office of Justice Programs Coordination Group on Women.

Vaux, A., Phillips, J., Holly, L., Thomson, B., Williams, D. and Stewart, D. (1986) 'The social support appraisals (ssa) scale: Studies of reliability and validity', *American Journal of Community Psychology*, 14: 195–219.

Veysey, B.M. (1998) 'Specific needs of women diagnosed with mental illnesses in U.S. Jails', in B.L. Levin, A.K. Blanch and A. Jennings (eds) *Women's Mental Health Service: A public health perspective* (pp. 368–89). Thousand Oaks, CA: Sage.

Walker, L.E. (1993) 'The battered woman syndrome is a psychological consequence of abuse', in R.J. Gelles and D.R. Loseke (eds) *Current Controversies on Family Violence* (pp. 133–53). Newbury Park, CA: Sage.

Wolfe, D.A. (1999) *Child Abuse: Implications for Child Development and Psychopathology*. Thousand Oaks, CA: Sage.

Zweig, J.M., Schlichter, K.A. and Burt, M. (2002) 'Assisting women victims of violence who experience multiple barriers to services', *Violence Against Women*, 8 (2): 162–79.

Chapter 5

Responding to drug and alcohol problems: innovations and effectiveness in treatment programmes for women

Margaret Malloch and Nancy Loucks

Introduction

This chapter considers contemporary responses to women in the criminal justice system with drug and/or alcohol problems. Attempts to develop appropriate responses within the criminal justice system have often led to a general approach to 'addicted offenders', to the neglect of women's needs and preferences for service provision. The chapter examines innovative attempts to address the needs of women with addiction issues, focusing specifically on the 218 'Time Out' Centre (Scotland) which aims to provide a holistic alternative to custody for women, including both residential and community-based options (Loucks *et al.* 2006).

International context

Increasing numbers of women are incarcerated in prisons throughout the world (Cook and Davies 1999; Taylor 2004; Home Office 2004; National Offender Management Service 2005; Scottish Executive 2006). The number of women in prison as a percentage of overall prison figures remains relatively small (around 5% in Scotland and Canada; 6% in England and Wales, and New Zealand; 7% in Australia and just under 9% in the United States of America; International Centre for Prison Studies 2005). Nevertheless, in most countries, the number of women in prison has increased dramatically in recent years, significantly outstripping increases in the number of male prisoners and with particular consequences for minority ethnic, black and aboriginal women, who constitute disproportionate levels of female prison populations in many countries including Canada, Australia, the UK and the USA.

Internationally, more women are being sent to prison for drug-related offences and crimes motivated by poverty (Home Office 2004; Taylor 2004). A significant number of women in prison are drug users, with a high proportion imprisoned for offences directly related to problem drug use (Malloch 2000; Scottish Executive 2002). In Scotland, between 90–100% of women prisoners reported being drug users on reception to prison (HM Inspectorate of Prisons for Scotland 2004 and 2006). Similarly, other countries report high rates of illicit drug use among female prisoners prior to sentence (Department of Correctional Services 2002; Ramsey 2003). Problem alcohol and tranquiliser use is also reported to be high among women involved with the criminal justice system (Ramsey 2003). Universally, rates of drug use among women prisoners appear to exceed those for male prisoners (EMCDDA 2001).

Drug-related offending has a considerable impact on the number of women imprisoned for offences such as shoplifting, fraud and other property offences (Home Office 2004) and such offences have contributed to the dramatic rise in the number of women in prison (McIvor 2004a). Nevertheless, the largest group of female prisoners in Scotland in 2005 were detained for drug offences (Scottish Executive 2006).

Internationally, criminal justice systems are increasingly expected to meet the needs of growing numbers of individuals with drug/alcohol related problems. Evidence that 'coerced treatment' can be effective has been used to increase treatment options as alternatives to custody, but also strengthens arguments for the provision of resources within prisons. However, the success of prison programmes in reducing reoffending is mixed, and significant variations are evident in the content and quality of programmes for substance users in prisons at national and international levels (EMCDDA 2001; Home Office 2003; Ramsey 2003; MacDonald 2004).

The context and delivery of services is important in order to provide a response to the wider context of prisoners' lives. Recent research for the Home Office (Cann 2006) on the effects of prison-based cognitive skills programmes for women in England and Wales showed no statistically significant differences in reconviction rates between participants in matched comparison groups. Similar findings were evident for adult males and young offenders. Changing cognitive patterns is of little benefit if the structural realities of an individual's life remain unchanged.

For female drug users, a gender-specific application of rehabilitation/ recovery is necessary – but not unproblematic – and is increasingly recognised and adopted as part of programme formats (Bloom and Covington 1998; Hume 2001; Covington and Bloom 2004; Bloom 2005; Drugscope 2005). Programmes often focus on assertiveness training and self-esteem. While these may be of benefit in some cases, they tend to operate from a theoretical basis which suggests the individual woman is in some way 'inadequate' and that this can be 'treated'. Similarly, counselling provides an appropriate alternative only when underwritten by a feminist analysis in which individuals' experiences are linked to wider structural issues (Malloch 2000; 2004a; 2004b).

While initiatives in Scotland such as Drug Treatment and Testing Orders and Drug Courts are intended to lessen the number of drug users sentenced to custody, their success depends on available community resources (Howard League 2000; Eley et al. 2002; Malloch et al. 2003; McIvor et al. 2006). Regional variations can result in a geographical lottery in accessing services, which is clearly of importance where criminal justice agencies refer clients to external service-providers (Audit Commission 2002; Effective Interventions Unit 2002; Scottish Drugs Forum 2003).

Evaluations of the Glasgow and Fife Drug Courts in Scotland identified the importance of comprehensive service provision (Eley et al. 2002; Malloch et al. 2003, McIvor et al. 2006). In particular, Treatment and Supervision staff identified the need for increased rehabilitation services, specifically rehabilitation and community-based services that met the needs of women, and for follow-up support and after-care (Effective Intervention Unit 2002). Drug Court clients indicated a need for some form of 'after-care' to support them after the supervision of the court (and thereby the treatment team) had ended.

The Audit Commission in England and Wales (2002) noted that little emphasis was given to reviewing the needs of women systematically within and outwith the criminal justice system, with women generally considered to be a priority only when pregnant or having child-care issues. 'Women-only' services are significantly lacking, particularly for residential treatment, and places for women with children are very limited. If these services are not in place, courts are likely to have little success in fast-tracking women into them.

Developing programmes for women

The most effective approaches to treatment for drug and alcohol problems differ between men and women (Bloom *et al.* 2003). This clearly needs to inform the provision of resources in the community and criminal justice systems. Academics and practitioners have identified key components for effective programme content and the extent to which interventions relating to substance use and offending behaviour require an acknowledgement of the broader contexts of the lived experiences of men and women. This has allowed some key characteristics crucial to effective programme development to be identified (Koons *et al.* 1997; Fowler 2001; Bloom *et al.* 2003; Ramsey 2003; Covington and Bloom 2004; Addaction 2005; Holloway *et al.* 2005; McCampbell 2005), namely:

Gender

- That programmes are 'gender-responsive' in design and delivery, from assessment to aftercare;

- That theoretical knowledge about women's pathways into the criminal justice system is used to inform services for women;

- That women-only groups are a feature of services, especially for primary treatment.

Services

- That assessments and services are based on multi-agency co-operation, particularly in terms of the integration of mental health and substance abuse services;

- That treatment is individualised, and care plans are developed to meet individual needs, identified through comprehensive assessment.

Relationships

- That staff are gender-responsive and gender-sensitive, caring and available to clients, as far as possible have some shared experiences, and are able to take an holistic approach to the lives of the women with whom they are working;

- That training for staff is ongoing.

Environment

- That therapeutic environments are created to provide a 'safe' environment for service delivery;

- That aftercare forms a key element in service provision.

Developing a service in Scotland

Recent developments in Scotland afford an opportunity to examine the development of a service for women based on these characteristics. The recognition of a need for innovative practice followed a period of crisis surrounding the imprisonment of women and raised questions around the criminal justice system response to women. The developments which ensued illustrate the importance of locating programmes within an environment that enables effective and meaningful work to take place.

During the late 1980s, criminal justice responses to women began to attract increasing attention from policy makers and practitioners in Scotland for a number of reasons. First, the number of young women appearing before the courts increased, largely attributable to an increased incidence of drug misuse (primarily heroin) among young women. Second, as the number of women charged with offences increased, academics, practitioners and policy makers began to question the appropriateness of existing sentences and associated interventions for women (Dobash and Gutteridge 1986; Carlen 1990; Gelsthorpe and Morris 1990).

Third, and perhaps most influentially, a series of seven suicides in 30 months at HMP and YOI Cornton Vale (between 1995–1997), Scotland's only prison for women, resulted in a wide-ranging review of the use of imprisonment and non-custodial sentences for female offenders. Although no single reason for the suicides emerged from the subsequent fatal accident enquiries, a history of drug misuse and withdrawal problems shortly after being incarcerated was a common experience among the women who died.[1]

These factors resulted in a wide-ranging review of the use of imprisonment and non-custodial sentences for women in Scotland. The review, *Women Offenders: A Safer Way* (Social Work Services and Prisons Inspectorate 1998), concluded that 'the backgrounds of women in prison are characterised by experiences of abuse, drug misuse, poor educational attainment, poverty, psychological distress and self-harm'

(1998: 13). It also produced a number of recommendations aimed at keeping women out of prison where possible and at improving the conditions for those who were, by necessity, detained. It concluded that the backgrounds of women who offend and the circumstances which lead to their offending meant that prison was, for the most part, an inappropriate and potentially damaging disposal for this group.

Following the recommendations in *A Safer Way*, an Inter-Agency Forum was set up to establish services for women in the criminal justice system. The Inter-Agency Forum recommended, among other things, the creation of 'Time Out' Centres to provide residential and non-residential support services for women, focusing primarily on those with addictions. The underlying principle was that women should be able to get 'time out' of their normal (and often chaotic) environment without resorting to 'time in' custody, where many of them were being placed. A Ministerial Working Group on Women's Offending subsequently took forward the work of the Forum. The Ministerial Group's report, *A Better Way* (Scottish Executive 2002), recommended greater emphasis upon alleviating the social circumstances that lead some women to offend, intervening early to ensure that women's needs could be met without recourse to imprisonment, promoting the use of the full range of community disposals (including 'Time Out' Centres) and shifting the penal culture away from punishment and towards rehabilitation and 'treatment'. The 'Time Out' Centre, or 218 as it is now called after its location at 218 Bath Street in Glasgow, was established in August 2003 and opened its doors to women in December 2003.

Implementation issues

218 was designed to address the needs of women involved with the criminal justice system in Glasgow, a high proportion of whom have issues with addictions. In particular 218 was intended to provide a service for women who would otherwise have been imprisoned. Research in Cornton Vale (Loucks 1998) found that women in prison in Scotland shared characteristics of abuse, drug misuse, poverty, poor education, psychological distress, and histories of self-harm. In this sense they are similar to female prisoners internationally (Loucks 2004).

The original emphasis of 218 was on alleviating the social circumstances that lead some women to offend, early intervention to meet the needs of women (with addiction prominent among these), and promoting the use of the full range of community disposals, with the ultimate aim of reducing reoffending and consequently the number of women who end up in custody. Specifically, its objectives are to:

- provide a specialist facility for women subject to the criminal justice system;
- provide a safe environment for women in which to address offending behaviour;
- tackle the underlying causes of offending behaviour;
- help women avert crises in their lives;
- enable women to move on and reintegrate into society.

As such, 218 was an innovative project responsible for providing services for women in a relatively unique way. Initial funding was comparatively generous to ensure that the Centre made the planned services available to women in-house. This created benefits to service users, who were able to access support from different agencies in one location, and a number of difficulties in the staffing and managerial structures, some of which have yet to be resolved. These difficulties generally related to multi-agency working and the management of multi-professional teams – problems not unique to 218 (Eley *et al.* 2002; Malloch *et al.* 2003; Popham *et al.* 2005).

Workers from a range of agencies are located within 218, providing a unique feature of the service. They include a Health Team leader, responsible for co-ordinating health services in 218; a number of health professionals, including additional nursing staff; a District Nurse; two Community Psychiatric Nurses; a psychologist; an Occupational Therapist; a Women's Health nurse; and part-time services contracted in by 218 from GPs, a physiotherapist, an acupuncturist, a dietician, a dentist, and a psychiatrist. A solicitor from the Public Defence Solicitors Office (PDSO) visited the residential unit once a week to give advice to clients who had no other representation.

Most workers in the 218 project had some sort of experience in the field of addictions, counselling, and social care before coming to 218, including a number who had previously worked for Turning Point Scotland[2]. At the outset, all staff (including those from outside agencies) had four weeks' residential training in counselling skills and trauma, followed by six weeks of programme development. Ongoing training included Solution Focused Therapy, Cardiopulmonary resuscitation (CPR), and training on new systems of paperwork as they developed. All members of staff were also trained to give ear acupuncture (found to be effective in controlling withdrawal symptoms) and Indian Head Massage as a relaxation technique. Many were pursuing further qualifications in counselling skills.

At least as important as training was an expectation of certain attitudes amongst the staff hired at 218. One member of staff described it like this:

> I think we share a value system. We share values and share goals ... Personal honesty matters, ... consistency matters. And ... non-judgment matters. And I think that is a rare thing to achieve in an institution ... that's the indefinable 'other'-ness about the project ...

Another staff member described things like this:

> ... we were all brought on because of our attitude, because of the people we were, rather than the skills we had. Although we are all very skilled at lots of different things, there were lots of levels of ... education and experience and all that. But it was the type of people we were ... feisty and having attitude and not just going with the flow. It was about fighting for stuff and fighting for clients.

This emphasis on relationships came out strongly in clients' assessments of the value of 218 as a service. Equally, physical conditions reflect the value a service places on its clients, intentionally or otherwise (Wood 2005), and the new service at 218 excelled in creating a comfortable and welcoming atmosphere.

Referral

218 was set up to provide a service for women in the criminal justice system aged 18 years or over who are particularly vulnerable to custody or re-offending and who may have an addiction. Women access 218 from courts, from prison, as part of a court order, through a referral from other agencies (criminal justice or otherwise), or through self-referral,[3] as long as they had been in custody (including police custody) at some time within the last year. In practice clients were indeed referred from a variety of sources. While many of these were not direct referrals from criminal justice agencies, the majority

were related to criminal justice services in some way. Some women needed to be referred a number of times before they engaged in the service. The initial court assessment and a three-stage formal process of assessment were designed to determine which women were ready to engage in the service. The women referred to 218 were all clearly vulnerable women at (usually immediate) risk of physical and psychological harm. The characteristics of service users replicated those of women who end up in prison in Scotland, indicating that the target group for referral and engagement was being identified appropriately.

Referrals from pivotal criminal justice sources such as sentencers did not begin until 218 had been operating for over a year. This meant that initial referrals often related to women whom stakeholders considered to be 'on the path' to custody rather than at immediate risk. Women who referred themselves to 218 often defined themselves in this way too or, more often, believed they were likely to die without some sort of meaningful help:

> When I went there ... the state my health was in ... I got took
> in right away because I was, em, what do you call that ...
> Interviewer: Dying?
> Aye well (laughter) ... 'high priority'.

As the service developed, the proportion of direct criminal justice referrals increased, with more women accessing the service as a direct alternative to custody. However the service was initially developed to prevent reoffending, to provide alternative methods for dealing with women who offend, and to tackle the underlying causes of offending behaviour.

The 343 women referred to 218 between 1 April 2004 and 31 March 2005 were 30 years old on average and came predominantly (but not exclusively) from the Glasgow area. Two-thirds (67%) had at least one child, though only 15% were primary carers on entry to 218. Few had experience of employment, and educational achievements were low. Clients suffered from poor physical health, 83% suffered from depression, and 45% had self-harmed or attempted suicide. Almost half (44%) had no fixed address or were in temporary accommodation. Of women who engaged with 218, 84–97% had used heroin, and 52% had problems with alcohol. The average cost of their substance use was £61 per day[4], though ranged from 0–£500 per day. The highest proportion of women (70%) had committed offences of shoplifting or other theft. While all had been in police custody at some point, only

40% had been remanded or sentenced to custody. About half (49%) had been or were currently on probation.

One hundred and forty three women (42% of those referred) engaged with 218 at least once. Levels of engagement were highest among women referred by non-criminal justice agencies; levels of engagement were highest among women referred by non-criminal justice agencies (e.g. organisations supporting women to exit prostitution). The suggestion that people who self-refer may be more likely to benefit from the service was not a consistent view but was one that both staff and clients shared.

Reasons women did not engage with services at 218 were not always clear. Women sometimes failed to turn up for one or more of their assessments, despite repeated attempts from the assessment team to encourage contact. Clients themselves said people did not engage until they were ready to do so and that the three assessments were a useful means of determining who was ready.

Service provision

218 is a distinctive service which provides 'holistic' care for women involved with the criminal justice system. Services include health care, prescribing, psychological and psychiatric services, alternative therapies such as acupuncture and massage, as well as access to relevant self-help resources such as Alcoholics Anonymous or Narcotics Anonymous, emotional and practical support on an individual and group basis, and structured programmes. Services were available on a residential basis or as a day programme, depending on the needs of the individual client. Importantly for the clients, timing for services were flexible. Programmes could take into account the personal circumstances of the women, and other agency providers recognised the importance of the broad remit of services at 218:

> Well, the overall thing is to try and deal with root causes of women's offending and substance use. Whether that be mental health problems or housing, poverty or any relationship issues or whatever. It's to try and address and tackle the root causes ... (Health professional)

Staff perceived client input as a means both of empowering women and of building relationships with them:

... we are supposed to be taking a person centred approach and involved in negotiation and communication, it's not 'right come in, sit down, I'll do this up for you and here's what you're going to do'. It wouldn't help to build relationships if we came at it from that side, so yes, the woman should be involved all the way along in the process and have a say, have an opinion, and is entitled to all that. (Residential staff member)

A number of factors seemed to set 218 apart from other services. For the most part this centred on the quality of the relationship between clients and staff. This is not to say that quality relationships do not develop elsewhere; rather, relationships comprised the main focus of the service at 218. Another difference was its focus on women. Literature on female offenders continually emphasises the need for programmes designed specially for women rather than merely adapted from a male-centred treatment model or 'added on' to programmes for men (see for example Bloom *et al.*. 2003; Covington 1998). The programme at 218 was designed with this in mind, building on work that had been started in the Turnaround[5] project for women with addictions. The emphasis was both on delivering a programme designed specifically for women and, at least as importantly, creating a safe environment in which to deliver it.

A 'women only' service

Responses from clients were slightly mixed on the need for an all-female environment. Criticisms referred to the 'bitchiness' of an all-female environment and the need for a male presence to temper this. In contrast, some women indicated that their time at 218 had provided the first opportunity to develop meaningful relationships with other women. Overall, both clients and staff were supportive of a women-only service (see also Rumgay 2004). One client commented that '... a lot of the women are quite vulnerable when they are coming off drugs, and the guys know that, and they take advantage of that', while a member of residential staff said that 'apart from anything else, it gives the women time ... to concentrate on themselves.' Relationships with the (few) men who worked at 218 were particularly important in this context, as one client described:

> With it being a women only project, because I have got a lot of issues with men, which makes this place so much better, and so much safer, which I think a lot of people have to be honest with you. That's why I think it works so well, because it's all women ... They keep it to a minimum of men on the staff as you know, and even then the male staff are fine, I don't know, they seem to hand pick them ...

Women actively praised the regime at 218 and believed it addressed their needs. Some criticism was made of policies regarding family contact and time out of the building for residential service users, but most women also understood and accepted reasons for restrictions. Staff also believed the support at 218 was appropriate and that its strength lay in the emphasis on relationships with service users. Some members of staff were concerned that a time-limited service relegated the residential unit to crisis intervention, though longer-term support was available through the day programme.

The support available to help women address problematic substance use, from both health and addiction workers, was seen as a crucial component of the service. The availability of ongoing support was important in the prevention of relapse. Interviews with all respondents illustrated the important correlation between substance use and offending. Notably, 52 women (83% of those interviewed) said their drug use and/or alcohol use had decreased or stopped (mostly the latter) at the time of interview. Reducing or ending substance use was considered an important way of reducing or ending offending behaviour, as other research suggests (Hough *et al.* 2003; McIvor 2004b). This also had a significant impact on other areas of the women's lives, with 42 women (67% of those interviewed) providing specific examples of direct improvements to their health and well-being as a result of attending 218.

Childcare issues

While 218 can access facilities for children while women attend day-programmes, the residential unit had no provision for children. The literature is divided regarding assistance with childcare for women in treatment. Bloom and McDiarmid (2000) note that engagement with families, particularly with children, can be highly effective in programmes for women. Chapple (2000: 34) states that 'involving the children of a female offender in a residential program often helps to keep the woman in treatment', in which case the woman herself should retain primary responsibility for her children, and any residential facility must be designed to serve the children as well as the mother. Critics of this approach (i.e. respondents interviewed in Fairweather, Loucks and McIvor 2003) expressed concern about the disruption for children. If a woman fails to complete a programme, for example, the child as well as the mother must leave, and the child may feel he or she has somehow failed.

Other authors, such as Jacobs (2000), argue that women need to focus on themselves first, then move gradually towards reunification with their children. Non-residential programmes tend to be organised in this way. Some programmes offer childcare on site, though other service providers believe this is too distracting for programme participants (see discussion in Fairweather, Loucks and McIvor 2003). Other programmes provide childcare allowances for the women. The Asha Centre for Women in England, for example, gives women the option of an on-site crèche or an allowance to arrange their own childcare (Rumgay 2004). The on-site crèche enables staff to watch the children's behaviour and to offer mothers information and assistance.

The logic behind 218's decision not to provide facilities for children was based on a number of practical considerations. First, the staff noted that the women who come to 218 need time to concentrate on themselves rather than on dealing with their children. Second, they believed childcare facilities should be designed specifically for children and not as an 'add-on' to a facility designed to address criminal justice issues: the belief was that children should have support in their own right rather than because of the status of their parents. Child protection was a concern here, not least because of the chaotic and unpredictable behaviour of the client group. Perhaps surprisingly the clients agreed with this approach, and only one expressed difficulty in making arrangements for her children.

Linking women with other services

Creating a holistic service to address the needs of female offenders is an ambitious prospect and not without its difficulties. Awareness of 218 initially seemed limited amongst agencies that were expected to have a keen interest in the programmes there. Staff were required to increase the profile of 218 while, at the same time, attempting to link women in with other services. This situation gradually improved, and

218 staff continue to make active attempts to inform key agencies and services of their work.

Links with services to enable women to move on from 218 were generally good. Twenty-one of the women interviewed indicated that they had been referred to other services from 218, including counselling, training or other support. More consistent problems existed in terms of finding suitable housing for service users and to some (often related) extent, accessing community-based prescribing services and addiction workers. Nevertheless sixteen women said that 218 had helped them find stable accommodation, when it had previously been unstable. Problems which arose were generally due to difficulties ensuring appropriate provision was available where and when it was needed, often at fairly short notice.

Outcomes and effectiveness

The effectiveness of a service like 218 is often difficult to measure in quantifiable terms, particularly in light of its broad remit and changes in its structure over the course of the initial evaluation. Statistics regarding changes in sentencing patterns and criminal justice outcomes were not available during the evaluation, as any meaningful attempt to establish reconviction data requires a two-year follow up period. Nonetheless, interviews with sentencers and prosecutors showed that they make use of 218 and value it as a resource. In individual cases, referrals to 218, through diversion from prosecution or direct bail, often successfully prevented female offenders from entering custody, at least in the short term, and women who engage with services at 218 will likely avoid custody in the short and longer term. Importantly staff at 218 viewed relapse as a normal part of recovery and worked to re-engage the women rather than label them as failures.

The absence of measurable outcomes made cost-effectiveness impossible to assess during the course of the evaluation. Comparisons of costs, however, determined that the average cost per engagement at 218 (£7,701), equalled the cost of 2.6 months in prison. The average length of stay at 218 was 2.6 months, but this is based only on those cases where complete information was available. Data on the length of time spent at the project were missing or incomplete for just over half of the women, often because they were still engaged with the project. This evaluation and other previous research demonstrated numerous benefits associated with the range and level of services provided at 218 which are not offered over the course of short-term custodial sentences. However, limiting measurements to quantifiable and immediate criminal justice outcomes misses the contribution 218 was likely to make to longer-term crime prevention and to the lives of the women.

Conclusions

Research clearly shows that substance misuse is often central to women's offending, but also that this cannot be addressed in isolation from the contextual factors that both initiate and perpetuate this. Addressing women's addictions is critical both to reduce their involvement in offending and to address the overarching chaos in their lives. The context of women's lives differ significantly from many men's and consequently requires different approaches in the development of appropriate services.

Projects such as the 218 Centre in Glasgow demonstrate the value of a woman-centred approach to the clients who use it, even where its impact is difficult to measure in quantifiable terms. The centrality of relationships in engaging women with addictions, in conjunction with a flexible and comprehensive service, was crucial according to workers, women using the service and other agencies. Programmes in themselves are of little use unless they are located within a context that is conducive to engagement and meet the broader issues that appear to characterise the lives of women caught up in the criminal justice system, namely trauma, addiction, and family issues.

Notes

1 A further seven women have since died at Cornton Vale.
2 Turning Point is a non-governmental drug support service currently contracted to manage 218.
3 Self-referral is no longer possible due to increased emphasis on the criminal justice remit of the Centre.
4 This figure includes alcohol use, which tended to cost much less or be acquired through theft.
5 Turnaround was a specific project within Turning Point Scotland for female drug users in the criminal justice system.

References

Addaction (2005) *Aftercare Consultation 2005: The Service User Perspective.* London: Addaction.

Audit Commission (2002) *Changing Habits: The Commissioning and Management of Community Drug Treatment Services for Adults.* London: Audit Commission.

Bloom, B. (2005) *Creating Gender-Responsive Services for Women in the Criminal Justice System: From Research to Practice.* Paper presented at conference 'What Works with Women Offenders' University of Monash, Prato, Italy, July 2005.

Bloom, B. and Covington, S. (1998) *Gender-Specific Programming for Female Offenders: What is it and Why is it Important?* Paper presented at the 50th Annual Meeting of the American Society of Criminology, Washington, DC., November.

Bloom, B. and McDiarmid, A. (2000) 'Gender-responsive Supervision and Programming for Women offenders in the Community.' In *Responding to Women Offenders in the Community.* Washington DC: National Institute of Corrections.

Bloom. B., Owen, B. and Covington, S. (2003). *Gender Responsive Strategies: Research, Practice and Guiding Principles for Women Offenders.* US Department of Justice: National Institute of Corrections.

Cann, J. (2006) *Cognitive Skills Programmes: Impact on Reducing Reconviction Among a Sample of Female Prisoners.* London: Home Office Findings 276.

Carlen, P. (1990) *Alternatives to Women's Imprisonment.* Milton Keynes: Open University Press.

Chapple, K. (2000) 'Community Residential Programming for Female Offenders and Their Children.' In *Responding to Women Offenders in the Community.* Washington DC: National Institute of Corrections, USA.

Cook, S. and Davies, S. (eds.) (1999) *Harsh Punishment: International Experiences of Women's Imprisonment.* Boston, MA: Northeastern University Press.

Covington, S. (1998) 'Helping Women Recover', *Correctional Journal.* New York: Jossey-Bass.

Covington, S. and Bloom, B. (2004) *Creating Gender Responsive Services in Correctional Settings: Context and considerations,* Paper presented at 2004 American Society of Criminology Conference, Nashville, November 17–20.

Department of Correctional Services (2002). *Illicit Drugs and Correctional Services.* Issues Paper for South Australian Drugs Summit (unpublished).

Dobash, R. and Gutteridge, S. (1986) *The Imprisonment of Women.* London: Blackwell.

Drugscope (2005). *Using Women.* London: Drugscope.

Effective Interventions Unit (2002) *Integrated Care for Drug Users: Principles and Practice.* Edinburgh: Scottish Executive.

Eley, S., Malloch, M., McIvor, G., Yates, R. and Brown, A. (2002). *Glasgow's Pilot Drug Court in Action: The First Six Months.* Edinburgh: Scottish Executive.

EMCDDA (2001). *An Overview Study: Assistance to Drug Users in European Prisons.* Portugal: European Monitoring Centre for Drugs and Drug Addiction.

Fairweather, C., Loucks, N., and McIvor, G. (2003) *Airborne Initiative: Development of Programmes for Female Offenders.* Unpublished report prepared for the Airborne Initiative. Braidwood: Airborne Initiative.

Fowler, V. (2001). *Drug Services for Youth and Women in Prisons in Europe.* London: ENDSP and Cranstoun Drug Services.

Gelsthorpe, L and Morris, A. (1990) *Feminist Perspectives in Criminology.* Milton Keynes: Open University Press.

HM Inspectorate of Prisons for Scotland (2004) *HMP and YOI Cornton Vale.* Edinburgh: Scottish Executive.

HM Inspectorate of Prisons for Scotland (2006) *Report on HMP and YOI Cornton Vale.* Edinburgh: Scottish Executive.

Holloway, K., Bennet, T. and Farrington, D. (2005). *The Effectiveness of Criminal Justice and Treatment Programmes in Reducing Drug-Related Crime: A Systematic Review.* London: Home Office Online Report 26/05.

Home Office (2003). *The Substance Misuse Treatment Needs of Minority Prisoner Groups: Women, Young Offenders and Ethnic Minorities.* Home Office Development and Practice Report 8. London: Home Office.

Home Office (2004). *Statistics on Women and the Criminal Justice System 2003.* London: Stationary Office.

Hough, M., Clancy, A., McSweeney, T. and Turnbull, P. (2003) *The Impact of Drug Treatment and Testing Orders on Offending: Two Year Reconviction Results.* London: Home Office Findings 184.

Howard League for Penal Reform (2000). *A Chance to Break the Habit: Women and the Drug Treatment and Testing Order.* London: Howard League.

Hume, L. (2001). *Programming for Substance Abusing Women Offenders.* Canada: Correctional Services Canada.

Inter-agency Forum on Women's Offending (2001) *Second Year Report,* Edinburgh: Scottish Executive Justice Department.

International Centre for Prison Studies (2005) *World Prison Brief,* London: Kings College London, http://www.kcl.ac.uk/depsta/rel/icps/worldbrief

Jacobs, A. (2000) 'Give 'em a Fighting Chance: The Challenges for Women Offenders Trying to Succeed in the Community,' In *Responding to Women Offenders in the Community.* Washington DC: National Institute of Corrections.

Koons, B., Burrow, J., Morash, M. and Bynum, T. (1997). 'Expert and Offender Perceptions of Program Elements Linked to Successful Outcomes for Incarcerated Women', *Crime and Delinquency*, 43 (4): 512–32.

Loucks, N. (1998) *HMPI Cornton Vale: Research into Drugs and Alcohol, Violence and Bullying, Suicides and Self-Injury, and Backgrounds of Abuse*. Occasional Paper 1/98. Edinburgh: Scottish Prison Service.

Loucks, N. (2004) 'Women in Prison', In G. McIvor (ed.) *Women Who Offend*. London: Jessica Kingsley Publishers, 142–58.

Loucks, N., Malloch, M., McIvor, G. and Gelsthorpe, L. (2006) *Evaluation of the 218 Centre*. Edinburgh: Scottish Executive.

Malloch, M. (2000) *Women, Drugs and Custody: The experiences of women drug users in prison*. Winchester: Waterside Press.

Malloch, M. (2004a) 'Women, Drug Use and the Criminal Justice System'. In G. McIvor (ed.) *Women Who Offend*. London: Jessica Kingsley Publishers Research Highlights 44.

Malloch, M. (2004b) 'Missing Out: Gender, Drugs and Justice'. *Probation Journal*, 51 (4): 295–308.

Malloch, M., Eley, S., McIvor, G., Beaton, K. and Yates, R. (2003) *The Fife Drug Court in Action: The First Six Months*. Edinburgh: Scottish Executive.

McCampbell, S. (2005). *Gender-Responsive Strategies for Women Offenders*. Washington DC: US Department of Justice/National Institute of Corrections.

McDonald, M. (2004) *A Study of Existing Drug Services and Strategies Operating in Prisons in Ten Countries from Central and Eastern Europe*. Warsaw, Poland: Cranstoun Drug Services, Central and Eastern European Network of Drug Services in Prison.

McIvor, G. (ed) (2004a) *Women Who Offend*. London: Jessica Kingsley Publishers.

McIvor, G. (2004b) *Reconviction Following Drug Treatment and Testing Orders*. Edinburgh: Scottish Executive Social Research

McIvor, G., Barnsdale, L., Eley, S., Malloch, M., Yates, R. and Brown, A. (2006) *The Operation And Effectiveness Of The Scottish Drug Court Pilots: Final report to the Scottish executive justice department*. Edinburgh: Scottish Executive.

National Offender Management Service (2005) *Population in Custody*, July 2005. London: Home Office.

Popham, F., Brown, A., Eley, S., Malloch, M., McIvor, G., Murray, C., Piacentini, L., Walters, R., Murray, L., Christie, A. and Ruffell, R. (2005) Evaluation of the Hamilton Sheriff Youth Court, Report to the Scottish Executive Justice Department. Edinburgh: Scottish Executive.

Ramsey, M. (ed.) (2003) *Prisoners' Drug Use and Treatment: Seven Research Studies*. London: Home Office Research Study 267.

Rumgay, J. (2004). *The Asha Centre: Report of an Evaluation*. London: London School of Economics.

Scottish Drugs Forum (2003) *Submission to the Scottish Executive Review of Treatment and Rehabilitation Services*, Edinburgh: SDF.

Scottish Executive (2002). *A Better Way: The Report of the Ministerial Group on Women's Offending*. Edinburgh: Scottish Executive.

Scottish Executive (2006) *Prison Statistics Scotland, 2005/06.* Edinburgh: Scottish Executive.

Social Work Services and Prisons Inspectorate for Scotland (1998) *Women Offenders – A Safer Way: A Review of Community Disposals and the Use of Custody for Women Offenders in Scotland.* Edinburgh: Scottish Office.

Taylor, R. (2004). *Women in Prison and Children of Imprisoned Mothers: Preliminary Research Paper.* Geneva: Quakers United Nations Office.

Wood, T. (2005) 'The Importance of Small Things'. Paper presented at *Tackling Reoffending in Scotland.* MacKay and Hannah in association with Napier University, 23 May 2005, Carlton Hotel, Edinburgh.

Chapter 6

Offending behaviour programmes for women offenders

Sue Pearce

Introduction

In the National Probation Service for England and Wales only offending behaviour programmes accredited by the independent Correctional Services Accreditation Panel are delivered to offenders. Whilst most such programmes have been adapted for use with women and have subsequently been accredited for use with women offenders, the programmes have generally been based on research into the criminogenic need and most effective ways of working with male offenders and there has been debate on their suitability for women. Recent initiatives have looked at the emerging evidence base of criminogenic need for desistence in female offenders and the development of programmes specifically for women. However practical difficulties make delivery of such programmes in the community challenging.

This chapter is based on a paper delivered at the conference 'What works with women offenders' in Prato, Italy, June 20–22, 2005 (Kennedy and Pearce, 2005). The paper examined some of the practical issues involved in delivery of the 'What Works' agenda to women offenders in the community in England and Wales. The paper outlines the arrangements for accrediting programmes for women offenders in England and Wales, emerging information from the Offender Assessment System (OASys) in relation to women offenders and some of the 'unintentional negative consequences' of seeking to deliver gender specific programmes for women offenders in England and Wales.

The Probation Service

The Probation Service of England and Wales is responsible for both managing the offender in line with national standards (both subject to a community sentence and for those with longer custodial sentences on release on licence) and delivering a range of interventions (sometimes delivered in partnership with other organisations). A community sentence can include one or more specified requirements, for example a requirement to attend an offending behaviour programme accredited by the Correctional Services Accreditation Panel. All offenders are assessed pre-sentence using OASys (Offender Assessment System – an assessment tool developed to provide a common offender assessment, risk management and sentence planning system in the correctional services for adults in England and Wales.):

> Criminogenic needs are ... dynamic attributes of an offender that, when changed, are associated with changes in the probability of recidivism. Non criminogenic needs are also dynamic and changeable, but these changes are not necessarily associated with the probability of recidivism (Andrews and Bonta 1994: 176 in Hollin and Palmer 2003).

From this analysis a sentence plan is developed to reduce the risk of harm posed by the offender, and the likelihood of reoffending, by addressing the criminogenic need and enhancing protective factors. One method of delivery of some targets for change in the sentence plan is the offending behaviour programme. Non-criminogenic needs may also be addressed in the sentence plan, for example if they are associated with the ability to access the programme.

Accredited programmes

The Probation Service in England and Wales has been strongly committed to the 'What Works' agenda for many years. The Correctional Services Accreditation Panel (CSAP) is an independent panel of international academics and experts in the criminal justice field that exists to assess the quality of programmes submitted to it by the prison and probation services against published criteria of what is most likely to achieve effective reduction in re-offending.

The criteria include:

- A clear model of change: an explicit model explaining how the programme is intended to bring about relevant change in the offender group (the theoretical basis of the programme);

- How offenders will be selected as suitable for this particular programme and the characteristics of those not be suitable and how these would be identified;

- Targeting a range of dynamic risk factors: how these have been identified as likely to impact on offending for this particular group of offenders;

- The use of effective methods: how these have been demonstrated to be effective with this offender group;

- That the programme is skills orientated;

- How the programme will be sequenced with other interventions, its density (how many sessions a week are delivered) and duration (how long the programme takes to complete);

- How offender engagement and motivation will be addressed;

- How the programme and learning from the programme will be reinforced as part of the wider community order by the offender manager or others;

- How programme integrity is to be maintained. Programmes are manualised and must be delivered as designed. All sessions are videoed so that a treatment manager can quality assure delivery by the tutors. Tutors undergo specific training to deliver the programme and only those so trained may deliver it;

- How the programme will be subject to ongoing evaluation. Ongoing pre- and post-programme psychometrics are used as a proxy measure of outcome with targeted reconviction studies.

The Correctional Services Accreditation Panel will not accredit programmes that do not 'demonstrate in relation to the full range of the accreditation criteria that appropriate consideration has been given to diversity issues'.

The Probation Service is committed to ensuring that all offenders are treated fairly and with respect. This includes ensuring that female offenders are able to appropriately access the full range of sentencing options available to the courts including offending behaviour programmes. However equality of access is not sufficient; making equality of outcome a reality that may need different approaches and/ or additional support. The Probation Service also works closely with Her Majesty's Prison Service (HMPS) and other partner organisations to deliver services to offenders.

What works for women offenders?

The Probation Service is therefore committed to the development of offending behaviour programmes firmly based in the 'What Works' literature, that is they are based on a sound evidence about what is most likely to achieve change and desistence. However, much of the research into the effectiveness of offending behaviour programmes is based on meta-analyses of studies of male offenders. The criminogenic needs have in the main been identified for male offenders and there is debate as to whether the criminogenic needs for female offenders are the same (Hollin and Palmer, 2003).

Until recently the evidence base on the uniqueness of 'criminogenic needs' for women has been limited compared to that of men. This has resulted in a trend to 'adapt' programme material in a bid to make programmes more responsive to the needs of female offenders. However generally speaking women's patterns of offending can be demonstrated to be different from that of men. Analysis of national (England and Wales) data establishes that they are less likely to commit crime or be involved in the criminal justice system or to serve a custodial sentence, and are proportionately less likely to be convicted of other types of offence (Home Office, 2002). There may be different pathways into and out of offending evidenced by the age of first conviction, being more likely to be convicted only once and to have shorter criminal careers. This together with the differences in criminogenic need would suggest that different factors should be prioritised as treatment targets. There may be differences within each need as compared to men, suggesting different treatment targets within specific interventions, and there may be gender specific needs suggesting specific additional interventions, for example with experience of victimisation, as women report high levels of childhood and adult abuse.

OASys provides a structured clinical and actuarial assessment of twelve areas of criminogenic need and identifies likelihood of reoffending by a range of static and dynamic risk factors, and risk of harm indicators. The trained assessor assigns a score to many of the questions, guided by extensive documentation, and the total score for each domain (area of need) can be calculated. Analysis of data in 2005 of distribution of the eleven criminogenic need indicators showed many similarities but some variation between male and female offenders:

- The most frequent criminogenic needs of female offenders were education, training and employability; and relationships and emotional well-being;

- Female offenders had greater frequencies of criminogenic need than males in relationships and emotional well-being, and to a lesser extent in education, training and employment, financial management and drug misuse;

- Male offenders had greater frequencies of criminogenic need in offending information; based on criminal history, alcohol misuse, thinking and behaviour and to a lesser extent attitudes;

- While female offenders had a slightly higher mean number of needs, these tended to be in areas less associated with recidivism, resulting an a lower mean score on OASys predictor of reconviction.

'It is plausible that there are factors solely associated with offending by women' Criminogenic factors among women offenders (Hollin and Palmer, 2003). With this in mind, the prison service and the National Probation Service have been working together, since 2003, on a shared commitment 'to enable female offenders to participate in a range of accredited programmes in custody or the community or a combination of both settings' (Joint HMPS and NPD Strategy Paper, 2003).

The Government's Strategy for Women Offenders was published for consultation in 2000 and a report on the consultation was published in September 2001. The report identified a range of factors that affect women's offending:

- Health
- Housing
- Carer issues (especially child care)
- Substance misuse
- Histories of abuse
- Poverty

Table 6.1 Criminogenic needs by sex of offender (from OASys completed 2003/2004)

Section	% of offenders with criminogenic need	
	Female	Male
1 and 2: Offending information	33	57
3: Accommodation	36	34
4: Education, training and employability	61	56
5: Financial management and income	31	23
6: Relationships	59	35
7: Lifestyle and associates	37	39
8: Drug misuse	37	29
9: Alcohol misuse	24	37
10: Emotional well-being	60	39
11: Thinking and behaviour	44	55
12: Attitudes	18	25
Mean scores		
Total needs	4.41	4.29
Total needs excluding section 1 and 2	4.08	3.72
Total weighted score	56.7	63.8

The Home Office is committed to ensuring closer joint working across government departments to tackle women's offending and encourage the development of more 'women specific' programmes.

The innovative 'Women's Programme' developed by T3 Associates (Fabiano, VanDieten and Pororino) for the National Probation Directorate of England and Wales was the first programme to be developed for accreditation specifically for women and is delivered by female tutors. The programme is constructed very differently from programmes accredited for men and is designed to integrate cognitive behavioural methods with motivational enhancement techniques in order to maximise effectiveness. It is delivered in three phases reflecting motivational states:

> Phase one: Pre contemplation to contemplation;
> Phase two: Contemplation to action;
> Phase three: Action to maintenance;

It also includes tools specific to the programme including a virtual 'group of six' based on the lives and experiences of some of the initial women offenders going through the pilot programme. Feedback from tutors and offenders experiencing the programme has been very positive. Completion numbers however are still too low to draw many conclusions in terms of outcome.

Whilst understanding gender difference is important in reducing women's offending there are a number of tensions in programme development for women that require careful decisions to be made in order to offer the best programme provision to women offenders. All programmes accredited for delivery in the community by the probation service in England and Wales have been accredited for delivery to women and are available to women offenders except sex offender programmes, domestic abuse programmes for perpetrators, and one of two anger management programmes. Evaluation of the programmes is on-going. Although completion numbers are small, analysis in 2005 of pre- and post-psychometric data (General Offending Behaviour Programmes, Interventions Unit, National Offender Management Service, England and Wales) on women offenders completing offending behaviour programmes in the community indicated that they were achieving change in the positive direction at least as much as and on some measures were doing better than, their male counterparts.

Implementation issues

The commitment to an evidence-based practice for programmes for women offenders, and emerging evidence based on offending by women and problems of scale, give rise to dilemmas around what is best practice for working with women offenders. Whilst the programme may be excellent, if we agree that preferred practice in 'What Works' for women offenders is the development of programmes on what is currently known of the evidence base, and implementation of programmes specifically for women, there remain pragmatic decisions to be made.

There are environmental factors which impact on the delivery of women-only programmes. Outside large urban areas there are limited numbers of female offenders for women-only groups. There are also issues of geography, availability of transport and carer responsibilities. Some probation areas have creatively addressed these issues but

Table 6.2 Evaluation measures used

Treatment Target	Measure
• Poor decision making • Lacking of alternatives/ consequential thinking • Personal skills enhancement, development and maintenance • Skills for expanding connections and building healthy relationships	• Social problem Solving Inventory (D'Zurrilla *et al.*, 2003) • Impulsivity Scale (Barratt *et al.*, 1999) • Emotional Control Questionnaire (Roger and Najarian, 1989)
• Poor self management	• Impulsivity Scale (Barratt *et al.*, 1999) • Emotional Control Questionnaire (Roger and Najarian, 1989)
• Pro-social attitudes and values	• Crime-Pics (Frude *et al.*, 1994)
• Enhancing motivation for change • Encouraging personal responsibility	• Stages of Change Questionnaire (McConnaughy *et al.*, 1983) • Locus of Control of behaviour (Craig *et al.*, 1984)

they continue to impact on the delivery of women-only offending behaviour programmes. Issues and challenges include:

- extending waiting time to start a gender specific programme may lead to potential loss of motivation to complete, contributing to treatment delay and the likelihood of new offences in the 'waiting time' and consequent custodial sentence;

- extended travelling time, increasing the punishment component and sometimes difficult to accommodate for some women who are the prime carers of children at school;

- Some women may not share the professional's construct of the value of women only groups and do not want to be denied access to the first available group programme, believing that mixed gender is preferable to a long delay;

- Some professionals may not refer women offenders to programmes believing that the enforced delay to start women only programmes/ extended travel discriminates against the woman;

- Lack of referral may be linked to beliefs of 'setting the woman up to fail' either due to the factors above or by underestimating her ability to manage her other commitments in such a way as to start and successfully complete the programme.

Pragmatically this suggests that, due to problems of scale, it may not always be practical to run groupwork programmes developed specifically for women everywhere, or even to deliver programmes in women-only groups. To seek to do so in the face of these contextual factors may have unintended negative consequences, including custodial sentences for further offences or breach of the order of the court, and lead to women offenders experiencing less positive outcomes than their male counterparts, not necessarily from a lesser impact of the programme but from the implementation of the programme.

In some probation areas the flexibility provided by the accredited One to One programme, developed for National Probation Directorate (Priestly, 2002) while based on the criminogenic needs of male offenders is responsive to a range of diverse needs, and has been valuable in providing access to an accredited programme, where it may not be possible to provide a single gender group.

It is however important that those involved both in decisions about programme development for women and implementation of such programmes in the community do not make unacceptable compromises. Kennedy (2004) identified that the crucial balance is between 'What Works' and 'what can be appropriately implemented' in order to achieve the most effective approach to reducing offending by women. In a joint prison and probation service paper Kennedy (2004) identified four main areas of conflict.

Homogeneity versus heterogeneity

Women offenders are not an homogenous group. They may have different ethnic backgrounds, may be lesbian or heterosexual, have different cultural and religious beliefs, be of different ages, or have needs in relation to disability or as carers. For some women one or more of these characteristics may be more important to how they experience service delivery than their gender. For example an older woman may be more comfortable, and therefore perceive herself to be in safer learning environment, in a group including older men than in a single gender group where all other participants are much younger. The actual number of women offenders (as compared to men) supervised in the community is small (less than ten per cent) and will be at different stages in their sentence; thus, division in terms of diversity produces very small numbers in any one probation area giving rise to real problems of scale. It may be appropriate for some women to receive women-only group provision in custody followed by individual or mixed gender provision in the community. Programmes must demonstrate appropriate consideration to a full range of diversity issues. A minimum requirement for programmes should be appropriate responsivity of tutors and materials to minimise the likelihood of people feeling (and being) excluded.

Evidence versus opinion

There are a number of opinions on models of programme development for women. Some argue that entirely different programmes are needed; others that programmes developed in relation to the evidence base for men will work effectively for women if gender responsive tutors and materials are used. These strongly held views must be balanced against the emerging evidence. There are currently some shared criminogenic needs identified (see above) but no certainty that the need is comparable for men and for women. The impact of past and present victimisation is an issue here.

However it is not acceptable to offer no service or offer no opinion on the likelihood that a programme will impact on reoffending. Similarly it is not acceptable for unsupported opinion to be the basis for the development of programmes for women.

Expert opinion must be based on the current empirical evidence but there is a role for plausible hypothesis carefully tested. New evidence will give rise to better developed programmes

Theory-driven versus pragmatism

Interventions for women may need to address additional treatment targets (for example, experience of domestic abuse/continued victimisation as an adult) and some existing treatment targets in programmes for men may not be relevant for women. There may be training needs for staff in gender awareness if a programme developed for men is to be modified for delivery to women. In practice the only available and relevant accredited offending behaviour programme may be one that has been developed in relation to the evidence base for men. In the community it may only be practical for women to participate in accredited programmes as part of a mixed gender group. If there is a likelihood of negative impact, women should not be required to attend. However it is acceptable for a woman to attend a programme that does not address the full range of dynamic risk factors known to be associated with her risks of repeat offending. Addressing a sufficient range of desistence factors for women attending such programmes should be in the context of the wider sentence plan and referral made to local community groups providing gender specific services.

Programmes versus systems and structure

Unless programmes begun in the custodial setting cross over into the community delivery it is unlikely that large numbers of women serving shorter sentences will have the opportunity to participate in an accredited programme whilst in custody or in a woman-only programme at all. The evidence base however already indicates that programmes are more effective when there is post-programmes support and opportunities to revisit the learning. This requires supervising offender managers (probation officers) to be aware of gender issues to provide this follow up support.

In addition the offender manager will need to have access to information about the range of services available locally to women which may address criminogenic needs/dynamic risk factors and preventative factors that are not treatment targets for the programme.

For some women access to appropriate assistance with care responsibilities may be the overriding factor in a successful outcome. For others the provision of a mentor/volunteer to enhance self-efficacy and provide a bridge from the programme to the wider community resources may be a significant factor in achieving a successful outcome.

The overriding criteria must be equity of outcome. Some decisions about how offending behaviour programmes will be delivered to women offenders whilst intended to be in the offender's interest may have unintended negative impact. It is not acceptable to deny women access to accredited programmes if these are demonstrated to have some positive impact or to insist on attendance if this disadvantages them (for example, de-motivating by delivery in an unresponsive manner; not supporting carers of children to access suitable childcare). Offending behaviour programmes must be implemented thoughtfully to reflect the needs of women.

Conclusion

'What works for women offenders' is therefore problematic both in terms of content of programmes for women (treatment targets based on criminogenic need), providing a safe learning environment, but also in implementing such programmes so that women can access them appropriately.

In order to provide the most effective resources for women offenders to reduce offending the following points have been established for the probation service:

- Women should be enabled to access, where appropriate, a range of accredited programmes to address their needs. Issues of responsivity in delivery and materials must always be considered and carefully implemented;

- Outcomes should be carefully considered in terms of gender and race and other relevant issues of diversity;

- Where need is identified, specific programmes for women offenders should be developed with consideration of practical delivery and follow up issues across both the custodial and community settings;

- All staff delivering and supporting programmes for female offenders should attend gender awareness training to better equip them to responsively implement programmes for women;

- Obstacles to attendance and completion of programmes for women offenders should be actively addressed. This should include both delivery schedules and the wider supporting environment;

- Given the prevalence of women offenders as victims of abuse the importance of providing a safe learning environment should always be considered. This does not necessarily mean women only groups but may do so on some circumstances;

- Women offenders should be encouraged to utilise the wider community resources available to address long term, gender specific needs e.g. domestic abuse advocacy projects, rape crisis etc.

Throughout England and Wales women offenders are able to access a range of accredited programme in the community based on the 'What Works' principles. Selection is based on targeting and suitability criteria established for each programme. Current evaluation data and feedback from the female completers is showing positive outcomes but numbers are too low at the moment for meaningful conclusions to be drawn.

In practice five probation areas in England and Wales currently deliver the 'Women's Programme'. Whilst some women would prefer and benefit from female only provision others, for a diverse range of reasons, would prefer the opportunity to attend mixed groups. Most probation areas provide access to accredited programmes in 'mixed gender' groups (ensuring that whilst women may be in the minority they are not the only woman in the group and that tutor pairs include a woman at all times) or in single gender groups with female only tutors, sometimes in specifically 'female friendly environments, for example, in a local community women's centre. The wider issues around long term support for gender specific need are addressed through the sentence plan objectives.

References

Blanchette, K. (2002) 'Classifying female offenders for effective intervention: Application of the case-based principals of risk and need'. Forum on Correctional Research, 14, (1), Correctional Service of Canada, http://www.csc-scc.gc.ca/text/pblct/forum/e141/e141h_e.shtml

Barratt, E., Stanford, M., Dowdy, L., Liebman, M. and Kent, T. (1999) 'Impulsive and premeditated aggression: a factor analysis of self-reported acts', Psychiatry Research, 86 (2): 163–73.

Chesney-Lind, M. (1997) The Female Offender: Girls, women and crime. California, USA: Sage Publications.

Craig, A., Franklin, J. and Andrews, G. (1984) 'A scale to measure locus of control of behaviour', British Journal of Medical Psychology, 57 (2): 173–80.

D'Zurilla, T., Chang, E. and Sanna, L. (2003) 'Self-esteem and Social Problem Solving as Predictors of Aggression In College Students', Journal of Social and Clinical Psychology, 22 (4): 424–40.

Fabiano, E., Van Dieten. M. and Pororino, F. (2003) 'A Women's Programme: A Programme for Acquisitive Female Offenders'. London: National Probation Directorate.

Farrington, D. and Painter, K. (2004) Gender Differences in Offending: Implications for Risk Focused Prevention. London: Home Office Online Report 09/04.

Frude, N., Honess, T. and Maguire, M. (1994) CRIME-PICS II Manual. Cardiff: Michael and Associates.

General Offending Behaviour Programmes Interventions Unit, The National Offender Management Service, England and Wales.

Her Majesty's Prison Service and National Probation Directorate, England and Wales (2003) *Strategy paper on programmes for women offenders in custody and the community*. London: HM Prison Service.

Hedderman, C. (2000) *Evidence base for a programme for women involved in acquisitive crime*, paper prepared for London: National Probation Directorate.

Hollin, C. and Palmer, E. (2003) *Criminogenic Factors Among Women Offenders. A Literature Review*. London: HM Prison Service.

Home Office (2002) *Statistics on Women and the Criminal Justice System*. London: Home Office.

Kennedy, S. (2004) 'Joint Prison/Probation: Programme development and delivery for female offenders', paper presented to Correction Services Accreditation Panel, Oxford, England.

Kennedy, S. and Pearce, S. (2005) 'An effective and coherent approach to working with female offenders in custody and in the community in England and Wales' paper presented at the international conference *What Works with Women Offenders*, Prato, Italy, 20–22 June, 2005.

McConnaughy, E., Prochaska, J. and Velicer, W. (1983) 'Stages of change in psychotherapy: Measurement and sample profiles', *Psychotherapy*, 20: 368–75.

Priestly, P. (2002) 'One to One programme', manual developed for the National Probation Directorate, England and Wales.

Roger, D. and Najarian, B. (1989) 'The construction and validation of a new scale for measuring emotion control', *Personality and Individual Differences*, 10 (8): 845–53.

Chapter 7

Parole and probation

Chris Trotter

Introduction

This chapter is about probation and parole for women. It discusses the terminology used to identify probation and parole services and the nature of those services. It provides a general discussion about the effectiveness of parole for women, and discusses the general literature about what works in probation and parole supervision. In doing so it canvasses the very limited literature about the differences in effective practices for men and women. Finally, the chapter outlines a project that looked at the effectiveness of parole for women who were released from prison in Victoria, Australia, during 2003.

Terminology

The term probation generally refers to a type of court order that imposes supervision by a probation officer for a period of time on a convicted offender. The period of time generally varies from one to three years. Parole refers to an order that is imposed by a statutory Parole Board which permits a convicted offender to serve part of their prison sentence in the community whilst under the supervision of a parole officer. The proportion of time of their sentence that a convicted individual may spend on parole is generally pre-determined by the sentencing court. Whether or not the prisoner is released on parole, however, is determined by a statutory Parole Board, which in Australia are usually chaired by a Judge of the County Court or Supreme Court.

The terms used to describe these court orders vary across countries and within countries. Probation, for example, is often referred to as a Community Corrections Order, and an offender may be placed on a Community Corrections Order under the supervision of a Community Corrections Officer. Probation may also be referred to as Supervision, with offenders placed under the supervision of a probation officer or a community corrections officer. There is more consistency in the use of the term parole although there may be variation in who determines whether or not someone is released from prison and placed on parole.

What happens to individuals placed on probation and parole orders also varies across countries and within countries. In some jurisdictions, individuals on probation may rarely, if ever, see their probation officer. They may simply be required to sign in at the probation service on a regular basis. Or, they may be required to wear an electronic tag, which allows their whereabouts to be monitored by the probation service with little direct supervision being offered. In other jurisdictions, individuals on probation and parole might receive much higher levels of contact. Intensive probation or parole supervision might involve almost daily contact with the probation or parole service.

The nature of probation and parole

The nature of probation or parole supervision also varies. Probation and parole in the 1970s and 1980s in Australia, when I worked as a probation officer, involved interviewing clients for twenty minutes or so once a week, once a month or once every three months, depending on the stage of the statutory Order. The probation officer would also assist clients to find work or to find accommodation, and give advice about problems with their families. Individual clients were often referred to other agencies for more extensive assistance.

Contemporary Probation Orders in Australia are more wide ranging. They can involve special conditions attached to the order that require the individual to undertake community work, cognitive behavioural group programmes, educational programmes or drug and alcohol treatment. The last decade has seen a great increase in the use of group and individual programmes based on cognitive behavioural principles, offered as part of probation orders, what Vanstone (2004) refers to as the cognitive behavioural revolution in probation in the UK. Whilst in many cases the same programmes are offered to both men and women, there are also specific programmes offered to women. An example of this is the British Home Office Programme 'the real women program' which addresses women's 'relationships, roles, duties, self-esteem and problem solving skills' (Home Office, 2004:1).

The increased use of groupwork programmes in probation and parole has not been without controversy. It has been suggested that the rise of groupwork has been used as a means of social control (e.g. Vanstone, 2004). Certainly it has occurred at a time of increasing use of imprisonment around the world, particularly of women, and at a time when politicians regularly seek to gain political advantage by supporting harsher sentences.

Women and probation and parole

Probation and parole services are offered to both women and men, to juveniles and adults. While women represent a small proportion of the prison population around the world, for example around 9% in the USA (Walmsley, 2006) the proportion of women on community supervision programs is much higher, around 22% in the USA (Festervan, 2003). However, concern has been expressed about increasing use of imprisonment of women in the UK and the insufficient use of probation for women (Gelsthorpe, 2003).

Effectiveness of probation and parole services for women

The research in relation to the effectiveness of probation and parole supervision is equivocal. A number of reviews of studies in the 1970s and 1980s suggested that offenders who received supervision in the community were no less likely to reoffend than those who did not receive supervision (e.g. Martinson *et al.* 1975; Whitehead and Lab, 1989). Some studies have found that prisoners released with supervision have done worse than equivalent prisoners who were released without supervision. Cass and Nelson (1998) found, for example, that young offenders released from residential facilities in Florida, with aftercare, had higher rates of reoffending than those released directly, without aftercare. Moreover, intensive supervision programmes implemented in the 1980s and 1990s in the United States did not show the positive outcomes, in terms of reduced recidivism, which had been hoped for (Petersilia and Turner, 1993). More recent research conducted in the UK has also found that intensive supervision programs are ineffective in reducing recidivism (Moore, Gray, Roberts, Taylor and Merrington, 2006).

Yet, whilst the overall impact of probation and parole supervision may be seen to be minimal, there is increasing evidence that probation and parole can be effective in reducing recidivism in some circumstances. The debate has thus moved in recent years from 'nothing works' to 'what works'. In particular it is argued that if probation and parole officers use certain skills, and if programmes are developed for clients that are based on effective practice principles, they can be successful (Dowden and Andrews, 2004; Trotter, 1996; 2006). There is evidence that programmes offered to individuals on probation and parole that include cognitive behavioural treatment and drug treatment may be effective in reducing reoffending (e.g. Wilson, Bouffard and Mackenzie, 2005).

These studies have generally focused on males or on a general cohort of offenders which may include a small proportion of female offenders. There is however support for the value of probation and parole services for women offenders. As a group, they often face severe problems with accommodation, employment, children and families, poverty, sexual abuse, self-harm, and drug use (see Loucks, 2004 for discussion about the characteristics of female offenders). Some research suggests that women may benefit from supervision which addresses these particular issues. Zanis, Mulvaney and Coviello (2003) found that recidivism was lower (22% compared to 34%) for women with a history of drug use if the women were given early parole to a community based drug treatment facility, compared to women who were paroled directly into the community because of prison overcrowding. Holtfreter, Reisig and Morash (2004) found that community corrections officers who helped women with their housing needs had clients who offended less often. Pearl (1998) also found that women on parole who made use of social services after their release had lower recidivism. A study undertaken in the USA of more than 2000 individuals on probation found that women in this cohort were less likely to be rearrested, when compared to the men in the study, although they acknowledged the paucity of research on this issue (Olsen Alderden and Lurigio, 2003).

A recent study undertaken by the editors of this book found further support for the value of parole for women (Trotter, Sheehan and McIvor, 2006). Several references are made to this study throughout this chapter and thus some details about the study are provided here.

One hundred and thirty-eight women with sentences of three months or more who were due for release from prison in Victoria, Australia, during 2003, were interviewed before leaving prison. The women who were interviewed constituted 58% of the 237 women with sentences of three months or more, who were released from prison in the period of the project. Research officers conducting the interviews gathered information about the women's participation in prison-based welfare programmes and sought their permission to interview the women again approximately three months after their release from prison and again after twelve months. The research officers also sought the written permission of the women to access their police records twelve months after their release. The research officers conducted interviews with 83 women one to three months after their release, and 69 women were interviewed twelve months after their release. The women were released either from the Women's Correctional Centre situated on the outskirts of metropolitan Melbourne or from Tarrengower Women's Prison situated in a rural area about 136 kilometres from Melbourne.

Of the women in the sample, 64 were released on parole and 74 were released without parole. When released on parole, the women were expected to report to the parole officer within 48 hours of their release from prison. In all cases, those women who were given parole undertook intensive parole for the first three months of the parole period. This involved visiting the parole officer twice per week and undertaking one day per week unpaid community work (unless the women had children or full time work). The parole officer also often arranged an early visit to the Social Security agency.

Many of the women had special conditions and were legally required to be involved in programmes such as drug treatment, psychiatric treatment or cognitive behavioural programmes. While access to parole is at the discretion of the Parole Board, no women in the sample were denied parole.

Table 7.1 shows that only one (4%) of the women on parole, who allowed research officers access to the police records, was sentenced to a period of imprisonment within an average of twenty months following her release from prison. On the other hand, 42% of the women who were released without parole, who allowed access to their records, were sentenced to a period of imprisonment in the period following their release.

Although the numbers in the study are relatively small, the differences in recidivism in percentage terms are stark and it is clear from the statistical analysis that this is not a chance occurrence. The

Table 7.1 Imprisonment after release and relationship to parole

	Imprisoned
Paroled	1/25 (4%)
No Parole	14/33 (42%)

Pearson chi square 11.921 p.003

study also used a number of other measures including number of further offences, number of court appearances and self-report, which confirm that the women who received parole had lower recidivism at statistically significant levels. Further analysis of the data suggested that these differences were not related to factors such as prior drug use, prior criminal history, or their age.

It is acknowledged that this study has limitations. In particular, the fact that only 59 women agreed to allow their police records to be examined. Furthermore, access to Corrections Victoria records was not available for the study; hence assessment of risk is dependent on data extracted from the 59 police records. Nevertheless there are a number of factors, which suggest that the results may reflect the benefit of parole for women.

The women on parole received more, and earlier, supervision. On average, the women on parole indicated that they saw their parole officer at least one day after their release. On average, women not on parole saw a welfare worker on average two and a half days after release. Women who received parole indicated, in the interviews twelve months after their release, that they had had more contact with welfare agencies since their release than women who were released without parole (on average, 16 times for those women who received parole; 12 times for those women released without parole) and that they now had fewer problems for which they needed help (34% – 11 out of the 32 women on parole; 66% – 19 of the 29 women not on parole). The women who received parole were also more likely to have accessed welfare services in prison.

The women in this study appeared to be medium to high risk offenders: 71% of women's police records showed evidence of prior illegal drug use; the average number of prior offences was 67; on average the women had received three prior periods of imprisonment; and 88% of the women in the initial prison interview identified multiple problems which could lead to reoffending, from drugs to friendships. The women on parole may also have done well based on the risk principle referred to above, that intensive services were delivered to medium to high risk offenders. Certainly it seems that women particularly benefit from supervision in the community on parole or probation orders.

What works

The notion of 'what works' refers to the idea that reoffending by offenders placed on probation or parole can be reduced by providing supervision and services which research has shown to be effective. 'What works' is part of the terminology and ethos of many probation services around the world.

What does the research say about 'what works'? Much of the knowledge about 'what works' has come from meta-analyses of correctional studies, in particular the work of Andrews and Bonta (2003). The 'what works' principles can be summarised to include: first, a focus on high risk offenders; second, focus on criminogenic needs, in other words helping the offenders to deal with problems which may have led to their offending; third, the provision of opportunities for offenders to learn from pro-social models and reinforce clients' pro-social comments and actions; fourth, a balanced approach by the worker to the dual roles of social control and helping; and, fifth, the provision of relevant programmes.

Focus on high risk

Much of the literature talks about the importance of focusing on high risk offenders rather than low risk offenders. It is argued that there is a relatively large group of offenders who are unlikely to reoffend and are unlikely to benefit from intensive intervention, whereas there is a smaller group of medium to high risk offenders who are more likely to reoffend and more likely to benefit from supervision (see for example Gendreau, 1996; Andrews and Bonta, 2003). For this reason it is important to assess risk levels and to focus resources on medium to high risk offenders.

The issue of risk assessment is a complex one and it has its critics (see Robinson, 2003 for a discussion about the issues). One problem is that while there are clear advantages in providing additional levels of welfare and support services to high risk offenders' risk levels are sometimes used to provide additional punishment. They may be used as part of a sentencing process, which involves increased penalties to high risk offenders, or as part of a post-sentencing process to provide higher levels of surveillance. An offender who is homeless, without family support, with a drug or alcohol addiction, and without employment might receive a harsher sentence or intervention than someone, who does not have these problems but has committed a similar offence. This criticism of risk assessment may apply particularly to women offenders who commonly have multiple problems (Loucks, 1998).

Nevertheless there is some research support for the benefit of concentrating welfare or human service resources on higher risk individuals (Andrews and Bonta, 2003). To this end a number of risk assessment profiles have been developed for use by corrections services. One of the most popular ones is the LSIR (Level of Supervision Inventory Revised) developed over many years by Andrews and Bonta (2003). It is in use in many probation and community corrections services in many English speaking countries, for example, Canada, USA, Australia and the United Kingdom. The LSIR, as well as providing a risk assessment, also helps to identify criminogenic needs, which can inform the problem solving process.

While the LSIR and other risk assessment tools have been developed with mixed populations some studies have suggested that the risk principle applies equally to women offenders and that the LSIR may in fact be more effective in predicting reoffending for women than it is for men (Raynor and Miles, 2006; Andrews and Dowden, 2006).

Pro-social modelling and reinforcement

There is considerable evidence that probation and parole officers who model pro-social values and who reinforce pro-social values in their clients have clients with lower reoffence rates (for example Gendreau, 1996; Andrews and Bonta, 2003: Raynor 2003b; McNeill, 2003; 2005; Trotter, 1990; 1996; 2006). Probation officers do better if they are fair, optimistic, punctual, reliable, honest, do what they say they will do, support their clients' pro-social pursuits such as non-criminal friends, good family relations and work, and are optimistic about the rewards which can be obtained by living within the law. Effective probation and parole officers reinforce pro-social values in their clients. They may also challenge pro-criminal expressions and actions of their clients. The relationship between the use of these practices by workers and improved outcomes has been evident in studies with both male and female juvenile offenders (Trotter, 1990) male and female adult offenders (Trotter, 1996) predominantly female child protection clients (Trotter, 2004) and female ex-prisoners (Trotter, 2006).

While the use of pro-social modelling and reinforcement has been shown to relate to improved outcomes for both male and female offenders there is little support in my studies for the use of confrontation or challenging female offenders. In the study outlined previously, of women after prison, there was no support for services which challenged the client, focused on the offences, or the things that the client does badly (Trotter, Sheehan and McIvor, 2006). Similarly in the child protection study referred to, challenging clients was only effective if it involved suggesting more positive ways of dealing with the situation, acknowledging that the clients' negative feelings were justified or exploring the reasons why the clients felt and acted in the way they did (Trotter, 2004). It is acknowledged that the child protection situation is different to probation and parole nevertheless they do have much in common and the effective practice principles often apply across both situations (Trotter, 2006).

Problem solving/criminogenic needs

Effective interventions in corrections, including probation and parole services, address issues which have led individuals to become offenders. As mentioned earlier the literature reviews and meta-analyses often refer to the concept of criminogenic needs. Criminogenic needs are those needs or problems which are related to offending but which it is possible to change. Obviously age, gender and prior criminal history relate to offending. They cannot, however, be changed. On the other hand, employment, family relationships, drug use, peer group associations, housing, finances, pro-criminal attitudes, may all relate to offending and can be changed. These are criminogenic needs. It is argued that criminogenic needs do not include intra-psychic issues such as anxiety, self-esteem or depression, factors which cannot easily explain offending behaviour (Gendreau *et al.* 1996; Andrews and Bonta, 2003).

There seems little doubt that effective practice in work with offenders involves addressing the client's offence-related problems or needs. At the same time it seems clear that a problem solving process will be more successful in reducing offending if the workers and the clients reach agreement on the problems to be addressed and what is hoped to achieve. This is evidenced in Trotter (1996; 2006) and the general counselling literature is replete with research studies which point to the importance of working with the client's view of their problems (see for example, Hepworth, Rooney and Larson, 2002 for more detail on this issue).

The women after prison study referred to above confirms this finding. The effective services, both in terms of the women's satisfaction with services and the reoffence rates were characterised by: 'dealing with all of the women's problems; being accessible, understanding the women's point of view; and working together with the women' (Trotter, Sheehan and McIvor, 2006:1).

A balanced approach – social control and problem solving

The research consistently suggests that interventions, which focus exclusively on punishment or scare tactics, lead to increased offending (e.g. Gendreau, 1996; Andrews and Bonta, 2003). Similarly interventions which focus exclusively on developing insight or which focus exclusively on the client-worker relationship are unlikely to be helpful (Trotter 1990; 1996).

Much of the work with offenders involves what Rooney (1992) and Jones and Alcabes (1993) refer to as client socialisation or what Trotter (2006) refers to as role clarification: in other words helping the client to accept that the worker can help with the client's problems even though the worker has a social control role. This involves exploring the client's expectations, helping the client to understand what is negotiable and what is not, the limits of confidentiality, and the nature of the worker's authority. The stage is set for effective work once the client begins to accept that the worker can help and once the worker and client begin to reach agreement on the goals of the intervention. This idea is also supported in the women after prison study (Trotter, Sheehan and McIvor, 2006). When the women believed that their worker knew what they (the client) wanted from the service, when the women felt that the purpose of the service was clear, and when they were clear about how information which was given to the worker could be used, the women were more likely to believe that they were helped with their problems and they were less likely to reoffend.

Programmes

As discussed earlier a number of meta-analyses have suggested that structured learning programmes based on cognitive behavioural principles are effective in reducing re-offending (Andrews and Bonta, 2003). Many probation and parole services around the world offer group and individual programmes based on cognitive behavioural principles. These programs, according to Raynor (2003a: 79) 'put together a series of planned and sequential learning opportunities into a cumulative sequence covering an appropriate curriculum of skills and allowing plenty of opportunity to reinforce learning through structured practice' (the Cognitive Centre Foundation website www. cognitivecentre.com describes a range of structured programmes based on the 'what works' principles). Research conducted on the 'reasoning and rehabilitation programme', has shown promising results with male offenders (Raynor and Vanstone, 1996; Pearson et al., 2002).

The value of these programmes for women has, however, been questioned (Cann, 2006). Studies of cognitive behavioural programmes have predominantly focused on male samples with negligible attention to the study of women. Nevertheless, the British Home Office (2004) examined the effectiveness of prison based programmes and found no significant differences in one and two year reconviction rates for 180 women who participated in the programmes when compared to those who did not participate. This was regardless of risk levels of the women. It was apparent however that the services were often delivered to low risk offenders and there were implementation problems with the programmes. It is suggested however, that women have different needs to men and that their problems with mental health, histories of abuse, substance misuse, family relationships and welfare dependency, may be more important factors in their criminality than cognitive behavioural deficits.

Other factors

The literature refers to a number of other practices. For example 'multi-modal' approaches, which rely on a range of intervention methods, are likely to be more effective than those which rely on only one method (Gendreau, 1996). There is also some support for working with families of young offenders (see Corcoran, 2000 for a review of the evidence), for intervention methods which are implemented exactly as designed, and for matching workers and clients according to learning style and personality (Gendreau, 1996; Chui, 2003).

What works with women offenders

It seems therefore that many of the effective practice principles, which apply to work with male offenders, often also apply to work with female offenders. Unfortunately there is very little research in relation to effective practices in the supervision of female offenders. Fergus McNeill and his colleagues (2005) provide a comprehensive review of key practice skills in reducing reoffending and while acknowledging the limited research they point to certain principles which the literature suggests may apply to work with women. They refer to holistic approaches, approaches which focus on specific needs of women such as relationship issues, family and substance abuse and the importance of the worker/client relationship. While these are presented as propositions rather than research findings there is some support for these ideas in the Australian study of women after prison (Trotter, Sheehan and McIvor, 2006). Even though the study focused on specific services such as drug treatment or housing, for example, as well as on the effectiveness of parole, there was a strong tendency for the women to describe the effective services in the same way regardless of whether they were parole or other services.

One interesting finding from the study was the importance the women attributed to their professional workers. At the final interview, one year after the women's release from prison, 64 of the 69 women had either been on parole or had had some contact with welfare agencies since their release. The people they found most supportive

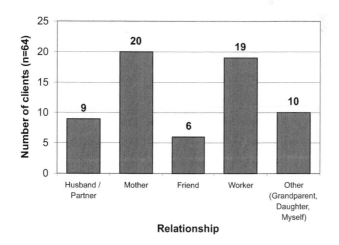

Figure 7.1 Women's responses to who they found the most helpful to them, in the twelve months after release from prison

were other family members, in particular their mother, as shown in Figure 7.2. Nineteen of the 64 women identified a professional worker, whether this was a parole officer, a counsellor or other workers, as the person who had been most helpful to them since their release from prison. This perhaps helps to explain the apparent impact which some workers are able to have on the lives of their clients.

It was apparent from the study that most of the women accessed welfare services of some sort whether or not they were placed on parole. The women were asked at the three month interview if they had contact with welfare agencies since their release and 95% (79 of the 83 women) indicated that they had. Forty-six of the women had seen three or more agencies. The women were asked to nominate the agency they first contacted and the agency that they had most contact with. The agencies that the women were most likely to access, other than Community Corrections, where many were required to attend for supervision, were housing agencies and material aid agencies.

The women indicated that they found the personal support services most helpful as shown in Figure 7.2, which rates how helpful the women found each type of service.

Most of the women felt that the help they received was in the form of support and simply 'being there' rather than any more specific assistance as detailed in Figure 7.3.

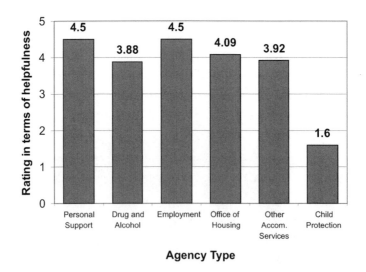

Figure 7.2 Women's ratings of the helpfulness of services after prison

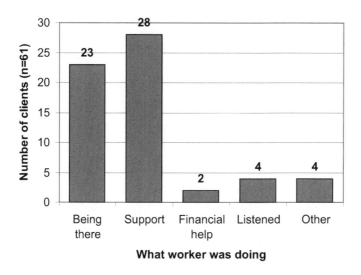

Figure 7.3 What is the worker doing that is helping you?

The women were asked at the final interview to comment on the characteristics of the services and their views about the extent to which the services helped with their problems and reduced the likelihood of reoffending. Table 7.5 refers to the characteristics of the services as assessed by the women and the relationship between these characteristics and whether or not the women reoffended. The results would seem to support comments at the outset of this chapter about 'what works'.

More significant associations were evident between what the women said about their workers and the women's view that the service had helped with their problems and reduced their chances of reoffending.

Conclusion

This chapter has considered probation and parole services for women. It is apparent that at least in some places considerable use is made of community based supervision for women with proportionately fewer women than men receiving sentences of imprisonment. There is some evidence that women may benefit from parole in particular and that the multiple problems which women offenders face may make them

Table 7.2 Women's views about the service and how this relates to re-offending (significant associations in order).

Purpose of service and what worker was aiming to achieve was clear
Worker understands my problems
Worker knew what I wanted from the service
I made maximum use of this service
Worker focused on all the issues that were concerning me
Worker focused on the problems as I described them

Table 7.3 Factors that were associated with women's views that the service had helped with their problems and reduced their chances of re-offending

Service was accessible
Worker and I worked together to decide how we would address my problems
Worker did what they said they would do
I made maximum use of service
Worker focused on all the issues that were concerning me
Worker did practical things for me
I like the worker
Worker was punctual
Worker was concerned about my feelings and my understanding of my own behaviour
Worker understands my problems
Worker focused on the problems as I described them
Worker encouraged me when I said non criminal and positive things
Purpose of service and what worker aimed to achieve was clear
Worker believes that I will not re-offend
Worker is a friend
Worker knew what I wanted from the service
Worker is friendly
Authority worker had and how it might be used was clear
Worker has a sense of humour
Worker believed I can I change
Worker comments on the things I do well

particularly suitable for community based supervision. The evidence about what works in probation and parole supervision has been presented in the chapter and for the most part the principles appear to apply to both men and women. There is some support for the view, however, that women may benefit from a more relationship oriented style of supervision which provides personal support, and a holistic approach to the many problems which women offenders face.

References

Andrews, D.A. and Bonta, J. (2003) *The Psychology of Criminal Conduct.* Cincinnati, USA: Anderson Publishing.

Andrews, D. and Dowden, C. (2006) 'The risk principle of classification in correctional treatment: A meta-analytic investigation', *International Journal of Offenders Therapy and Comparative Criminology,* 50 (1): 88–100.

Cann, J. (2006) *Findings 276 Cognitive skills programmes: Impact on reducing reconviction among a sample of female prisoners.* London, UK: Home Office.

Cass, E. and Nelson, R. (1998) *Juvenile aftercare effectiveness in Florida.* Tallahassee, Florida, USA: Florida Department of Juvenile Justice.

Chui, W.H. (2003) 'What Works in reducing reoffending: Programmes and principles', in W.H. Chui and M. Nellis (2003) *Moving probation forward: evidence arguments and practice.* Harlow, UK: Pearson, Longman.

Corcoran, J. (2000) *Evidence based social work: A lifespan approach.* New York, USA: Springer Publishing Company.

Dowden, C. and Andrews, D.A. (2004) 'The Importance Of Staff Practice In Delivering Effective Correctional Treatment: A meta-analytic review of the literature', *International Journal Of Offender Therapy And Comparative Criminology,* 48 (2): 203–14.

Festervan, E. (2003) *Women probationers: Supervision and successes.* Maryland, USA: American Correctional Association.

Gelsthorpe, L. (2003) 'Theories of Crime', in W.H. Chui and M. Nellis (eds) (2003) *Moving probation forward: evidence, arguments and practice.* Harlow, UK: Pearson, Longman.

Gendreau, P. (1996) 'The principles of effective intervention with offenders in Harland AT' in P. Gendreau (ed.) (1996) *Choosing Correctional Options that Work.* Newbury Park, California: Sage Publications.

Hepworth, D.H., Rooney, R.R. and Larson, J.A. (2002) *Direct Social Work Practice.* Pacific Grove, California: Brooks Cole.

Holtfreter, K., Reisig, M. and Morash, M (2004) 'Poverty, state capital, and recidivism among women offenders', *Criminology & Public Policy,* 3 (2): 181–216.

Home Office (2004) *Focus on female offenders: the real women program – probation service pilot.* London, UK: Home Office.

Jones, J. and Alcabes, A. (1993) *Client Socialisation: the achilles heel of the helping professions.* Connecticut, USA: Auburn House.

Loucks, N. (2004) 'Women in Prison', in G. McIvor (2004) *Women Who offend.* London, UK: Jessica Kingsley.

Martinson, R., Lipton, D. and Wilks, J. (1975) *The effectiveness of correctional treatment: A survey of treatment evaluation studies.* New York, USA: Praeger Publishers.

McNeill, F. (2003) 'Desistance Focused Probation Practice' in W.H. Chui and M. Nellis (2003) *Moving probation forward: evidence arguments and practice.* Harlow, UK: Pearson Longman.

McNeill, F., Batchelor, S., Burnett, R. and Knox, J. (2005) *21st Century Social Work Reducing Offending Key Practice Skills.* Edinburgh, Scotland: The Scottish Executive.

Moore, R., Gray, E., Roberts, C., Taylor, E. and Merrington, S. (2006) *Managing Persistent and Serious Offenders in the Community,* Devon, UK: Willan Publishing.

Olson, D., Alderden, M. and Lurigio, A (2003) 'Men are from mars: Women are from Venus but what role does probation play in probation recidivism?', *Justice Research and Policy,* 5 (2): 33–54.

Pearl, N. (1998) 'Use of community-based social services to reduce recidivism in female parolees', *Women and Criminal Justice,* 10 (1): 27–52.

Pearson, F., Lipton, D., Cleland, C. and Yee, D. (2002) 'The effects of behavioural/cognitive behavioural programs on recidivism', *Crime and Delinquency* 48 (3): 476–96.

Petersilia, J. and Turner, S. (1993) 'Intensive probation and parole' in M. Tonry, M. (ed.) *Crime and Justice: A Review of Research.* Chicago, USA: University of Chicago Press.

Raynor, P. (2003b) 'Evidence Based Probation and its Critics', *Journal of Community and Criminal Justice,* 50 (4): 334–45.

Raynor, P. (2003a) 'Research in probation; From nothing works to what works', in W.H. Chui and M. Nellis (eds) (2003) *Moving probation forward: evidence arguments and practice.* Harlow, UK: Pearson, Longman.

Raynor, P. and Miles, H. (2006) 'Evidence based probation in a microstate: the British Channel Island of Jersey', paper presented at the 6th Annual Conference of the European Society of Criminology, 2006, Tubingen, Germany.

Raynor, P. and Vanstone, M. (1996) 'Reasoning and Rehabilitation in Britain: The results of the straight thinking on probation (STOP) programme', *International Journal of Offenders Therapy and Comparative Criminology,* 40 (4): 272–84.

Robinson, G. (2003) 'Risk and risk Assessment', in W.H. Chui and M. Nellis, (eds) (2003) *Moving probation Forward Evidence Arguments and Practice.* Harlow, UK: Pearson, Longman.

Rooney, R. (1992) *Strategies for Work with Involuntary Clients.* New York: Columbia University Press.

Trotter, C. (1990) 'Probation Can Work, A Research Study Using Volunteers', *Australian Journal of Social Work,* 43 (2): 13–18.

Trotter, C. (1996) 'The Impact of Different Supervision Practices in Community Corrections', *Australian and New Zealand Journal of Criminology,* 29 (1): 29–46.

Trotter, C. (2004) *Helping Abused Children and Their Families.* Sydney: Allen and Unwin.

Trotter, C. (2006) *Working with involuntary clients.* Sydney, NSW: Allen and Unwin.

Trotter, C., Sheehan, R. and McIvor, G. (2006) *Women After Prison.* Caulfield, Victoria, Australia: Department of Social Work, Monash University.

Vanstone, M. (2004) 'A history of the use of groups in probation work: Part two – from negotiated treatment to evidence-based practice in an accountable service', *The Howard Journal*, 43 (2): 180–202.

Wilson, D., Bouffard, L. and Mackenzie, D. (2004) 'The quantitative review of structured group oriented cognitive behavioural programs for offenders', *Criminal Justice and Behaviour*, 32 (2): 172–204.

Walmsley, R. (2006) *World Female Imprisonment List.* Kings College, London: International Centre for Prison Studies.

Whitehead, J. and Lab, T. (1989) 'A meta-analysis of juvenile correctional treatment', *Journal of Research in Crime and Delinquency*, 26 (3): 276–95.

Zanis, D., Mulvaney, F. and Coviello, D. (2003) 'The effectiveness of early parole to substance abuse treatment facilities', *Journal of Drug Issues*, 33 (1): 223–35.

Chapter 8

Responding to the mental health needs of women offenders

James Ogloff and Christine Tye

Introduction

> Female inmates are among the most marginalised groups in society ... The prevalence of childhood and adulthood sexual and violent victimisation, poverty, and poor educational and employment attainment reported by female inmates is nothing short of alarming (Nicholls, Lee, Corrado and Ogloff, 2004:179).

An alarming trend has emerged in recent years: the rate of growth among women in custody has far surpassed the growth rate for male prisoners. The most recent data available from the United States, in a report published in November 2006, shows that in the ten years ending 2005 the number of women in prisons in the United States has risen from 68,468 to 107,518 (Harrison and Beck, 2006). This represents an increase of 57% for women, compared to a growth rate of 34% for men during the same period. Even more alarming, perhaps, is the fact that the increase in those women sentenced to a period of more than one year has increased almost 50% from 1995 to 2005 (Harrison and Beck, 2006). These results show that the number of women in prisons has increased dramatically and they are being incarcerated for longer sentences. Similar findings exist in Australia, where research shows that the number of women in prison increased by 66% from 1991 to 1999, while it increased by 24% for men during the same period (Cameron, 2001).

Another recent study, confirming previous work, found that the rate of self-inflicted deaths among female prisoners was higher than for male prisoners, and that the rate is significantly greater than for people in the general community (Leese, Thomas and Snow, 2006). The study examined all the self-inflicted deaths among prisoners in England and Wales from 2000 to 2002. The rate for women was 2.27 per 1000 compared to an overall rate of 1.14 per 1000 for prisoners. The rate for women was even greater than the rate for males on remand, which was 1.86 per 1000. The rate of self-inflicted deaths in prisons is approximately nine times greater in the United Kingdom than in the general community (Leese et al. 2006). This is similar to the discrepancy between prisons and the community in the United States, but in Canada and Australia, the likelihood that prisoners are more likely to die by self-inflicted means is reduced to 3.5 and approximately 2.5 respectively (Leese *et al.* 2006).

It has been recognised from the early days of women's imprisonment that rates of mental disorder and distress among this group are high (Nicholls *et al.* 2004). However, the majority of the research about prisoners' mental health needs was confined to that of male prisoners for most of the twentieth century. In the 1980s a body of literature emerged focussing on female prisoners' mental health. This culminated in several key studies in the mid-1990s (Maden *et al.* 1994; Jordan *et al.* 1996; Teplin *et al.* 1996). Since this time, a large body of literature has emerged outlining the rates of mental disorder and the mental health needs among women in prison.

In this chapter, we explore the prevalence of major mental illnesses among female prisoners. We then discuss the need to address the mental health concerns of women offenders both in the prison and upon their return to the community. Effective models for mental health services in correctional services require systematic approaches to intake screening for mental illness through to community reintegration and mental health services (Nicholls *et al.* 2004; Ogloff, 2002; Welsh and Ogloff, 2003). We turn now to an overview of the prevalence of mental illness among female prisoners.

The prevalence of mental illness among female prisoners

Clear and incontrovertible evidence now exists internationally which demonstrates that the proportion of people in prisons with major mental illnesses is very high (Ogloff, Davis, Rivers and Ross, 2006). But, just how high are the rates? Perhaps most important, how do they compare to the rates of major mental illnesses in the general community? We begin this section by presenting a particularly important study conducted by Brugha and colleagues in Britain and Wales (Brugha, Singleton, Meltzer, Bebbington, Farrell, Jenkins, Coid, Fryers, Meltzer and Lewis, 2005). Most previous studies have investigated the rates of various mental illnesses in populations of prisoners. While useful, this research makes it difficult to directly compare the rates of mental illness that exist in prison populations with the community. Only when direct comparisons are made can we be sure of the relative rate of mental illnesses in prisons compared to the community.

Brugha *et al.* (2005) used the *Schedules for Clinical Assessment in Neuropsychiatry* (SCAN) to compare more than 3,000 remanded and sentenced male and female prisoners in Britain and Wales and more than 10,000 household residents from the community in Great Britain. The SCAN was developed by a joint task force of the U.S. Alcohol, Drug, and Mental Health Administration and the World Health Organisation (Wing *et al.* 1990). The SCAN is administered as a semi-structured interview to identify Axis I psychotic and non-psychotic illnesses, substance use disorders and organic brain disorders. The overall results revealed that the rate of psychotic illness over the past year for those in the community was 4.5 per 1,000 (.045%) compared with a rate of 52 per 1,000 in prisons (5.2%). While the ten-fold increase in prevalence from the community to the prisons was remarkable, the results revealed further that the prevalence rate of psychotic illness for female prisoners was an astonishing 110 per 1,000 (11%), compared to 50 per 1,000 for males (5%).

The work by Brugha *et al.* (2005) is an important introduction to this area of research. Their work shows convincingly that the prevalence of mental illness is many times greater in prisons than in the general community when the incidence of mental illness is ascertained in the same manner. Moreover, the rate of mental illness among female prisoners is more than twice the rate for male prisoners. Unfortunately, they did not present comparisons of the prevalence of mental illness among female remand and sentenced prisoners. Other research, which has investigated this matter, is summarised below.

Given the growing body of research that exists investigating the prevalence of mental illness among female prisoners, the literature will be summarised here, through the use of tables found in the Appendix as well as an overview of findings presented below. Generally this research can be grouped according to broad methodological categories:[1]

1 Studies that have investigated rates of mental disorder amongst male and female prison populations (Brinded *et al.* 2001; Herrman *et al.* 1991; Maden *et al.* 1994; Simpson *et al.* 1999).

2 Studies that have focussed on sentenced female prisoners (Brinded *et al.* 1999a; Brinded *et al.* 1999b; Daniel *et al.* 1988; Jordan *et al.* 1996; Keaveny & Maden *et al.* 1994; Zauszniewski, 1999).

3 Studies that have focussed on female prisoners who are on remand or in prison (Parsons *et al.* 2001; Singer *et al.* 1995; Teplin *et al.* 1996).

4 Studies that have investigated rates of mental disorder amongst both remand and sentenced prisoners (Denton, 1995; Tye and Mullen, 2006), with some of these studies comparing the two prisoner populations (Hurley and Dunne, 1991; O'Brien *et al.* 2003; Wright *et al.* 2006).

5 Studies that have focussed on new receptions (Daniel *et al.* 1988; Mohan *et al.* 1997; Nicholls *et al.* 2004 ; Parsons *et al.* 2001; Singer *et al.* 1995), or that have compared receptions with a cross-sectional sample of prisoners (Butler *et al.* 2005; Wright *et al.* 2006).

6 Studies that have compared rates of mental disorder amongst women in prison with rates amongst women in the community (Butler *et al.* 2005; Daniel *et al.* 1998; Jordan *et al.* 1996; Teplin *et al.* 1996; Tye and Mullen, 2006).

Methodological considerations

Many of the above studies fit into more than one of the above categories, indicating considerable overlap. However there are also discrepancies between the populations investigated in the above studies. Some of the discrepancies are due to differences in the prison systems in America versus Australia, New Zealand and Great Britain. In the Commonwealth countries remanded and sentenced prisoners tend to be housed in the one facility. In the United States, gaols provide custody for individuals arrested and detained for misdemeanours (typically for sentences up to one year) and for those awaiting trial for serious crimes, while prisons house those serving sentences for more serious crimes. As noted by Powell *et al.* (1997: 429), the differences between the gaol and prison populations have resulted in '... two related but unintegrated bodies of research which provide little insight into one another'.

If these populations are as distinct as Powell *et al.* (1997) suggested, what do studies set in gaols tell us about the prison context and vice versa? Furthermore, how do we apply recommendations from these studies to the Australian context? Perhaps part of the resolution of these methodological issues is the most recent wave of research in the area which has compared new receptions with remanded and sentenced female prisoners (Butler *et al.* 2005; Wright *et al.* 2006).

A second important methodological consideration in interpreting the research on rates of mental disorder amongst female prisoners is the distinction between narrow and broad definitions of mental disorder. Some of the studies that will be discussed have used a broad definition of mental disorder, which has included drug and alcohol-related disorders and/or personality disorders. In contrast, other studies have used a narrow definition of mental disorder, where only major mental illnesses are included. Not surprisingly, it has been found that narrow definitions of mental disorder provide very different prevalence rates when compared to broad definitions of disorder (Corrado *et al.* 2000).

Comparing rates of mental disorder amongst male and female prisoners

It is acknowledged that women in prison have higher rates of mental disorder than their male counterparts; however, only a handful of studies have directly examined this phenomenon. Citing some of the earlier studies investigating this issue (Gibbens, 1971; Gunn *et al.* 1978), Maden *et al.* (1994: 173) noted that 'gender differences are not clear cut'.

In their study, Maden *et al.* (1994) compared a 25% sample of sentenced women prisoners in England and Wales with a 5% sample of sentenced male prisoners. They found no significant gender differences in rates of psychosis, but found that the female prisoner group had a significantly higher prevalence of neurosis, personality disorder, mental handicap and drug abuse when compared with the male prisoner group. These results contrast with those of Brugha *et al.* (2005), summarised at the outset of this section. It is also in contrast to the work by Herrman *et al.* (1991) who found that male and female sentenced prisoners had similar rates of current mood disorder, and that the female prisoners had higher rates of current psychotic disorder than the men.

Perhaps one of the reasons why the gender differences are not always consistent in the literature is that the numbers of male prisoners is vastly greater than that of female prisoners, making meaningful comparison difficult. This inherent difficulty has led to a focus on female prison populations, in an effort to better understand their mental health needs.

The general female prisoner population

Many studies investigating rates of mental disorder among female prisoners have combined the remand and sentenced populations. The methodological design of these studies has either been a reception study, where consecutive new receptions to the prison are interviewed (Mohan *et al.* 1997; Nicholls *et al.* 2004), or a census design where all of the women in a prison at one point in time are interviewed (Brinded *et al.* 1991; Denton, 1995; Hurley and Dunne, 1991; Tye and Mullen, 2006). Wright *et al.* (2006) considered both a reception sample and a cross-sectional sample of sentenced and remanded prisoners in their study.

The reception studies have found rates of substance-related disorders ranging from 58–65% (Mohan *et al.* 1997; Wright *et al.* 2006). Rates of current mental disorder in these studies have varied from 26%–62% depending upon whether the prevalence is based on the previous six or twelve month time frame (Wright *et al.* 2006; Butler *et al.* 2005). Even greater rates of co-morbid substance use disorders have been found for female patients in a forensic psychiatric hospital (74%) (Ogloff, Lemphers and Dwyer, 2004).

After substance use disorders, the most prevalent mental disorders amongst female prison receptions have been found to be affective disorders, particularly major depression, and anxiety disorders, with post-traumatic stress disorder the most prevalent anxiety disorder (Butler *et al.* 2005).

Anecdotal reports would suggest higher rates of mental disorder amongst women recently arrived at prison, when compared with those who have been in prison for some time. When they compared a sample of new committals with a cross-sectional sample of remanded and sentenced women, Wright *et al.* (2006) found higher rates of all categories of mental disorder among the cross-sectional group. The exceptions were psychosis and substance use which were similar for the two populations. This supports the view that prison precipitates mental illness, or at the very least exacerbates pre-existing mental illness. In their study, Hurley and Dunne (1991) found no support for this view when they found no difference in female prisoners' scores on a range of measures of psychological disturbance at time one and at time two (four months later).

Due to the relatively small numbers of women in prison in Australasia, many of the studies from this region have combined sentenced and remanded prisoners using a census design. In their census of female prisoners in New Zealand, Brinded and his colleagues (2001) found that 17% of female prisoners met the criteria for post-traumatic stress disorder in the month prior to interview, while 11% met the current criteria for major depression. They found a current rate of schizophrenia of 4%. Rates of drug and alcohol abuse and dependence were considerably lower than other studies (at 4% for alcohol abuse and 4% for other substance abuse) perhaps partly due to the narrow definition of 'current' rate, where prevalence was based on disorder in the preceding month.

Tye and Mullen (2006) investigated twelve month prevalence rates of mental disorder amongst female prisoners in Victoria, Australia. Using a broader definition of 'current' disorder, they found considerably higher rates of all disorders investigated compared to Brinded *et al.* (2001). In particular, 63% of women were found to have had a drug-related disorder in the twelve months prior to imprisonment, while rates of anxiety disorders (52%), and depressive disorders (45%) were also high. When compared to a community sample, the female prisoner group had a significantly higher prevalence of all disorders except obsessive compulsive disorder and harmful alcohol use.

The above studies have combined remanded and sentenced groups of female prisoners. As noted earlier in this discussion, some commentators in the area have argued that these two groups may constitute quite distinct populations (Powell *et al.* 1997). With this point in mind, the literature on the mental health needs of remanded women and sentenced women in prisons will now be considered separately.

The female remand prison population

The largest study to investigate rates of mental disorder amongst women on remand was conducted by Teplin and her colleagues (1996) at Cook County Jail, Chicago, USA. Drawing on a random sample of 1,272 female gaol detainees awaiting trial, Teplin et al. (1996) investigated six month and lifetime prevalence rates of a range of mental disorders and compared these prevalence rates with community rates. Using a broad definition of mental disorder, where antisocial personality disorder and substance disorders were included, they found that 70% of their sample met the criteria for a mental disorder in the past six months. Apart from substance disorder and antisocial personality disorder, the most prevalent current disorders were post-traumatic stress disorder (22%) and major depressive episode (14%). With the exception of schizophrenia, the women on remand had a higher prevalence of all disorders when compared with a community sample.

In their study, Parsons et al. (2001) interviewed 382 women remanded at H.M. Holloway and H.M. New Hall in England. In findings consistent with Teplin et al. (1996), Parsons et al. (2001) found that the most prevalent disorders in this group were drug/alcohol dependence and personality disorders. Anxiety disorders and mood disorders were also prevalent at 30% and 33% respectively.

The female sentenced prison population

In a study with a similar methodology to Teplin et al. (1996), but this time set in North Carolina, USA, Jordan et al. (1996) interviewed 805 sentenced women entering prison. They found that 46% of sentenced women interviewed met the six month diagnostic criteria for any mental disorder. This is somewhat lower than the six month prevalence rate found in the remand population (Teplin et al. 1996). Replicating the pattern in the above studies, Jordan et al. (1996) found that the most prevalent diagnoses in the sentenced population were drug dependence at 30% and personality disorder, with 28% of women meeting the criteria for borderline personality disorder. By contrast, prevalence estimates for the anxiety disorders were relatively low (in the range of 1–5%).

In their study of 100 sentenced women consecutively admitted to the Missouri, USA, correctional system, Daniel *et al.* (1988) found consistently low rates of panic disorder (at 2%). In a comparison of rates of disorder amongst sentenced female prisoners and women in the community, Daniel *et al.* (1996) found significantly higher rates of all disorders amongst the prisoner group compared to the community group. The only exceptions were anxiety disorders and mania where there were no significant differences.

In summary, the above studies investigating either female remand prisoners or sentenced prisoners consistently found that the most prevalent disorders in these two populations were drug/alcohol disorders and personality disorders. Rates of depression and anxiety disorders were also high in most of the studies reviewed. Another consistent finding is of higher rates of current mental disorder in the studies of the remand population compared to rates found in studies of the female sentenced prison population.

Comparing rates of mental disorder: female prisoners compared to women in the community

An obvious conclusion from studying the data on mental disorders in female prisoners is that for most disorders, the prevalence rates amongst the prisoner group are considerably higher than generally accepted prevalence rates in the community. A select group of studies have statistically compared female prison samples and female community samples with respect to rates of mental disorder (Butler *et al.* 2005; Daniel *et al.* 1988; Jordan *et al.* 1996; Teplin *et al.* 1996; and Tye and Mullen, 2006). Some of these studies have matched women from the community and prison samples according to socio-demographic characteristics such as ethnicity, age, education level, geographic location and/or income (Butler *et al.* 2005; Jordan *et al.* 1996; Teplin *et al.* 1996), thereby reducing the likelihood that any difference in the prison group could be explained by socio-economic disadvantage alone.

The overwhelming conclusion from this group of studies is that women in prison have a significantly greater prevalence of most mental disorders when compared with women in the community. This pattern holds even when the impact of socio-economic factors is controlled for. Not surprisingly, given the consistently high rates of these disorders in the prison population, some of the largest differences between the community and prison samples have been found for drug abuse/dependence and personality disorders (Teplin *et al.* 1996; Tye and Mullen, 2006).

Female prisoners' psychiatric treatment history

Given the high current and lifetime prevalence rates of mental disorder amongst women in prison, an important consideration in the literature has been the extent to which this group have received mental health treatment in the community. In Australia, Herrman *et al.* (1991) matched the names of the 31 female prisoners interviewed with the Victorian Psychiatric Case Register (a database of past contacts with psychiatric services that was in use at the time of the study). They found that 61% of the women had a match with the database. While a proportion of these women had had past contact for substance abuse treatment alone, 48% had received inpatient psychiatric treatment in the past. This methodology is strong because the study relied upon objective means to analyse past contacts with psychiatric services, rather than relying on self-report alone.

Jones *et al.* (1995) used a similar methodology when they matched the names of all women incarcerated in Tasmania between 1981 and 1990 (n = 210) on Tasmania's mental health services database. They found that 35% of their sample had a past psychiatric history.

More recent studies from the United Kingdom have found consistent results using self-report and verification from collateral sources where possible. O'Brien *et al.* (2003) found that 40% of their sample of remanded and sentenced women had a history of mental health treatment prior to imprisonment. Wright *et al.* (2006) found rates of past psychiatric treatment in the community of between 34–40% among their sample of female prisoners in Ireland.

Although these rates of past psychiatric treatment amongst female prisoners are relatively high, they are considerably lower than the rates of overall current and lifetime mental disorder reported in the literature. There could be several explanations for this discrepancy. One is that women in prison are not receiving adequate mental health services in the community. Another is that women's mental health problems are exacerbated by the prison experience (an area that is still unclear in the literature although there is little doubt that for some women incarceration leads to a reduction in mental state).

Summary

Although the number of studies of the prevalence of mental illness among female prisoners is lower than that available for men, the results of the vast majority of studies point to the same conclusion: that the prevalence rate of mental illnesses, including major mental illnesses, among prisoners is very high. Moreover, most properly conducted studies have found that the prevalence of mental illnesses is much higher amongst female prisoners than male prisoners.

There is little doubt that the process of incarceration has some detrimental effect on people's mental state. There is no evidence, though, that incarceration explains or causes mental illness in prisoners – male or female. The fact that most studies show that rates of mental illness are actually greater in remand populations rather than populations of sentenced prisoners convincingly shows that mental illness rates do not in fact increase over time. Relatively higher rates of mental illnesses in remand populations suggest that women with mental illnesses are likely to be arrested and incarcerated sometimes as a result of the mental illness and its nexus with offending behaviour. This is particularly true for relatively minor infractions for which, arguably, people with mental illnesses should not be incarcerated but should perhaps be hospitalised. In the next section of this chapter, we turn to a discussion of the need to respond to the mental health needs of female prisoners.

Responding to the mental health needs of female prisoners

The need for diversion from the criminal justice system

Although the aim of this chapter is to discuss the prevalence of mental illness among female prisoners and to reviews ways for responding to their mental illnesses, one cannot go past the need to divert women with mental illnesses from the criminal justice system wherever possible. It is beyond the scope of this chapter to discuss diversion on detail, but we would be remiss if we did not mention it as a critical element of any sensible systematic approach to reducing mental illness in the criminal justice system and in jails and prisons in particular.[2]

Five specific goals of pre-trial diversion programs flow from the rationale behind pre-trial diversion, the assumptions that underlie it, and the need for mental health services for women with mental illnesses who come into contact with the criminal justice system (Ogloff, 2002):

1   To reduce recidivism, thereby lowering the crime rate.

2   To decongest the criminal justice system, thereby improving cost-effectiveness and allowing prosecutors and judges to attend to more serious offenders who pose greater threats to the community.

3   To provide necessary services (e.g. psychiatric and psychological services, job training) to individuals to better prepare them for the demands of society.

4   To reduce the coercive, punitive social control of the criminal justice system by removing many less-serious offenders from the system.

5   To avoid the negative stigma and labelling (as a 'criminal') that occurs in the formal criminal justice system.

Given the prevalence of mental illness among offenders, the non-violent and minor nature of many mentally disordered offenders' (MDOs') offences, and the lack of appropriate community treatment and residential facilities for MDOs, it is not surprising that many cycle back and forth between the mental health and criminal justice systems. What is needed is an alternative for apprehending and releasing MDOs to the community without appropriate treatment. It is recommended that systematic attention must be paid to developing programs to 'divert' mentally ill offenders out of the criminal justice system, ideally at some point before arrest, or immediately following arrest once they have been screened for mental illness (Ogloff *et al.* in press). Tragically, though, many women with serious mental illnesses make their way into gaols and prisons. For them, it is critical that appropriate mental health services be provided. We turn, then, to a discussion of a systematic approach to the identification and treatment of mental illness among women in custody.

A model for the identification and treatment of mental illness among women in custody

Rather than providing a prescriptive template for mental health services for female prisoners, we provide here a general model of the services necessary to identify and treat the mental health needs of women prisoners. Care must be taken in developing services for particular prisons or correctional services to consider the unique needs and circumstances of the female prisoners.

Before presenting the proposed mental health plan, it is important to review the guiding principles and goals that were considered in developing the plan. Steadman, McCarty, and Morrissey (1989) developed five planning principles after conducting a national study of 43 jails in 26 of the United States. These principles have been considered and expanded upon elsewhere (Ogloff, 2002; Ogloff, Tien, Roesch and Eaves, 1991). The principles are sufficiently broad to encompass the concerns that normally occur when considering the concerns and needs of providing mental health services in jails for women. Therefore, these principles are critical for planning mental health services programmes for prisons:

1   Women in custody with mental illnesses must be treated with dignity and be provided with mental health services consistent with those enjoyed by others in the community.

2   Women with mental illnesses have unique needs compared to their male counterparts. As such, services developed must be tailored toward the unique needs of women.

3   Prison mental health services must be considered a community issue given that prisons, in fact, are part of the community, and prisoners are from the community and are released back to the community.

4   Prisons are and should remain correctional facilities and not specialised mental health institutions. This is not to say that specialised services for mental health assessment and treatment should not be implemented in prisons.

5   There is a need for professional services in every prison, and this includes medical as well as mental health professionals.

6   Traditional boundaries that separate government ministries and agencies must be crossed to ensure that mental health services are provided to those women in need, and to stop women with mental illness from cycling continuously through health, mental health, forensic and criminal justice systems.

7   The core elements of mental health services in corrections include: screening for mental health services (including suicide risk assessment and the identification of dangerous prisoners), assessment, treatment, crisis intervention, as well as institutional and post-release community planning and case management.

8   All people who work with women prisoners with mental disorders must play an active role in the identification and management of them (this includes correctional officers, chaplains, and other staff); thus, it is important to provide training to staff to enable them to identify and manage MDO's.

9   While it is necessary to establish minimum standards of mental health care in prisons, there is no single blueprint for creating a prison mental health programme. Indeed, differences in geography, size of the facility, availability of local resources, and other factors will need to be considered separately for each facility.

10 Programme evaluation should be an integral part of the mental health plan and the information generated by the evaluation will be used to determine the extent to which the plan meets its goals and to help identify areas that may benefit from adjustment and further refinement.

The core elements of mental health services for women in custody include: screening, assessment, treatment, crisis intervention, as well as institutional and post-release community planning and case management. The elements of such a programme will be reviewed below following which some particulars of the programme will be discussed.

Under some circumstances, women in custody may need acute mental health services that are not available in correctional facilities. To determine whether a prisoner is so mentally ill that she should be transferred to a mental health facility, the mental health professional generally conducts an evaluation to identify the existence and severity of any psychopathology (Ogloff, Roesch and Hart, 1993). If the clinician recommends that the prisoner be transferred to a secure mental health institution, a transfer should be arranged in consultation with the corrections staff. This typically involves certifying the woman for involuntary treatment under the jurisdiction's mental health act. Where a prisoner apparently suffers from a mental disorder that is not serious enough to warrant transfer, the goal of the assessment should be to determine whether she would benefit from a programme initiated within the corrections branch.

Given the large number of women offenders who enter prisons, it is not necessary or cost effective to perform a complete mental health assessment on every prisoner. Thus, the model advanced uses a two-tier mental health evaluation process. The first step involves a brief mental health screening for every inmate, once upon admission and then periodically during the prisoner's sentence. Second, those prisoners identified as being mentally ill are referred to mental health professionals for a more complete mental health review.

Most mental health screening in prisons is conducted at the time of admission or following a crisis in which an inmate displays acute psychological problems (Nicholls, Roesch, Olley, Ogloff and Hemphill, 2005). However, inmates may develop mental health problems after incarceration (or their problems may intensify) but before experiencing a crisis episode, fall between the cracks. Therefore, the mental health programmes ultimately adopted by individual institutions must provide mechanisms for monitoring the mental health status of offenders throughout their stay in the institution.

The model for the mental health plan advocated in this report consists of six separate components: intake screening; ongoing monitoring/screening of prisoners; comprehensive psychodiagnostic assessment of MDOs; mental health treatment; gradual/post-release monitoring/supervision and continuity of services; and research evaluation of the program. Each of these components is briefly discussed below.

Intake screening

Given the prevalence of mental illness among female prisoners, and the stress and anxiety that can follow incarceration, all prisoners should be screened for mental illness soon after admission to a correctional facility. The screening should be brief, with the purpose of identifying prisoners who are suffering from mental illness (Ogloff et al. in press). The *Jail Screening Assessment Tool (JSAT;* Nicholls et al. 2005) was developed to screen people being admitted to gaols and prisons for mental illness, as well as self/harm risk and risk of harm to others. The JSAT is designed to be administered by psychiatric nurses or other mental health professionals. Validation data reported by Nicholls and colleagues (2005) indicated that the JSAT has a very high degree of validity. Indeed, 100% of those identified as having psychotic illnesses, obsessive compulsive illnesses, or suicide risk, were subsequently referred to a mental health program. The JSAT has been validated specifically for use with female offenders (Nicholls et al. 2004).

The interviews are brief (i.e. approximately 20 minutes), but provide sufficient information to make initial decisions about the mental health needs of incoming prisoners. The screening procedure includes a brief semi-structured mental status interview and the *Brief Psychiatric Rating Scale*. The interview covers seven content areas: personal/demographic information, suicide risk, orientation to time and space, criminal history, recent social adjustment, recent mental status, and mental health history.

The screening should normally be completed within the first day of admission to prison. The purpose of this screening is to detect serious mental disorder requiring rapid management, treatment, or further evaluation. It is desirable to minimise false negative errors at this screening stage (inmates who have a mental disorder that is not detected). It will allow those prisoners who do have a mental illness to be evaluated further.

Ongoing monitoring/screening of prisoners

The model places heavy emphasis on prevention and early intervention. Therefore, an essential component is a formal process for ensuring that prisoners are monitored, both formally and informally. The system also should encourage self-referrals to facilitate access to treatment services. In addition to formal assessment, those correctional officers who are in frequent contact with prisoners should be trained to recognise signs of mental disorder. Correctional officers should be in a position to detect early signs of mental health problems and to refer these problems to mental health professionals. Because training correctional officers to detect symptoms of mental disorder is inexpensive, ongoing screening and evaluation is feasible in all gaols (Ogloff, 2002). However, once officials detect mental illness, mental health professionals must be available for further assessment and treatment.

In addition to corrections officers, other staff, particularly chaplains, teachers, and others should be drawn upon to assist with monitoring prisoners who have been identified with mental health problems. Moreover, they also should help with the identification of prisoners who have not yet been identified as being mentally ill, but who may develop problems during incarceration.

Comprehensive psychodiagnostic assessment of MDOs

In many cases, of course, an individual's time in prison may be too brief for any further assessment of her mental condition. The purpose of more comprehensive assessment, where possible, though, is to determine mental status and treatment needs of prisoners who are flagged as potentially mentally ill during the initial screening or subsequent monitoring process. Again, the emphasis of all mental health assessments is to obtain the information needed to make decisions about appropriate classification and treatment services. In larger correctional facilities, mental health professionals are employed or contracted and are located in the institution; however, in small prisons, or sentenced facilities with a small number of mentally ill inmates, it is often more feasible to have mental health professionals from nearby community mental health centres attend the prison on an 'as need' basis (Ogloff and Roesch, 1992). Through such an arrangement, a community mental health centre (or equivalent) could provide assessment and treatment services while the woman is incarcerated and services following release if the woman remains in the local community.

In addition to 'routine' comprehensive reviews of women identified as possibly mentally ill and referred to mental health professionals, on occasion there will be a need to give a comprehensive psychodiagnostic examination to women prisoners to determine whether they are acutely mentally ill and whether they should receive treatment in the institution or be transferred to an inpatient treatment facility. In some instances, of course, women prisoners will be identified as seriously mentally ill, in need of psychiatric treatment, and at risk of harm to themselves or others. In such cases, the women can be involuntarily hospitalised and transferred to a psychiatric unit or hospital.

Where indicated, the diagnostic examination also determines what mental illness a woman has and provides a more functional assessment of her specific problems. For example, a diagnosis of schizophrenia, by itself, gives little direction to treatment providers or corrections staff. However, knowledge that a woman prisoner experiences delusions or has difficulty controlling aggressive impulses allows treatment officials to engage in specific interventions designed to ameliorate these problems. It also provides important information to corrections staff about the woman's classification and management needs. Therefore, the assessment of women referred from intake or ongoing screening should include an assessment of their specific behavioural problems.

Mental health treatment

Once a prisoner is assessed with a mental illness that requires treatment, he or she should be referred to an appropriate treatment program within the correctional facility or correctional system if possible and practical. The size of the gaol and its mandate affects the type of service available. While a number of treatment programs have been designed specifically for gaol inmates, the reality is that most gaols currently provide little treatment.

Although a thorough discussion of the treatment of mentally ill offenders in gaol is beyond the scope of this chapter, it is important to note that there has been considerable development in this area (Welsh and Ogloff, 2003). The general program was developed to last approximately 20-weeks. The program is designed on a three-tiered treatment approach with an emphasis on the treatment and management of the offender's illness as well as the interruption of the offender's crime cycle. Treatment sessions are divided across three distinct phases: intake assessment and monitoring; intensive treatment; and reintegration preparation. The objective of a tiered-system approach to treatment is to present information and teach skills in manageable modules for the offenders. The tiered-system approach also allows skills to be presented in a progressive fashion, with basic skills being taught early in the program setting a foundation for future learning. Each of the stages is briefly highlighted below.

Phase 1: Intake assessment and monitoring. The purpose of the initial stage of the program is twofold: 1) to conduct a comprehensive assessment to determine the individual's mental status and treatment needs; and 2) to stabilise the individual with psychotropic medication. Monitoring and assessment of prisoners will occur immediately upon admission and will be performed by qualified mental health care personnel.

Phase 2: Intensive treatment. Consistent with the empirical literature, the treatment modalities will reflect a multi-disciplinary approach incorporating both a bio-psycho-social model and an educational approach. This phase of the program is also progressive such that prisoners will acquire skills in each module that will assist them in the next phase of their treatment plan. Consistent with this approach, early treatment modules focus on basic skills (e.g. symptom recognition, medication use) with each subsequent module building upon those skills. Finally, the specific treatment sessions will focus both on issues related to mental illness and criminal offending.

Eight short-term treatment modules will also be offered in this phase. As previously discussed, a growing body of research has demonstrated that a combination of social skills and vocational training with mentally disordered individuals can result in profound improvements in several outcome areas including symptoms, social adjustment, public safety, and happiness (see, e.g. Liberman *et al.* 1998; Wallace, Liberman, MacKain, Blackwell, and Eckman, 1992). Based on this body of research, four modules from the UCLA Social and Independent Living Skills Program were used for this phase of the program (Welsh and Ogloff, 2003).[3]

Phase 3: Reintegration preparation phase. The goal of this phase is to prepare the individual for release into the community. At this phase, the prisoner is transferred from the secure facility to the open facility of the prison as a first step in preparing towards release into the community. Building on the general skill training of Phase 2, programming is focussed on more specific skills such as relapse prevention and finding residency upon release. In addition, prisoners work closely with a staff reintegration worker in an effort to connect the prisoner with appropriate services in the community prior to release.

Gradual post-release monitoring/supervision and continuity of services

Few would contend with the assertion that treatment that begins in gaol should continue post-release in the community (Ogloff and Roesch, 1992). Many treatment programs initiated in prisons terminate once the individual is released. The transition back to the community is often difficult, as evidenced by high recidivism rates. It is essential that the assessment and intervention process that begins in prison continue after release, in cases where this is deemed appropriate. Nonetheless, despite increased efforts at providing and maintaining mental health services for women in custody, the continuity of treatment on a post-release basis is rare. Limited correctional resources make it difficult to connect MDOs with appropriate services in the community (Dvoskin and Steadman, 1989). Service needs for mentally ill women leaving prison include initiating psychiatric treatment and psychosocial services with a community mental health agency, locating housing, and finding employment. However, the criminal justice system is often unable to provide these services to all MDOs leaving prison. Moreover, some MDOs released into the community may refuse referral, may not keep appointments, may not be compliant with medications, may not abstain from substance abuse, and may refuse appropriate housing placements.

Several factors have been linked to successful community case management (Edens, Peters and Hill, 1997; Veysey, Steadman, Morrissey and Johnsen, 1997):

1 Upon release, contact should be made with clients in their homes.

2 Attention should be made to the practical problems of daily living.

3 Assertive advocacy should be conducted on the client's behalf.

4 Employ the services of 'transitional coordinators' whose primary responsibility is to identify and link prisoners with other institutional or community resources (e.g. mental health/ intellectual impairment services, Alcoholics Anonymous groups).

5 Community mental health services should be used.

6 A liaison-model approach to community case management should be employed. That is, community treatment teams should reflect a multi-disciplinary approach and be comprised of individuals from a variety of social assistance backgrounds (e.g. probation officer, psychiatrist, therapist).

7 Pre-release should include opportunities for transfer to transitional centres and sometimes require placement in these transitional settings (i.e. lower levels of security).

8 Manageable caseload size and long-term commitment to clients.

Unfortunately, continuity of treatment, on a post-release basis, is rare. In those prison/community programs that are effective in assimilating MDO's back into society, one consistent factor seems to be associated with their success: the existence of a core person responsible for managing the interactions of mental health, prison, and judicial personnel. Also known as a 'boundary spanners' (Steadman *et al.* 1989), this individual has responsibilities that reach into all areas of the rehabilitation process, to ensure that prison and community services programmes provided the needed services. Regardless of this core person's title or professional qualifications, it is essential that such individuals have the responsibility of ensuring that the two systems interact effectively and efficiently.

This model can be applied to the integration of mental health services in prison and community services, making continuity of treatment more likely. The only problem with implementing such a program is the fact that prisoners are released into communities all around a jurisdiction. Thus, many boundary spanners would be needed to apply this model to the correctional system. As noted in the 'systems issues' section discussed previously, efforts must be made at both the provincial and local levels to coordinate services between corrections and other agencies, including those in the community. Such relationships are important to develop linkages with service agencies that can help women with mental illness obtain services in the community: services that will help decrease the likelihood that she will reoffend and return to the correctional system.

Programme evaluation

Given the complexity of mental health services in prisons, it is critical that programmes are evaluated on an ongoing basis (e.g. Elliot, 1997). Such evaluations are as important as the other components in achieving assessment and delivery of mental health services. Also, wherever possible, assessment must be linked with treatment. Mental health professionals conducting the evaluations can make recommendations for treatment based on their assessment of an individuals needs. These recommendations are based on perceived need and on the availability of services. Often the most appropriate treatment will not be available or the inmate will not be incarcerated long enough to take advantage of treatment programs. Compromises often must be made. It is all the more important that ongoing evaluations of the effectiveness of the assessment/treatment decisions are built into the system. Evaluation informs decision-makers about the outcome of their decisions. Over time, this feedback can lead to improvements in the assessment, referral, and treatment phases of the model. Data on the base rates of mental disorder among women in custody – and the number of female prisoners who fall into the MDO categories – also can prove valuable in planning for future treatment needs.

Conclusions

It must be noted that, as with many male prisoners, but to an even greater extent for female prisoners, the increase in the representation of mentally ill people in custody is being driven by the same socio-political forces that are responsible for the general increase in imprisonment rates (Ogloff, Davis, Rivers and Ross, in press). Garland (2001) identifies a series of changes in late modern communities that are associated with a decline in traditional 'penal-welfare' approaches and the rise of punitive sanctions and expressive justice. The key change is that offenders who in the past were at the margins of custody (especially non-violent, recidivist and drug dependent offenders) are now routinely imprisoned, and average periods of imprisonment have increased. Female offenders, and particularly those with mental illnesses, are particularly vulnerable to these changes.

With the dramatic increase in the number of women entering prisons, and the high rate of mental illnesses among them, it is incumbent on society to begin to address the underlying causes of increases in offending among women. Doubtless, greater focus on the mental health needs of women in the community would begin to show benefits by ultimately reducing the number of women with mental illnesses entering into custody. Once they are in custody, though, it is critical that a systematic programme that includes the identification and treatment of mental illness among women be implemented. Without such a programme, the revolving door phenomenon will persist and women with major mental illnesses – whose mental health needs will go unmet – will continue to cycle between the community and prison ending, perhaps, in great tragedy.

Notes

1 The methodologies of the key studies referenced below are summarised in greater detail in the Appendix.
2 For a more complete review of diversion in the context of criminal justice mental health services, see Ogloff (2002).
3 For a complete discussion of a mental health treatment program for people in custody, see Welsh and Ogloff (2003).
4 'Schizophrenia' includes related disorders, ax = abuse, dx = dependence, OCD = obsessive-compulsive disorder, PTSD = posttraumatic stress disorder
5 In the United States of America, jails receive remand prisoners and prisoners serving short sentences for misdemeanours

References

Brinded, P.J.J., Stevens, I., Mulder, R.T., Fairley, N., Malcolm, F., Wells, J.E. (1999a) 'The Christchurch prisons psychiatric epidemiology study: Methodology and prevalence rates for psychiatric disorders', *Criminal Behaviour and Mental Health*, 9 (2): 131–43.

Brinded, P.J.J., Mulder, R.T., Stevens, I., Fairley, N., Malcolm, F. (1999b) 'The Christchurch prisons psychiatric epidemiology study: Personality disorders assessment in a prison population', *Criminal Behaviour and Mental Health*, 9 (2): 144–155.

Brinded, P.M.J., Simpson, A.I.F., Laidlaw, T.M., Fairley, N. and Malcom, F. (2001) 'Prevalence of psychiatric disorders in New Zealand prisons: A national study', *Australian and New Zealand Journal of Psychiatry*, 35: 166–173.

Brugha, T., Singleton, N., Meltzer, H., Bebbington, P., Farrell, M., Jenkins, R., Coid, J., Fryers, T., Meltzer, D. and Lewis, G. (2005) 'Psychosis in the community and in prisons: A report from the British National Survey of Psychiatric Comorbidity', *American Journal of Psychiatry*, 162: 774–80.

Butler, T., Allnutt, S., Cain, D., Owens, D. and Muller, C. (2005) 'Mental disorder in the New South Wales prisoner population', *Australian and New Zealand Journal of Psychiatry*, 39: 407–13.

Cameron, M. (2001) 'Women Prisoners and Correctional Programs', *Trends and Issues in Crime and Criminal Justice*, 194, Canberra, ACT: Australian Institute of Criminology.

Corrado, R.R., Cohen, I.M., Hart, S.D. and Roesch, R. (2000) 'Diagnosing mental disorders in offenders: Conceptual and methodological issues', *Criminal Behaviour and Mental Health*, 10: 29–39.

Daniel, A.E., Robins, A.J., Reid, J.C. and Wilfley, D.E. (1988) 'Lifetime and six-month prevalence of psychiatric disorders among sentenced female offenders', *Bulletin of the American Academy of Psychiatry and Law*, 16 (4): 333–42.

Denton, B. (1995) 'Psychiatric morbidity and substance dependence among women prisoners: An Australian study', *Psychiatry, Psychology and Law*, 2 (2): 173–77.

Dvoskin, J.A. and Steadman, H.J. (1989) 'Chronically mentally ill inmates: The wrong concept for the right services', *International Journal of Law and Psychiatry*, 12: 203–10.

Edens, J.F., Peters, R.H., Hills, H.A. (1997) 'Treating prison inmates with co-occurring disorders: An integrative review of existing programs', *Behavioural Sciences and the Law*, 15 (4): 439–57.

Elliot, R.L. (1997) 'Evaluating the quality of correctional mental health services: An approach to surveying correctional mental health systems', *Behavioural Sciences and the Law*, 15 (4): 427–38.

Garland, D. (2001) *The culture of control: Crime and social order in contemporary society*, Oxford: Oxford University Press.

Gibbens, T.C.N. (1971) 'Female offenders', *British Journal of Hospital Medicine*, September, 279–86.

Gunn, J., Robertson, G., Dell, S. and Way, C. (1978) *Psychiatric aspects of imprisonment*. London: Academic Press.

Harrison, P.M. and Beck, A.J. (2006) *Prisoners in 2005*. Washington, DC: US Bureau of Justice Statistics Bulletin NCJ 215092.

Herrman, H., McGorry, P., Mills, J. and Singh, B. (1991) 'Hidden severe psychiatric morbidity in sentenced prisoners: An Australian study', *American Journal of Psychiatry*, 148 (2): 236–39.

Hurley, W. and Dunne, M.P. (1991) 'Psychological distress and psychiatric morbidity in women prisoners', *Australian and New Zealand Journal of Psychiatry*, 25: 461–70.

Jones, I.J., Marris, B., Hornsby, H. (1995) 'Psychiatric characteristics of female prisoners in Tasmania', *Australian and New Zealand Journal of Psychiatry*, 29 (4): 671–77.

Jordan, B.K., Schlenger, W.E., Fairbank, J.A. and Caddell, J.M. (1996) 'Prevalence of psychiatric disorders among incarcerated women: II. Convicted felons entering prison', *Archives of General Psychiatry*, 53: 513–19.

Leese, M., Thomas, S. and Snow, L. (2006)'An ecological study of factors associated with rates of self-inflicted death in prisons in England and Wales', *International Journal of Law and Psychiatry*, 29: 355–60.

Liberman, R.P., Wallace, C.J., Blackwell, G., Kopelowicz, A., Vaccaro, J.V. and Mintz, J. (1998) 'Skills training versus psychosocial occupational therapy for persons with persistent schizophrenia', *American Journal of Psychiatry*, 155: 1087–91.

Maden, A., Swinton, M. and Gunn, J. (1994) 'A criminological and psychiatric survey of women serving a prison sentence', *British Journal of Criminology*, 34 (2): 172–91.

Mohan, D., Scully, P., Collins, C. and Smith, C. (1997) 'Psychiatric disorder in an Irish female prison', *Criminal Behaviour & Mental Health*, 7 (3): 229–35.

Nicholls, T.L., Lee, Z., Corrado, R.R. and Ogloff, J.R.P. (2004) 'Women inmates' mental health needs: Evidence of the validity of the *Jail Screening Assessment Tool (JSAT)'*, *International Journal of Forensic Mental Health*, 3(2): 167–84.

Nicholls, T.L., Roesch, R., Olley, M.C., Ogloff, J.R.P. and Hemphill, J.F. (2005) *Jail Screening Assessment Tool (JSAT): Guidelines for mental health screening in jails*. Burnaby, BC, Canada: Mental Health, Law & Policy Institute, Simon Fraser University.

O'Brien, M., Mortimer, L., Singleton, N. and Meltzer, H. (2003) 'Psychiatric morbidity among women prisoners in England and Wales', *International Review of Psychiatry*, 15: 153–57.

Ogloff, J.R.P. (2002) 'Identifying and accommodating the needs of mentally ill people in gaols and prisons', *Psychiatry, Psychology, and Law*, 9: 1–33.

Ogloff, J.R.P., Davis, M.R., Rivers, G., and Ross, S. (in press) *The identification of mental disorder in the criminal justice system*, Trends and Issues Report, Canberra: Australian Institute of Criminology.

Ogloff, J.R.P., Lemphers, A. and Dwyer, C. (2004) 'Dual diagnosis in an Australian forensic psychiatric hospital: Prevalence and implications for services', *Behavioral Sciences and the Law*, 22: 543–62.

Ogloff, J.R.P. and Roesch, R. (1992) 'Using Community Mental Health Centers to provide comprehensive mental health services to jails', in J.R.P. Ogloff, (ed.) (1992) *Psychology and law: The broadening of the discipline*. Durham, NC, USA: Carolina Academic Press.

Ogloff, J.R.P., Roesch, R. and Hart, S.D. (1993) 'Screening, assessment, and identification of services for mentally disordered offenders in prisons', in H.J. Steadman and H.J. Cocozza (eds) *Providing services for offenders with mental illness and related disorders in prison*. Seattle, WA, USA: National Coalition for the Mentally Ill in the Criminal Justice System.

Ogloff, J.R.P., Tien, G., Roesch, R. and Eaves, D. (1991) 'A model for the provision of jail mental health services: An integrative, community based approach', *Journal of Mental Health Administration*, 18: 209–22.

Parsons, S., Walker, L. and Grubin, D. (2001) 'Prevalence of mental disorder in female remand prisons', *The Journal of Forensic Psychiatry*, 12 (1): 194–202.

Pollock, J. (2002) *Women, crime and prison*. New York: Wadsworth.

Powell, T.A., Holt, J.C., Fondacaro, K.M. (1997) 'The prevalence of mental illness among inmates in a rural state', *Law and Human Behaviour*, 21 (4): 427–38.

Simpson, A.I.F., Brinded, P.M.J., Laidlaw, T.M., Fairley, N., Malcolm, F. (1999) *The National Study of Psychiatric Morbidity in New Zealand Prisoners*, 1–77, New Zealand: Department of Corrections.

Singer, M.I., Bussey, J., Song, L., Lunghofer, L. (1995) 'The psychosocial issues of women serving time in jail', *Social Work*, 40 (1): 103–13.

Steadman, H.J., McCarty, D.W., Morrissey, J.P. (1989) *The mentally ill in jail: Planning for essential services*. New York: Guilford.

Teplin, L.A., Abram, K.M. and McClelland, G.M. (1996) 'Prevalence of psychiatric disorders among incarcerated women: I. Pre-trial jail detainees', *Archives of General Psychiatry*, 53: 505–12.

Tye, C.S. and Mullen, P.E. (2006) 'Mental disorders in female prisoners', *Australian and New Zealand Journal of Psychiatry*, 40: 266–71.

Veysey, B.M., Steadman, H.J., Morrissey, J.P. and Johnsen, M. (1997) 'In search of the missing linkages: Continuity of care in U.S. jails', *Behavioral Sciences and the Law*, 15: 383–97.

Wallace, C.J., Liberman, R.P., MacKain, S.J., Blackwell, G. and Eckman, T.A. (1992) 'Effectiveness and replicability of modules for teaching social and instrumental skills to the severely mentally ill', *American Journal of Psychiatry*, 149: 654–58.

Welsh, A. and Ogloff, J.R.P. (2003) 'The development of a Canadian prison based program for offenders with mental illnesses', *International Journal of Forensic Mental Health*, 2: 59–71.

Wing, J.K., Babor, T., Brugha, T., Burke, J., Cooper, J.E., Giel, R., Jablenski, A., Regier, D. and Sartorius, N. (1990) 'Schedules for Clinical Assessment in Neuropsychiatry', *Archives of General Psychiatry*, 47: 589–93.

Wright, B., Duffy, D., Curtin, K., Linehan, S., Monks, S. and Kennedy, H.G. (2006) 'Psychiatric morbidity among women prisoners newly committed and amongst remanded and sentenced women in the Irish prison system', *Irish Journal of Psychological Medicine*, 23 (2): 47–53.

Appendix 8.1 Summary of studies investigating the prevalence of mental illnesses among women in custody

1. Prevalence studies of remand and sentenced women/reception studies

Author	N	Sample	Instruments	What was measured	Results
Hurley and Dunne (1991)	92	Population study of Brisbane Women's prison. RR=98%	- recent stressful life events questionnaire - general health questionnaire (GHQ-12) - Structured Clinical Interview for DSM-III-R (SCID) - Hamilton Depression-Rating Scale (HAM-D)	- psychological distress - psychiatric disorder - relationships between psychological distress and subject characteristics - role of recent stressful events in distress - changes in psychological and psychiatric distress over time	*Current (past month)* Adjustment disorder with depressed mood (18.5%) Depression (1.1%) Schizophrenia (paranoid) (2.2%) ASPD (19.6%) BPD (17.4%) DPD (1.1%) Any disorder (53.3%) Lifetime Heroin (28.3%) Alcohol (14.4%) Any psychoactive substance (55.4%) T1 reported. T2 no sig. diff.
Mohan, Scully, Collins and Smith (1997)	45	Randomly selected from all receptions over three months at an Irish prison RR=100%	The Schedule for Clinical Assessment in Neuropsychiatry (SCAN) - DSM-IV criteria applied to assign diagnosis based on current state	- prevalence of psychiatric disorder - factors associated with psychiatric disorder in these subjects past psychiatric history	Primary diagnosis substance dependence (58%) Additional axis I (24%) History of contact with psychiatric services in the past (40%)

				(6-month)	Committals	Cross-sectional
Wright, Duffy, Curtin, Linehan, Monks and Kennedy (2006)	94 newly committed 92 remand/sentenced	- Reception/cross-sectional sample of female prisoners in Ireland - 94 newly committed prisoners interviewed within 72 hrs - Cross-sectional sample of 24 remand and 68 sentenced (RR: 87.3%)	- SADS-L (Schedule for schizophrenia and affective disorders, lifetime version) - SOD-Q (severity of dependence questionnaire) - SAPAS (schedule for assessment of personality, screening-version)	- current, 6-month and lifetime prevalence rates of mental disorder - Drug and alcohol use and dependence (6-month, 12-month, current and lifetime diagnoses) - screen for personality disorder (committal sample only) - suicidal ideation and suicidal behaviour - medical, psychiatric and forensic histories	Psychosis Affective d/order Major depression Anxiety d/order Substance use Any mental illness	5.4% 14.0% 4.3% 8.6% 65.6% 25.8%	5.4% 20.7% 16.3% 15.2% 65.2% 39.1%

- 34.4% committals and 39.6% of cross-sectional subjects reported history of community psych. Treatment (as inpatient or outpatient)

Appendix 8.2 Prevalence studies of sentenced and remanded female prisoners' mental health

Author	N	Sample	What was measured	Instruments	Results		
					Disorder	*One month N (%)*	*Lifetime N (%)*
Denton (1995)	56	Midnight census of sentenced and unsentenced female prisoners in Victoria, Australia	- One month and lifetime prevalence rates of mental disorders	- The Structured Clinical Interview for DSM-III-R (SCID-R)			
					Schizophrenia	2(4)	2(4)
					Reactive psychosis	2(4)	2(4)
					Bipolar	3(5)	3(5)
					Major depression	4(7)	5(9)
					Substance dx	34(61)	38(68)
					Alcohol	5(9)	11(20)
					Opiate	28(50)	30(54)
					Benzodiazepine	16(29)	23(41)
Brinded, P., Simpson, A. et al. (2001) Simpson et al. (1999)	170	Census of female remand- and sentenced prisoners in NZ	- Current (one month prevalence rates of major mental disorder and personality disorder	- Demographics questionnaire - Composite International Diagnostic Interview, automated (CIDI-A) - Personality Diagnostic Questionnaire screener (PDQ-4+)	*Disorder[4] (DSM-IV)*	*N(%)*	
					Schizophrenia	7(4.2)	
					Bipolar	2(1.2)	
					Major depression	18(11.1)	
					OCD	7(4.3)	
					PTSD	27(16.6)	
					Alcohol abuse	7(4.3)	
					Alcohol dx	4(2.5)	
					Cannabis ax	6(3.7)	
					Other substance	6(3.7)	

[4]'Schizophrenia' includes related disorders, ax = abuse, dx = dependence, OCD = obsessive-compulsive disorder, PTSD = post-traumatic stress disorder.

Study	Sample	Setting	Instrument	Prevalence measured	Results	Reception %	Sentenced %
Butler, Allnutt, Cain, Owens and Muller (2005)	953 reception (165 women) 579 sentenced (108 women)	- Consecutive receptions screened at four male and one female correctional centre in NSW - Sentenced population randomly selected from 28 correctional centres across NSW	- CIDI-Auto (NSMHWB version)	Prevalence of mental illness - 12-month ICD-10 diagnoses	Psychosis	15.2	5.7
					Affective dx	*33.9*	*20.4*
					Depression	23.6	14.4
					Dysthymia	9.7	5.8
					Manic episode	7.9	1.9
					Anxiety d/order	*55.8*	*54.4*
					PTSD	43.6	43.8
					GAD	22.4	15.2
					Panic d/order	17.0	16.2
					Agoraphobia	3.0	5.7
					OCD	2.4	2.0
					Social Phobia	0.6	1.0
					Any Disorder	*61.8*	*59.2*
O'Brien, Mortimer, Singleton and Meltzer (2003)	187 remand 584 sentenced	- Part of the Office for National Statistics, London, survey of psychiatric morbidity among prisoners in England and Wales (1997). - Two stage model: 1. Initial interview 2. Random 1 in 5 sub-sample completed follow-up clinical interview	- SCID-II - SCAN - AUDIT - CIS-R	- Prevalence of personality disorder - 12-month prevalence psychosis - Neurotic symptoms and disorders in the week prior to interview - Alcohol and drug use disorders (year pre-prison) - Self harm, suicide ideation - Past mental health treatment history	- Women on remand-higher CIS-R (neuroses) scores than sentenced women (11% v 6%) - PD=50%; ASPD: 31%; BPD: 20%, PPD:16% - Mental health treatment pre-prison = 40% - Hazardous drinking pre-prison=38% - Drug dependence pre-prison= 54% (remand), 41% (sentenced) - Functional psychosis in last year = 14%		

Appendix 8.3 Prevalence studies of sentenced female prisoners

Author	N	Sample	Instruments	What was measured	Results Six month	Lifetime
Daniel, Robins, Reid and Wilfley (1988)	100	- Consecutive admissions at the Missouri correctional system. RR=100%	- Diagnostic Interview Schedule (DIS) for DSM-III	- Lifetime and 6-month prevalence of psychiatric disorder - Comparison with community data (St. Louis site of ECA)	*Six month* Schizophrenia (7%) Depression (17%) Mania (2%) Panic disorder (2%) Phobia (20%) Alcohol (10%) Drug (26%) ASPD (29%) *Higher than general population except mania and the anxiety disorders	*Lifetime* 7%) (21%) (2%) (2%) (24%) (36%) (26%) (29%)
Jordan, Schlenger, Fairbank and Caddell (1996)	805	Census of women felons entering prison in North Carolina (94%) Remainder (6%) random sample of newly entering felons	Stage 1: - Composite International Diagnostic Interview (CIDI) - Diagnostic Interview Schedule (DIS) (ASPD-module) - Impact of events scale - Diagnostic Interview for Personality Disorder (BPD module)	- 6-month and lifetime prevalence of psychiatric disorder - Comparison with community prevalence rates (ECA data) - Risk factors - Outcomes - Role of trauma discussed	*Six month* Depression (10.8%) GAD (1.4%) Panic disorder (4.7%) Alcohol (17.1%) Drug (30.3%) ASPD (11.9%) BPD (28.0%) Any current disorder (46.3%)	

Study	N	Aim	Method	Results
			Stage 2: - Follow up interview with 25% sample to validate two measures	*Lifetime* Depression (13.0%) GAD (2.7%) Panic disorder (5.8%) Alcohol (38.6%) Drug (44.2%) ASPD (11.9%) Any lifetime disorder (64%) Antisocial personality disorder = 39%
Brinded et al. (1999a)	50	The level of personality disorder in a prison population in Christchurch, NZ, using three different measures of personality disorder	Census of female prisoners at Christchurch women's prison (all sentenced) - The structured clinical interview for DSM-III-R Personality Disorders (SCID-II) (ASPD module) - The 'Four As - The temperament and character inventory	Four As: 'Asthenic personality' = 21% 'Anankastic personality' = 5% 'Antisocial personality' = 32% 'Asocial personality' = 13% Temperament and character: - high in novelty seeking and harm avoidance
Brinded et al. (1999)	50	The one month and lifetime prevalence rates of psychiatric disorders in the prison population	As above - demographics questionnaire - The Composite International Diagnostic Interview – Automated (CIDI-A)	(see table below)

Diagnosis	One month N(%)	Lifetime N(%)
Major depression	7(19)	18(48)
Schizophrenia	0(0)	0(0)
GAD		
Agoraphobia	2(5)	2(19)
Social phobia	4(11)	14(38)
OCD	0(0)	1(3)
Alcohol dx	7(19)	19(51)
Non-alcohol dx	7(19)	15(41)

Appendix 8.3 Prevalence studies of sentenced female prisoners *continued*

N	Sample	Instruments	What was measured	Results
62	Convenience sample of female prisoners	- The Coping Resource Questionnaire - The Social Readjustment Rating Scale (SRRS) - The State-Trait Anxiety Inventory (STAI) - Centre for Epidemiological Studies Depression Scale (CES-D)	- Life events experienced - Psychological wellbeing - Criminological and psychiatric characteristics - Diagnoses given according to ICD-9 diagnostic criteria	- Subjects experienced an average of ten life events in the twelve months prior to incarceration - Mean levels of depression and anxiety among female prisoners were significantly higher than community rates - There was a significant correlation between life events and depression
262	Representative, cross-sectional sample of 25% of sentenced female prisoners in England and Wales	- Semi structured interview (designed for the project and piloted on 50 prisoners) - The Clinical Interview Schedule (CIS)		*Disorder* *N(%)* Psychosis 4(1.6) Neurosis 40(16) Personality disorder 46(18) Alcohol ax/dx 24(9) Drug ax/dx 67(26)

Appendix 8.4 Prevalence studies of female gaol detainees / remand prisoners

Author	N	Sample	Instruments	What was measured	Results
Teplin, Abram and McClelland (1996)	1272	Randomly selected, stratified (by charge and race) sample of females awaiting trial in a Chicago gaol RR=90%	- National Institute of Mental Health Diagnostic Interview Schedule Version III-R (NIMH DIS-III-R)	- 6-month and lifetime prevalence rates of psychiatric disorder - Comparison with ECA community rates - Association of psychiatric disorder with current arrest charge	6-month Schizophrenia (1.8%) Manic episode (2.2%) Depression (13.7%) Substance (60.1%) Alcohol (23.9%) Drug (52.4%) PTSD (22.3%) ASPD (13.7%) Any of the above (70.3%) - lifetime and 6-month rates similar - non-hispanic whites: highest rates of most disorders
Singer, Bussey, Song and Lunghofer (1995)	201	Random sample of all new admissions at a Cleveland jail. Inmates who were actively violent, high risk for violence or floridly psychotic excluded from sampling pool	- Multidimensional scale of perceived social support - Brief Symptom Inventory (BSI) - Short Drug Abuse Screening Test (S-DAST)	- Needs of the population with the aim of developing appropriate services	Depression (59.2%) Anxiety (40.8%) Phobic anxiety (49.3%) Somatisation (26.9%) OCD (37.3%) Interpersonal sensitivity (48.8%) Hostility (36.3%) * % within the distress range on the BSI

[5] In the United States of America, gaols receive remand prisoners and prisoners serving short sentences for misdemeanours.

Appendix 8.4 Prevalence studies fo female gaol detainees[5]/remand prisoner *continued*

Author	Sample	Instruments	What was measured	Results
Parsons, Walker and Grubin (2001)	382 RR=89%	- Schedule for Affective-Disorders and Schizophrenia (SADS-L) - The CAGE questionnaire - The Severity of Dependence Questionnaire (SODQ)	Lifetime and current prevalence rates of mental disorder The efficacy of the prison health screen in detecting mental disorder	*Diagnosis (current)* *N(%)* Psychotic disorders 42(10.9) Schizophrenia/other 38(9.9) psychotic Affective psychosis 4(1.0) Mood disorders 127(33.2) Major mood disorders 53(13.9) Dysthymic disorder 67(17.6) Anxiety disorders 116(40.4) Personality disorders 175(45.8) Drug/alcohol dependence 206(54.0)
	All new remands at H. M. Holloway, and H. M. New Hall, over a 14 week period, in England			
Teplin et al. (1997)	1272 PR= 90%	- National Institute of Mental Health Diagnostic Interview Schedule (DIS), Version III-R - Gaol records and case files to determine whether mental health services received in prison	- The proportion of female gaol detainees that needed mental health services - What proportion received these services - What variables predicted receipt of services	- Of 116 subjects who 'needed mental health services; 23.5% received them during their prison stay - 10.4% of those 'not needing services' received them - Subjects with schizophrenia/ manic episode more likely, and those with major depression less likely to receive services compared with a reference group - This pattern mediated by comorbid drug abuse/ dependence - Psychiatric treatment history greatest predictor of receiving services
	Stratified (by arrest charge and race/ ethnicity), random sample of female gaol detainees, at intake			

Study	N	Sample	Method	Results
Steadman et al. (1991)	3684 1101 females studied	12% random sample of all inmates in the NY state prison system and all 360 persons in inpatient mental health beds in that prison system	- Adaptation of the 'Level of Care Survey' (LOCS)	- Comparison of mental health disability with the services actually received - Investigated the receipt of services in the last 30 days and in the last year	Receipt of services in past 30 days: - Little/no psych disability 11% - Significant psych disability 25% - Severe psych disability 44% - Different factors predicted receipt of services for male and female prisoners
Delle et al. (1993a)	196 'psychotic' population N=95	All (remand) receptions into the medical unit at Holloway Women's Prison, between April and October 1989. (Women allocated to the medical unit if doctor thought medical/psychiatric supervision was necessary upon examination at reception). Those admitted on medical grounds alone were excluded from the study	- Prison medical records - Questionnaires sent to psychiatrists - Questionnaires to courts - Three month postal follow up study re: women subject to hospital orders	- The treatment outcome for remand female prosiners diagnosed as psychotic by prison psychiatrists. - Followed up to sentence	Of the psychotic women: - 76% prescribed medication in Holloway - 45% hospital order - 12% probation - 5% prison sentence (less than five days) - 16% case dismissed - 22% other (non-custodial)

Appendix 8.5 Studies of mental health service provision untilisation in prison

Author	N	Sample	Instruments	What was measured	Results
Dell et al. (1993b)	96 'non-psychotic' women Pop'n n = 101	Refer to Dell et al. (1993a). This study-remanded women prisoners referred to outside psychiatrists/ for whom court reports were written/ with mental handicap.	- Refer to Dell et al. (1993b)	- Followed up to time of sentence	- primary diagnosis – majority drug dependence, personality disorder or mental handicap - 37 referred to outside psychiatrists with a view to obtaining a bed. - 18 (49%) of these women had a PD diagnosis. - Final outcome for referred women: - Hospital orders 27% (10) - Sentenced to 2–3 years 8% (3) - Released to community 65% (24)
Teplin (1990)	728	Randomly selected, stratified (by type of charge) sample of male jail detainees in a Chicago jail. All post arraignment detainees eligible to participate	- National Institute of Mental Health Diagnostic Interview Schedule (NIMH-DIS-DSM-III)	- The extent to which mentally ill gaol detainees are treated while in custody of the criminal justice system.	- False negative errors (62.5%) - False positive errors (4.6%) - Severely ill detainees (n=40); 15 (37.5%) were ever detected Predictors of treatment (in order of significance) - treatment history on records - overt symptoms on records - nature of current arrest - depressive symptoms on records - schizophrenia

Maden et al. (1994)	M=1751 F=258	Semi-structured interview designed for the project. - The Clinical Interview Schedule (CIS)	Prevalence of mental disorder	Treatment during current sentence

Random, 50% sample from each of four women's prisons in England and Wales. Compared with a similar 5% sample of the male sentenced population described in Gunn et al (1991).

Prevalence of mental disorder
- Behavioural social and criminological characteristics
- Previous psychiatric contact.
- Current need for psychiatric treatment

Treatment during current sentence

Type	Female	Male
Any medication	26% (68)	8% (131)
Psychological treatments 3%(60)	8% (21)	3% (60)

Recommendations	Female	Male
'Outpatient' in prison	56% (145)	76% (1334)
Therapeutic community	22% (56)	10% (179)
Transfer to hospital	5% (12)	3% (52)
Further assessment	9% (25)	5% (90)

Appendix 8.6 Studies of mental health service utilisation among prisoners, prior to imprisonment

Author	N	Sample	Instruments	What was measured	Results
Herman et al. (1994)	M=158 F=31	Random sample, stratified by sex and prison, of sentenced prisoners in Victoria	- The Victorian Psychiatric Case Register	- Previous use of state psychiatric services	Positive match with VPCR records: - men (34%) (54) - Women (61%) (19) - For substance abuse disorders alone (64%) (35M, 12F)
Jones et al. (1995)	210	All women prisoners incarcerated in Tasmania between 1981 and 1990 inclusive	- The Mental Health Services database	- Psychiatric, social and criminological characteristics of female prisoners in Tasmania	Inpatient treatment: - Men (16%) - Women (48%) Prior psychiatric history (35%) (73) ICD-9 diagnoses for women with psychiatric history (most prevalent summarised below) - Neurotic disorders (mainly depressive) 15% (11) - Personality disorders (27%) (20) - Alcohol dependence (10%) (7) - Non-dependent abuse of drugs (19%) (14)

Study	Sample			Findings
Maden et al. (1994)	M=1751 F=258	Refer to table 7	Refer to table 7	Refer to table 7
				Previous psychiatric treatment

Type	M	F	OR
None	64% (1125)	55% (143)	0.7
Child guidance only	17% (291)	9% (22)	0.5
Adult outpatient	11% (199)	24% (61)	2.4
Adult inpatient	8% (136)	12% (32)	1.7

All odds ratios significant at .05

| Chandler and Kassebaum (1994) | F=39 | Reception study of sentenced female felons from March – August 1991 in Hawaii. Compared with similar sample (n=157) of males | The SAI (see table 4) | - Patterns of drug abuse (see table 4) |

- History of abuse (see table 5)
- Psychiatric treatment history

- Treatment for both substance abuse and psychiatric problems (36%)
- Treatment only for substance abuse (23%)
- Treatment for only psychiatric problems (18%)

Chapter 9

Responding to the health needs of female offenders

Angela M. Wolf, Fabiana Silva, Kelly E. Knight and Shabnam Javdani

Introduction

Prisoners in the United States have a fundamental right to receive adequate health care. However, most prisoners in this nation face numerous obstacles when attempting to receive quality services. This is particularly problematic for female prisoners, who suffer from physical and mental health disorders at rates higher than incarcerated men, yet receive fewer targeted services.

In the United States, the state of California leads the nation in the number of women it incarcerates, second only to Texas. The vast majority of these women are in custody for non-violent, drug-related offences, and will likely return to their communities after relatively short prison stays. Female offenders commonly face a wide range of serious health problems including substance abuse, infectious disease, mental illness, hypertension, asthma, and diabetes. Although there is some overlap in the basic needs of male and female offenders, women have distinct needs and face unique challenges upon entering correctional facilities and returning to the community. Nevertheless, perhaps due to women's traditionally more limited representation in correctional facilities, their treatment needs have been neglected, with negative consequences – increasingly, women return to prison for parole violations related to substance use – a health related issue not adequately addressed in prison.

The provision of health care is problematic in a prison setting. With increasing numbers, the system has found it difficult to keep up. As such, it is typical for women to enter the system after a lifetime of neglected health only to have their health care needs exasperated by the incarceration experience.

This chapter presents the results of the National Council on Crime and Delinquency's Women in Prison Project. This project included ten interviews with incarcerated women, site visits to model health care programmes, and fifty interviews with key stakeholders who have an interest in issues related to incarceration practices and health care. In this chapter, we first examine the rise of female incarceration. This is followed by an analysis of women's pathways to crime and their health needs. We will describe the effects of incarceration on women and characterise the current health care delivery system. Finally, we will present current understanding of how to treat incarcerated women, and will outline a strategy to improve quality and access of health care within the system and during the transition back into the community.

Rise of incarcerated women

For the better part of the twentieth century, the rate of incarceration in the US remained fairly stable. Over the past 25 years, however, the prison population has exploded. A substantial portion of local, state, and federal budgets are now directed towards corrections (Hughes 2004). This prison population increase has been overwhelmingly due to tough on crime policies and legislation enacted as part of the war on drugs (Casey and Wiatrowski 1996). Corresponding cuts in social services, education, and employment opportunity have also been fundamental components of the extreme growth of prison populations.

These policies have affected women disproportionately and there has been a dramatic increase in female incarceration over the last three decades. The number of women in state and federal prisons rose nearly eightfold between 1980 and 2000, from 12,000 to more than 90,000. The increase in women's rate of incarceration has outpaced the increase for men each year since the mid-1980s. While the total number of male prisoners grew 77% between 1990 and 2000, the number of female prisoners increased 108% during the same period. In gaols the difference is even more pronounced. The total number of men in gaol increased 48% between 1990 and 2000, while the total number of females increased 89% during that same period (Bureau of Justice Statistics 2001a; 2001b). Women are particularly vulnerable to policy changes because they are more likely to be incarcerated for the drug-related or petty, nonviolent property crimes that are driving the high rates of incarceration (Owen and Bloom 1995). Before the advent of mandatory minimums for drug sentences, these crimes would probably not have led to imprisonment, but now judges usually have few options.

As one of America's leaders in the incarceration of women, California's female prison population increased dramatically, growing from 1,232 in 1979 to 11,462 in 2005 (California Department of Corrections and Rehabilitation, CDCR 2006a). On a typical day in California in 2005 there were over 10,000 women in gaol, 11,000 women in prison, and 12,000 women on parole (CDCR 2006b; CDCR 2006a). California has the second largest population of women prisoners in the nation, second only to Texas. California has four prisons for housing women, with one being the largest women's prison in the world (CDCR 2006a).

Women's pathways to crime

The crimes women commit cannot be separated from histories including serious mental illness, trauma, drug addiction, and struggles for economic survival. Incarcerated women are characteristically women of colour, poor, unemployed, unmarried mothers of young children, and survivors of physical and sexual abuse. Imprisoned women also tend to have a fragmented family history, other family members involved with the criminal justice system, significant substance abuse issues and multiple physical and mental health problems (Bloom, Owen and Covington 2003). Given that incarcerated women often find themselves in communities lacking in resources, it is not surprising that women with serious mental illnesses often find themselves incarcerated (Maeve 1998).

Women's substance abuse problems are not being addressed in prison and, therefore, contribute to future crime and parole violations. In 1998, more than half of the returns of women to prison for parole violations were for drug offences (Hall, Baldwin and Prendergast 2001). Drug abuse is a stronger predictor of crime for women than for men (Belknap 2001). Nearly 90% of incarcerated women developed substance abuse issues prior to committing any crime (Farabee, Joshi and Anglin 2001). Fifty-two per cent of women admitted to being under the influence of alcohol and/or drugs at the time of their offence; 40% were said they were under the influence of drugs (Greenfeld and Snell 1999). Drug testing of a random sample of women arrested revealed that 65% tested positive for one or more drugs (National Institute of Justice 2003). A 1999 study by the Bureau of Justice Statistics reported that nearly one in three women in state prison admitted to committing the offence which brought them to prison in order to obtain money to support their need for drugs (Greenfeld and Snell 1999).

Furthermore, the great majority of incarcerated women were struggling financially prior to their arrest. The highest level of educational attainment for most incarcerated women is a high school diploma, that is to say they have completed twelve years of schooling; or they complete the GED, a test of high school equivalency which does not require completion of high school (Bloom, Owen and Covington 2004). Without an education, many of these women have had few opportunities to participate in the legitimate work force. In comparison to men, more women were unemployed before they were arrested, and most leave prison without necessary job training. National figures reveal that only 40% of women had a fulltime job before they were arrested compared to 60% of men; women's jobs were mostly low-skill and low-pay, with almost 40% yielding incomes of less than US$600 per month (Greenfeld and Snell 1999). Furthermore, while 8% of incarcerated men were on welfare, 30% of women received aid before they were incarcerated (Greenfeld and Snell 1999). In a study of incarcerated parents, 18% of mothers reported having been homeless in the year before admission to state prisons (compared to 8% of fathers) (Mumola 2000). In a representative survey of women in California facilities, almost 40% of women had not finished high school and half of the women had never worked at any time (Owen and Bloom 1995). A study of incarcerated women in California found substance abuse to be the most cited reason (30%) for unemployment, followed by 'made more money from crime and hustling' and child-care responsibilities (Owen and Bloom 1995: 22).

The economic marginalisation of women is embedded in the factors that produce and perpetuate female criminality. Women's offences are largely income producing crimes to support drug addictions and pay for food, children's needs, housing, and other bills (Bloom et al. 2004). They reflect attempts at economic survival rather than enrichment; often with serious health consequences. The drug trade may appeal to women who have no adequate economic alternatives; nevertheless, many of these women end up with serious drug addictions (Henderson 1998). Sex work as an economic strategy also has serious health implications (Belknap 2001). Health treatment cannot ignore women's precarious economic situation; women with histories of substance abuse are more likely to relapse without a stable home and a steady source of income (Pelissier and Jones 2005).

Health status of female prisoners

Nationally, incarcerated women report more serious health conditions than women on the outside (Belknap 2001). Furthermore, female inmates in state and federal prisons reported having higher rates of medical problems after admission than men: 23% of women in state prisons compared to 16% of men and 25% of women in federal prison compared to 15% of men (Maruschak and Beck 2001). Mental health and reproductive health issues appear to be particularly problematic for women in relation to men (Auerhahn and Dermody Leonard 2000). Studies find that incarcerated women have high rates of sexually transmitted disease, depression, anxiety, dental disease, and diabetes (Greenfeld and Snell 1999; Auerhahn and Dermody Leonard 2000; Young 2000). Up to 40% of prisoners in California are positive for hepatitis C (Action Committee For Women in Prison 2003). In addition to the health issues listed above, California stakeholders interviewed as part of the Women in Prison Project mentioned the prevalence of asthma, heart disease, HIV/AIDS, and staphylococcus infections among incarcerated women.

These poor health outcomes are partly due to life circumstances, such as poverty, and risky behaviours like unprotected sexual intercourse. Prisoners who are homeless or unemployed report more medical problems than those who are not (Maruschak and Beck 2001). In general, women in prison did not have health insurance before entering prison (Kane and DiBartolo 2002) usually because they were poor, did not have jobs or were not provided with health insurance at the jobs they did have, and came from medically underserved areas (Marquart, Merianos, Cuvelier and Carroll 1996; Berkman 1995). As such, women often bring untreated health concerns to prison, such as sexually transmitted diseases, high blood pressure, asthma, and diabetes (Maeve 1999). Furthermore, incarcerated females often lack a fundamental knowledge of basic health care concepts and have not taken careful care of their health in the past (Maeve 1999). Incarcerated women in California interviewed as part of the Women in Prison Project admitted entering correctional facilities with very poor health circumstances: they discussed their homelessness and poverty as particularly problematic, and admitted to various unhealthy behaviours such as drug use and sex work.

Mental health

Incarcerated women suffer from a number of mental health issues, such as depression, anxiety, post-traumatic stress disorder, and personality disorders (Auerhahn and Dermody Leonard 2000). In California, almost a third of incarcerated women report mental health problems (Little Hoover Commission, LHC 2004). California stakeholders interviewed as part of the Women in Prison Project estimate these numbers to be considerably higher. They cite depression, anxiety, post-traumatic stress disorder (PTSD), and substance abuse as particularly prevalent among incarcerated women.

Trauma

Gender differences in mental health are informed by women's difficult histories of physical and sexual abuse. Incarcerated women are much more likely than men to have been physically or sexually abused; 55% of women in gaols, compared to 13% of men (James 2004) and 57% of women in state prisons, compared to 16% of men (Harlow 1999), reported suffering from physical or sexual abuse. Staff members in several individual institutions have estimated this figure to be a great deal higher (Radosh 2002). Many women who have suffered from physical and sexual abuse suffer from long-standing depression and chaotic lives (Maeve 1997). Victimisation contributes to mental health and substance abuse issues (Reed and Mowbray 1999). Post-traumatic stress disorder (PTSD) caused by past experiences of abuse is an especially common mental health problem for women behind bars (Stoller 2001). By and large, these women have received little treatment or support to assist them in coping with the trauma they have experienced (Kane and DiBartolo 2002). As such, these histories of abuse inform high rates of mental health problems among incarcerated women. Our interviews with incarcerated women found that these women's lives from a very young age were affected by victimisation; a number of women mentioned feeling they had grown up aware of the constant possibility of sexual abuse in their homes.

Substance abuse

Many incarcerated women find themselves addicted to substances, with significant impact to their health and criminal behaviour. This substance use often begins as a way for women to self-medicate their significant mental health issues and histories of victimisation (Belknap

2001). A 1999 study by the Bureau of Justice Statistics reported that about six in ten women in State prison admitted using drugs in the month before the offence, five in ten described themselves as daily drug users, and four in ten said they were under the influence of drugs at the time of the offence (Greenfeld and Snell 1999). Men had lower rates of drug use on all these measures.

Unsurprisingly, studies find that drug and alcohol abuse are harmful to women's overall health (Reed and Mowbray 1999). Women with substance abuse issues suffered from hepatitis, cirrhosis, higher risk for bone fracture, and anaemia (Reed and Mowbray 1999). Some practices associated with substance use were particularly harmful; among prisoners who had used needles to inject drugs or were alcohol dependent, health problems were more common (Maruschak and Beck 2001). One-third of prisoners studied by Snell and Morton (1994) had used illegal drugs, and an estimated 18% had shared needles. Furthermore, women who injected drugs were more likely to engage in risky sexual behaviour, such as having unprotected intercourse (Shearer 2003). In fact, women often resort to sex work to support their addictions (Belknap 2001).

As part of the Women in Prison Project, we found substance use to be an overwhelming issue. Incarcerated women and stakeholders cited the significant effects substance abuse had on women's lives, particularly their ability to take care of their families and away from the streets and negative behaviours. Incarcerated women discussed long histories of drug addiction and the difficulties they had faced in battling their substance use in the past.

Reproductive health problems

Incarcerated women are especially at risk for reproductive health problems due to histories of sexual victimisation and risky sexual behaviours, limited access to health care services, as well as unhealthy behaviours while pregnant. In California, 10% of women who enter gaols and prisons are pregnant and up to 15% are postpartum (Stoller 2001). Many of these pregnancies may be high risk; in one study of prenatal care for incarcerated women, results indicated that 71% of pregnant women had drug abuse problems, 70% smoked, and 21% had other medical problems (Acoca 1998).

Among state prisoners, nearly 5% of females were HIV positive in 2002 (compared to 2% of men) (Greenfeld and Snell 1999).

These findings were paralleled in the Women in Prison Project in California. Stakeholders expressed similar concern regarding women's reproductive health issues, and stressed that chlamydia had become a significant problem among incarcerated females, particularly young women.

Effects of incarceration on women's health

The current male-centered model of correctional facilities is the 'mega-prison': a facility designed to prevent escape, and punish and incapacitate violent offenders. This punitive approach, which undermines prisoner's self-value is especially ill-suited to female offenders, most of who are non-violent, drug-addicted, and have histories of abuse. Furthermore, it undermines women's ability to become agents of their own health, which is particularly important once they are released.

Mental health

Incarceration can have serious mental health effects, particularly for women with children and past histories of victimisation. The difficulties surrounding being sent to prison, and prison conditions themselves, compound depression for most women (Maeve 1998).

Researchers find that incarcerated mothers' separation from their children has significant negative consequences for both the mothers and the children (Maeve 1997; Auerhahn and Dermody Leonard 2000). Incarcerated women in California are more likely to be parents, to have multiple children, and to live with their children than incarcerated men (Powell and Nolan 2003). As such, they are more likely to have to confront the negative consequences their incarceration has on their children. Facilitating contact between children and their incarcerated parents has been linked with a reduction in the strain of separation (Women's Prison Association, WPA 1996) the promotion of family reunification upon release, improved mental health status and functioning for women and their children, reduced parental recidivism, and reduced disciplinary problems for children (Stanley and Byrne 2000). Nevertheless, prisons and gaols present many obstacles to family contact, particularly with regards to their remote locations, restrictive visiting policies, inadequate visiting facilities for children, and costs of phone communication (LHC 2004; Bloom 1995; WPA 1996).

Research indicates search and supervision practices in prisons can retraumatise women with histories of abuse, particularly if male guards are performing these practices (LHC 2004). It should be noted that changes in the California Department of Corrections and Rehabilitation within the last year have aimed to stop the practice of males patting down female inmates (Warren 2006). Furthermore, a study of a state prison system revealed that sexual victimisation rates in the female facilities were significantly higher than those for male facilities, especially with respect to abusive sexual contact between inmates (Wolff, Blitz, Shi, Bachman and Siegel 2006). A California study revealed high rates of sexual harassment and abuse of women by guards (Stoller 2001). Sexual victimisation can have a number of negative mental health effects, such as depression and unhealthy behaviours such as drug use (Wolff *et al.* 2006; Belknap 2001; Reed and Mowbray 1999).

Likewise, as part of the Women in Prison Project, stakeholders and incarcerated women highlighted the negative mental health effects of imprisonment on women. They stressed the suffering caused by separating mothers from their children, and detailed a number of problematic aspects of life within correctional walls, such as loss of personal freedom and sexual outlets. Stakeholders were particularly concerned that the many women with PTSD due to prior victimisation were particularly vulnerable to the abusive conditions within correctional facilities. Furthermore, they indicated concern that mentally ill women, whose symptoms are often labeled as illicit behaviour, were being isolated in Security Housing Units (SHU). Incarcerated women also stressed their displeasure with their seemingly excessive unscheduled time; one mentioned, 'all I can do is think, think, be inside my head; I'm going crazy!' Our study also found protective factors associated with having children. Our interviewees indicated that having a child gave incarcerated women 'something to go back to'. A woman in a Californian gaol shared that it would be easy to lose hope and to get caught up in the daily difficulties of life inside, but contact with her family helped her see that she had a life waiting outside for her, and helped keep her positive and motivated while inside.

Reproductive health

Pregnant women in correctional facilities face abrupt and rough treatment during their pregnancy and are quickly separated from their children after giving birth; all incarcerated women appear to be at risk of sexual victimisation. Before changes that occurred in the past year (Warren 2006), pregnant women in California were shackled for transport to outside hospitals; some even remained shackled during delivery (ACWP 2003). Women in prison are usually separated from their infants soon after birth and have very little contact with them during their incarceration (Acoca 1998). These children are often denied the health benefits of breast-feeding and typically suffer from a lack of attachment (Acoca 1998). Furthermore, a study of a state prison system revealed that sexual victimisation rates in the female facilities were significantly higher than those for male facilities, placing women at risk of sexually transmitted infections (Wolff *et al.* 2006). Stakeholders interviewed for the Women in Prison Project in 2005 confirm that pregnant women were treated roughly within correctional facilities, and worried that adoption agencies surfaced soon after women gave birth, bribing and manipulating women into parting with their children.

Physical health

With their lack of cleanliness and appropriate sanitation, as well as their over crowdedness, incarceration facilities often perpetuate physical health problems. A California study found that unintentional and usually preventable injuries, including broken bones and head injuries, were widespread in women's prisons (Stoller 2001). Stakeholders in the Women in Prison Project were particularly concerned about staphylococcus, which can be fatal, and is easily transmitted through unsanitary conditions; the risks of contracting it increase after surgery due to poor follow-up care. Incarcerated women were very concerned about their health exposure due to their unsanitary living conditions and sharing living quarters with so many women; one incarcerated woman in California spoke of sneaking cleaning supplies after the routine cleaning so she could try to maintain her area between the official cleanings. Women discussed having to live with women who were obviously sick and even had open wounds.

Health care in correctional facilities

A typical incarcerated woman lacks adequate health care prior to incarceration, receives inadequate care while incarcerated, and is released to medically underserved communities.

Access to health care

Process of access

Incarcerated women in California face numerous obstacles in accessing health care. Women must fill out a co-pay form, detailing their symptoms to schedule a non-emergency appointment; appointments are scheduled based on the relative importance of the request (ACWP 2003). Sick-call is designed to provide a woman with quicker, same-day treatment for pressing medical issues (ACWP 2003). Women go to the Medical Department, sign up on a waiting list, and wait outside, regardless of weather conditions, to be seen by a health professional; after being seen by a nurse, they must fill out a co-pay form (ACWP 2003). Additionally, sick-call is frequently cancelled; this is particularly problematic for women needing a medical 'lay-in' excusing them from work (ACWP 2003). Finally, to receive emergency care, a woman must convince a guard with no medical training of the seriousness of her condition. The guard, in turn, must convince medical staff that the prisoner requires immediate medical attention (ACWP 2003). However, studies find that staff tend to see women as manipulators who exaggerate their medical conditions; as such, they may ignore their pleas (ACWP 2003; Young 2000). It is not uncommon for medical staff to refuse to see a woman, regardless of the efforts of the correctional officers (ACWP 2003).

Women with limited communication skills and limited writing ability are often unable to communicate the scope or nature of their symptoms (ACWP 2003). Inmates who do not speak English are particularly vulnerable, as no official translation services are provided; in some cases, other prisoners will be asked to translate (ACWP 2003; Stoller 2001). Since women must convince guards and medical professionals of their need for all types of care, including emergency care, this can be particularly dangerous and problematic.

Stakeholders and incarcerated women interviewed for the Women in Prison Project reported similar circumstances. Stakeholders said women often waited outside during sick-call for hours before seeing a nurse; furthermore, they reported the deaths of women whose pleas were ignored by prison guards. Stakeholders told researchers that medical staff often used a 'proper' form of English difficult to understand for many incarcerated women. Meanwhile, incarcerated women described waiting in line for hours

Delays

The women Young (2000) interviewed reported frustrations related to long delays in receiving medical treatment. These delays occurred during sick-call, while waiting to see a medical provider, while providers figured out adequate treatment, and while women waited to receive treatment or medical equipment. The findings of the Women in Prison Project find similar delays for women in California. Stakeholders reported that appointment and services are frequently scheduled several months after inmates submit requests. Incarcerated women told the researchers that it was not worthwhile to ask for medical assistance unless they were suffering from a serious illness; by the time they finally got an appointment, they were no longer ill.

Medicine

Studies find that difficulties in obtaining medication are one of the biggest complaints for California's incarcerated women (ACWP 2003; Stoller 2001). In fact, women with medical problems requiring daily medication, such as heart disease, may experience delays for days at a time (ACWP 2003). These delays can exacerbate medical problems and create needless emergencies; for women with HIV and Hepatitis C it is particularly important to follow a timely treatment regimen. Women are not allowed to keep a variety of medications, referred to as 'hot meds', in their cells. Women with prescriptions for 'hot meds' are forced to stand in long lines two or three times a day, depending on their regimen, to receive their medicine. Sometimes, they must forego dinner and other activities while they wait in line (ACWP 2003). In addition, pain medication is notoriously difficult to obtain, even for women recovering from surgery or suffering from a terminal disease (ACWP 2003). As part of the Women in Prison Project, stakeholders reported that incarcerated women often complain of delays receiving their medication.

Five-dollar co-pay

California women must pay five dollars for each medical visit (ACWP 2003). Emergency care and follow-up services are exempt from this charge; however, women are often asked to pay for these as well, and can only challenge these charges through a lengthy and complicated appeals process (ACWP 2003). This co-pay charge discourages women from seeking treatment, particularly before their symptoms get very serious, presents an economic burden to poor incarcerated women, and has no demonstrated economic benefit to the California

Department of Corrections and Rehabilitation (Stoller 2001). Stakeholders and women incarcerated, interviewed as part of the Women in Prison Project emphasised the economic hardships and indicated that in some cases women are forced to make the decision between medical attention and other necessities such as sanitary products.

Gaps in health care

Incarcerated women and researchers typically described the health care they received as insufficient and inadequate (Belknap 1997; Ross and Lawrence 1998; Young 2000). Incarcerated women who spoke to Young (2000) felt the care they received was not thorough. Sometimes, these women felt that they were not given any options or input in the type of treatment they could receive, e.g. perhaps they were interested in trying exercise instead of only medication. Sometimes these women said only the bare minimum of care was provided.

Incarcerated women report insufficiency and inadequacy in all types of health services, such as dental health, particularly important for women who have experienced a lifetime of dental neglect and suffer from methamphetamine and other drug addictions that cause significant dental harm (Stoller 2001). Particularly problematic appear to be gender-responsive services, as well as the areas where women have unique health needs: reproductive and mental health services.

Medical Professionals

Studies find that incarcerated women feel that medical providers do not care about their well-being (Belknap 1997; Maeve 1999; Young 2000). Despite some positive comments about care received, the majority of women in Young's (2000) study felt their needs were not treated as important and that they were 'lumped together' and stereotyped as drug seekers, liars, responsible for their own health problems, and unworthy of quality care (p. 228). In addition, a number of the women felt the treatment they received was abrupt (Young 2000). One study found that women felt their care was intertwined with a punishment mentality (Maeve 1999). Vaughn and Smith (1999) report that sometimes medical care is withheld or delayed, or used to humiliate women prisoners. Medical care professionals expressed concern about their personal safety and the view that prisoners were exaggerating or even fabricating medical symptoms for personal gain (American Psychiatric Association 2000).

Stakeholders and incarcerated women interviewed as part of the Women in Prison Project described instances of hostile behaviour by medical staff towards women. A stakeholder described a sign hung in a clinic, mandating that patients complain about no more than two symptoms. Stakeholders reported a number of deaths that occurred as a result of critically ill women being refused treatment. Incarcerated women felt correctional and medical staff played favorites in helping women access medical services and medication.

Mental health and substance abuse treatment

Given the severity of women's treatment needs, mental health and substance abuse treatment appear to be insufficient and inadequate in correctional facilities. Studies find that instead of providing substantial counselling to address women's underlying issues, mental health treatment often consists of prescribing medication (Auerhahn and Dermody Leonard 2000; Maeve 1997). Access to substance-abuse treatment in prison is limited. At the national level, Sokoloff (2003) estimates that only 10% of incarcerated women with substance abuse problems are offered adequate drug treatment. In California, the in-prison substance abuse treatment only has beds for 18% of the female population considered in need (LHC 2004). Even when programmes are funded and well-attended, they are usually very limited in scope (Owen and Bloom 1995). For example, substance abuse programmes may only constitute weekly group discussions. In fact, the availability of formal treatment, as opposed to activities such as support groups, has decreased (Mumola 2000).

California stakeholders interviewed as part of the Women in Prison Project felt mental health treatment constituted the largest gap in prison health services. Stakeholders believe that prison staffs dismiss the significance and repercussions of mental health issues among prisoners. Further, stakeholders confirmed that some correctional facilities only have psychiatrists to prescribe medication: they do not have mental health counsellors. Incarcerated women mentioned waiting hours in line for a ten-minute appointment with a psychiatrist. With such a limited timeframe, the women did not feel they could discuss their life circumstances. Furthermore, both stakeholders and incarcerated women expressed concerns that psychiatric drugs were used to sedate and control incarcerated women. Stakeholders felt that women prisoners fearing punitive repercussions find it difficult to reveal their personal histories and speak truthfully to counsellors with correctional affiliations. Both stakeholders and incarcerated women report that counselling and intervention programs that address drug addiction can only serve an extremely limited number of the women who need such services.

Reproductive health

Women's reproductive health needs have been largely disregarded, and appear to point to a greater overall disregard of women's needs. Unfortunately, there is no systematic or routine administration of mammograms, pap smears, or comprehensive STD screening in California (ACWP 2003; Stoller 2001). Pregnant women receive inadequate health and prenatal care, little counselling, isolation, lack of parenting classes, lack of nutrition education, increased rate of caesarian delivery, and concurrent medical problems, all which combine to negatively affect the health of both mother and child (Stoller 2001). Concerns such as high blood pressure, lack of foetal heartbeat, and vaginal bleeding are often ignored; this has resulted in late-term miscarriages, premature deliveries, still births, and severe health problems for infants (ACWP 2003).

Unfortunately, stakeholders interviewed as part of the Women in Prison Project described reproductive health care as inadequate. They indicated pap smear requests can take over six months to fulfill. Despite the invasive nature of this procedure, stakeholders report that women cannot request treatment by female staff and that treatment by a largely male staff is rough and abusive with instances of using an over-sized speculum, and performing exams in abrupt forceful manners. One stakeholder described cases where women were subjected to gynecological procedures without their full knowledge and full consent; some of these procedures resulted in forced or coerced sterilisation. Furthermore, stakeholders mentioned that some pregnant women do not see obstetricians nor do they receive sonograms.

Lack of gender-appropriate services

There is significant evidence that women respond differently to community supervision, incarceration, treatment, and rehabilitation than men (Bloom *et al.* 2004). Importantly, gender is not considered in staffing decisions – for institutions or parole – and training is not provided to prepare staff to work effectively with female offenders (LHC 2004). The vast majority of programmes in the four women's prisons are identical to the programmes offered in the men's prisons (LHC 2004). In addition to two small programmes for pregnant or parenting female offenders, there is some gender-responsive programming including a parent and child development course, battered women support groups, and mental health groups focusing on surviving sexual abuse and other women's issues. However, the availability for such gender-responsive planning is severely limited, and only 2% of the female offender population is served at any given time (LHC 2004).

Continuity of health care

Chronic diseases, particularly cancer, have a profound effect on the physical health of incarcerated women. These negative effects are exacerbated due to the lack of continuity of care in California's facilities. Specifically, this lack refers to the inadequate and inefficient medical care provided to women at every stage of health care service continuum.

Prevention

There is no systematised routine screening approach in California's female prisons (ACWP 2003). This is particularly detrimental to women, whose physiological characteristics have greater need of routine assessments, such as mammograms and pap smears (Stoller 2001). Furthermore, women's interest in being tested and treated for HIV is limited due to confidentiality leaks and inadequate counselling (Stoller 2001). Stakeholders and incarcerated women interviewed as part of the Women in Prison Project said the correctional food had very limited nutritional value, and that women were not allowed sufficient opportunities to exercise.

Follow-up care

Follow-up care appears to be particularly problematic in California's women's correctional facilities. A study of California's women prisons cited instances where women who had reported breast lumps or abnormal bleeding to medical staff had to wait months before being tested and receiving care (ACWP 2003). This study found that abnormal test results are often either completely ignored or delayed sufficiently to significantly impact women's health; in some cases, they found these delays led to deaths (ACWP 2003). Furthermore, the researchers reported test results are often misfiled, and the prisoner, and sometimes even her doctor, are not informed of the results (ACWP 2003). Finally, the study revealed that women's needs were often neglected following surgery; women's bandages went unchanged and their incisions left open, often with very serious consequences to their health.

California stakeholders discussed similar faulty follow-up practices as part of the Women in Prison Project. Stakeholders reported that note-taking within files was inconsistent, making it difficult to track women's medical histories and to ensure appropriate follow-up care. Stakeholders reveal that lack of individual accountability is also a problem, as no specific staff member assumes responsibility for ensuring the completion of the doctor's recommendations.

Transitional care

Women face a multitude of issues upon release such as reuniting with their children, finding housing, and obtaining a job. All these factors affect women's ability to remain physically and mentally healthy, locate health care treatment, and remain substance free. Furthermore, it would seem as if women's highly regimented lifestyles in correctional facilities, particularly in regard to making choices regarding their health care, might hinder their ability to take care of their own health once released. As we have seen, women's recidivism is highly dependent on their success after returning to their communities. Furthermore, given incarcerated women's comparatively high rates of communicable diseases, the communities to which they return are put at risk if women do not access appropriate care.

Unfortunately, additional barriers further complicate California women's transition into the community. After release, California women often cannot obtain federal benefits, cannot obtain employment in certain occupations, and face a number of legal barriers in reuniting with their children if they have entered the child welfare system (LHC 2004; Sokoloff 2003). Furthermore, since prisoners cannot assess federally funded healthcare while incarcerated, women face a gap, ranging from days to months, before they can receive health benefits (Roberts *et al.* 2001). The policy of requiring parolees to return to the county in which they were convicted may interfere with relapse prevention efforts, as they return to the negative influences of their past (Hall, Baldwin, and Prendergast 2001). Finally, available programmes, such as substance abuse treatment for released women, can treat only a small portion of the women in need, and may not adequately address their needs (Hall, Baldwin and Prendergast 2001).

Stakeholders and incarcerated women interviewed as part of the Women in Prison Project discussed similar difficulties and concerns women faced after release. Most incarcerated women expressed optimism and excitement about their release; nevertheless, they worried about maintaining their substance-free lifestyle, particularly about feeling compelled to return to the street if their families did not provide them with a place to live. Reuniting with children and other family members, given the strained relation caused by their incarceration, was another concern. One woman admitted to feeling perplexed as to how she would go about earning money without resorting to "hustling." Stakeholders reported that medical records are often not transferred or at lost entirely when an incarcerated woman moves from one facility to another. Stakeholders said that after release, women were taken off their medications and could no longer access their medical histories. Furthermore, stakeholders report that women are sometimes released without proper identification documents, complicating their ability to access healthcare resources on the outside.

Causes of problematic health care

The findings from the literature review and the Women in Prison Project point to a few probable reasons for problematic healthcare in women's correctional facilities.

Lack of services

At 186% of capacity, female prisons in California are severely overcrowded (CDCR 2006a). Such overcrowding leads to reduced programming space, reduced programming, and inadequate staffing (Corrections Independent Review Panel 2004). Furthermore, as we have seen, such overcrowding can lead to unsanitary conditions; unsanitary conditions and being surrounded by many people put women at risk of contracting disease.

Adapted from a male model

Female facilities and treatment replicate that of males, with negative health consequences for women. The fact that women constitute a small portion of the correctional population has been used to justify a lack of adequate programming and treatment for them (Belknap 2001). Women's particular needs, such as counselling to address their histories of trauma, as well as the importance of creating a safe space for women are disregarded in favor of custodial concerns and medication. Similarly, this may explain the overwhelming disregard for women's reproductive needs. Interestingly, gender is not considered in staffing decisions – for institutions or parole – and training is not provided to prepare staff to work effectively with women under correctional care (LHC 2004).

Medical personnel appear to be staffed according to a male model

(Ammar and Erez 2000). However, women have unique medical needs and request more services than men (Ammar and Eerez 2000; Hyde, Brumfield and Nagel 2000; Ingram-Fogel 1991; Lindsquist and Lindsquist 1999). Indeed, a 1999 study by the Bureau of Justice Statistics reported that substance-abusing women inmates were more likely than their male counterparts to report receiving substance-abuse treatment (Greenfeld and Snell 1999).

As such, medical personnel may be particularly overworked and unprepared to work with women in prison, resulting in abrupt or delayed care (Belknap 1997; Young 2000). Interestingly, Morash, Haarr and Rucker (1994) found that despite women's high use of medical services, they had considerably less access to health services than did male prisoners. Reed and Mowbray (1999) reported the failure of medical professionals to understand the different ways women's health is affected by substance abuse. The co-occurrence of mental health and substance abuse issues, from which women are more likely to suffer, can obscure physical and mental ailments and complicate treatment (LHC 2004).

Custodial concerns

In a correctional setting, medical concerns appear to take the backseat to custodial concerns (Vaughn 1999). As such, it is considered preferable that women do not keep daily medications, even for serious illness such as HIV, and risk potentially serious health consequences, than to trust these women with medication. A study found that women felt their health care was intertwined with punishment, because it was provided through the corrections department (Maeve 1999). In California, at the time of the stakeholder interviews, a Medical Technician Assistant was a peace officer in addition to a medical professional (ACWP 2003). Sometimes, correctional officers undertake tasks intended for medical professionals (Vaughn and Collins 2004) or override the suggestions of medical staff (Ammar and Erez 2000). For example, Ammar and Erez (2000) described how a doctor's efforts to have a woman with serious heart problems transported to an outside specialist were thwarted by a correction officer's unwillingness to drive the woman in the fog.

Stakeholders interviewed as part of the Women in Prison Project and incarcerated women expressed concerns that psychiatric drugs were used to sedate and control incarcerated women. As such, even medical providers are seen as more interested in controlling the women than in improving their health conditions. Stakeholders reported that women prisoners fearing punitive repercussions find it difficult to reveal their personal histories and speak truthfully to counsellors with correctional affiliations

Cultural competency

Stakeholders and incarcerated women interviewed as part of the Women in Prison Project reported that medical staff are not representative of the ethnic distribution of the incarcerated female population; as such, cultural competency in attitude and practices is particularly important. Stakeholders indicated that they felt the medical professionals displayed racist attitudes and behaviours. Given incarcerated women report that they are treated according to pre-established stereotypes of prisoners as liars and drug-seekers, stakeholders hypothesised that medical staff stereotypes of other races helps them view women in correctional facilities as dishonest, dirty, unintelligent, and generally undeserving of adequate health care. Stakeholders suggested that ingrained racial stereotypes may make it more difficult for incarcerated women to trust medical and correctional staff. An increase in cultural awareness might improve the overall treatment received by incarcerated women, and create an awareness of the need for increased translation services and for health treatment that includes non-western medical practices.

Difficulties recruiting and the negative socialising of medical personnel

It can be difficult to recruit medical professionals because of the comparatively low pay (Acoca 1998; ACWP 2003), the typically remote, rural locations of prisons (Acoca 1998), and the considerable stigma attached to working within correctional facilities (Dabney and Vaughn 2000). Dabney and Vaughn (2000) found that physicians who work in correctional settings are perceived as inept. Furthermore, particular requirements of working in a correctional setting may be undesirable. For example, nurses in Ammar and Erez's (2000) study faced mandatory overtime. As such, nurses with undergraduate and more advanced degrees have more appealing and lucrative opportunities for employment elsewhere (Maeve and Vaughn 2001); prison doctors who may have had licensure problems are still employable within the prison system (Dabney and Vaughn 2000). Furthermore, it appears that correctional facilities may draw those health care providers who are attracted to the idea of controlling and punishing prisoners (Maeve and Vaughn 2001).

Furthermore, the correctional atmosphere, particularly the

'collective demonisation' of prisoners, can make it easier for medical providers to violate their ethical obligations (Vaughn and Smith 1999: 217). Maeve (1997) described her own experiences as a nurse in a correctional institution. She was instructed to distrust prisoners, that 'empathy would be your downfall', to stay distant, and to never touch a prisoner. In addition, in correctional settings, nurses most closely associate and socialise with officers and guards who practice from a different set of professional and moral principles (Maeve and Vaughn 2001).

Maeve found that health care providers were socialised to see prisoners as manipulators (1999). Given the relative scarcity of medical providers and the tendency for providers to dismiss inmate requests, there is a temptation for incarcerated women to exaggerate their symptoms to receive treatment (Maeve 1999). Furthermore, incarcerated women have the motivation to feign illness to obtain drugs for personal use (Lindquist and Lindquist 1999) or to use in the informal market within the correctional facility (Ammar and Erez 2000). Typically, these embellishments did not work and only promote the distrust among medical providers (Maeve 1999). Nevertheless, studies that review medical records show that the vast majority of female health visits were for legitimate health problems (Watterson 1996; Young 2000).

Administrative barriers

Women's health status and the treatment they receive are impacted on by bureaucratic barriers throughout their time in correctional facilities and after they have left these facilities. They must fill out co-pay forms to access care and appeals forms to protest problematic care, regardless of their level of literacy. Problematic note-taking and filing by medical professionals leads to inappropriate follow-up care. Inadequate protocols of care and clear guidelines for appropriate treatment services, makes it difficult to hold anybody accountable when problematic care occurs. Finally, women are released and face a number of barriers before they can obtain identification, access their medical records, and qualify for health services.

Recommendations and discussion

Though much more research is necessary to determine exactly how the unique health issues of incarcerated women should impact on their treatment, the findings in this study suggest a number of possible courses of action to improve incarcerated women's health status, the services women receive during their time in correctional facilities, as well as their transition back into the community. Furthermore, in this section we will present current 'best practices' for working with incarcerated women and women on parole.

Decarcerate and promote alternatives to incarceration

Incarcerated women are mostly low-level offenders, with histories of victimisation and with serious economic and health needs. Most do not represent a serious threat to their communities. Alternatives to incarceration could help put them back on a course towards becoming productive mothers and community members.

Community-based correctional facilities

In California, Governor Schwarzenegger recently called for the movement of 4,500 low-level non-violent women in prison into community-based correctional facilities. This would be a step towards the larger goal of moving most non-serious non-violent women (about 70% of the total female prison population) into community-based placement. Because community-based alternatives to incarceration operate on a smaller, more personal scale, and have stronger links to the community, these facilities are much more likely to provide appropriate services, including healthcare, than prisons. Further, community-based facilities are less likely to isolate women from their families and sources of support. The primary emphasis in prisons has been punishment and confinement, whereas community-based settings can emphasise treatment, service provisions, and community re-entry.

Sentencing reform

While NCCD supports the CDCR's female reform effort, it also strongly supports essential sentencing and parole reforms. Legislative reforms are necessary to affect the treatment of women involved in the criminal justice system. Particularly problematic legislation include: the three strikes laws, mandatory minimums, truth-in-sentencing, and parole revocation policies. These legislative policies unnecessarily place low-level non-violent women in short-term prison stints that do not address their needs, leading to high recidivism rates and exacerbating women's risk factors, including health issues.

Women need diversion, especially around drug treatment. Proposition 36, the Substance Abuse and Crime Prevention Act of 2000, is perhaps one of the most successful changes to sentencing and parole legislation. This public-enacted legislative reform allows people convicted of drug crimes or drug-related probation and parole violations to be sent to community treatment programmes instead of prisons. Correctional officials cite Proposition 36 as a large contributor to the 10% drop in the female prison population from 2001 to 2002 (Drug Policy Alliance 2002). Due to this Proposition and other efforts, from 2002 to 2003, only 17% of the 5,542 female parolee drug violations were sent to the Parole Board for a revocation hearing. Tellingly, support for this legislation appears to have grown since its passing. While 61% of people voted for this proposition in 2000, a 2004 poll showed that 73% of likely voters would vote in favor of Proposition 36 if it were put out to a vote again (Krisberg, Craine, and Marchionna 2004).

Improve services inside Correctional Facilities

Health care inside women's correctional facilities is insufficient and inadequate.

Prioritise medical services

It seems clear that custodial concerns are often prioritised to the detriment of medical concerns. Given the relation between women's health needs, such as drug addiction, and their success after release, as well as ethical and legal medical obligations, it appears this balance needs to shift to accommodate adequate health services. It might be sensible and cost-effective to move health care outside of the realm of correctional facilities, and make an outside agency responsible for health care delivery.

Improve access to care

Facilities should eliminate the co-pay, sick call, and hot meds policies, as they are particularly ineffective. As previously discussed, these services worsen health conditions by forcing women to fill out forms they may not understand due to language barriers and illiteracy, wait in long lines for extended periods of time, and be unable to advocate for their own well-being. Furthermore, these policies do not support positive patient-doctor relationships and are not conducive to the provision of adequate health care. Verbal and written translation services should be available to women who struggle with English.

Furthermore, women with low-literacy skills also require special assistance. Expanding the system's response to women's expressed health requests, particularly regarding a more holistic approach to health care, could help make women used to different forms of health treatment more comfortable and receptive to services within correctional facilities.

Increase prevention efforts

Prevention efforts should be expanded and improved. Specifically, exercise and nutritional needs must be addressed, routine screenings should be systematised, and voluntary testing for threatening or infectious disease must be made available and kept confidential. Furthermore, education could be a powerful prevention tool.

Improve follow up efforts

Medical staff must adopt standard record-keeping and note-taking systems, as well as protocols, to respond quickly to abnormal test results and to properly care for women after surgery.

Prioritise mental health and substance abuse treatment

Women suffer from mental health and substance abuse in large numbers; both of these issues are informed by histories of victimisation. As such, mental health services need to encompass appropriate counselling in addition to medication. Assuring confidentiality is crucial. Treatment should be responsive to the interrelation between substance abuse and mental health issues.

Prioritise reproductive status

Women's reproductive health services need to be expanded and improved, including prenatal care, regular feminine care, and routine screenings.

Improve quality of staff

Standards of hiring must be improved, and recruitment and retention incentives provided in order to assure that competent and well-intentioned staff are employed. Efforts should be made to hire females and people of colour to work in correctional facilities. Furthermore, quality training must be provided to ensure that the correct services are administered and positive, culturally and gender appropriate attitudes are exhibited; negative socialising should be curbed as much as possible. Medical staff should have clear guidelines by which they are held accountable.

Support continuity of care

The vast majority of women will be released from prison after a relatively short time and have to transition back into their communities upon release from prison. Incarcerated women face a number of challenges upon release, all which appear pressing: trouble finding housing, obtaining a job, and reuniting and caring for their children. As such, they may not prioritise health care. Nevertheless, adequate transitional health care is essential in ensuring that the women and the communities to which they return are healthy, that they achieve their main goals, and to curb recidivism.

Establish community linkages

Incarcerated women should be linked with community-based health organisations prior to their actual release from prison. This practice will also facilitate the efficient transfer of medical records. Research shows that a released female is more likely to stay on treatment if she has the following at the time of release (Roberts, Kennedy, Hammet and Rosenberg 2001):

- Medication to cover the gap before medical benefits are obtained;
- A copy of the prison medical summary;
- Schedules of follow-up appointments;
- Assistance completing applications for medical benefits;
- And connections to other re-entry services such as housing, cash benefits, and treatment for mental health and substance abuse, if necessary.

Assist drug addicted women

For the many incarcerated women with substance abuse issues, attendance at a community treatment programme, particularly a residential programme, can dramatically increase the likelihood of avoiding relapse and successfully discharging from parole (Prendergast, Wellisch and Wong 1996). Furthermore, providing women with more treatment options within their county where they were convicted, and allowing some to parole to another county, may help women avoid their drug-using areas (Hall, Baldwin and Prendergast 2001).

Reduce legal barriers to re-entry

The State should modify the ban on welfare funds for non-violent drug felons to improve housing, employment, cash, and substance abuse treatment opportunities; researchers suggest that women attending substance abuse treatment or who have been successfully discharged from parole be allowed to receive benefits (Hall, Baldwin, and Prendergast 2001). The ban on parolees' work opportunities in various sectors as well as the ban of former offenders as barbers and beauticians, should be re-examined. Furthermore, the State should ensure that all incarcerated women leave correctional facilities with proper identification documents. The Adoption and Safe Families Act should be modified to account for the particular restrictions of incarcerated women, perhaps extending the timeline for women to reunify with their children.

Provide gender-responsive services

Considering women's unique histories, needs, and pathways to crime, gender-responsive programming is essential at every level of the system. Some necessary improvements, such as follow-up of services and promoting community linkages, would be helpful to all incarcerated individuals. Nevertheless, it is not sufficient to improve services without paying attention to women's unique health issues and pathways to criminality.

Implement gender-responsive programming

The National Institute of Corrections' Gender-Responsive Strategies: Research, practice and guiding principles for women offenders report (Bloom, Owen and Covington 2003) documents the need for a new vision for the criminal justice system, one that recognises the behavioural and social differences between female and male offenders that have specific implications for gender-responsive policy and practice (Bloom, Owen and Covington 2003). They proposed the following guiding principles of a gender-responsive model:

- Acknowledge that gender makes a difference;
- Create and sustain an environment based on safety, respect, and dignity;
- Develop policies, practices, and programmes that are relationship-based and that promote healthy connections to children, family, significant others, and the community;
- Address substance abuse, trauma, and mental health issues through comprehensive, integrated, culturally-relevant services and appropriate supervision;

- Provide women with opportunities to improve their socioeconomic conditions;
- And establish a system of community supervision and re-entry with comprehensive, collaborative services.

Certain approaches have proven particularly promising in regards to working with incarcerated women, such as all-female programmes (Lockwood, McCorkel and Inciardi 1998), empowerment models (Richie 2001; Brown, Melchior and Huba 1999), integrated treatment for women with co-occurring disorders (Minkoff 1989; 2001), and the provision of supplementary services, such as vocational lessons, childcare, parenting, classes, and housing assistance (Hall, Baldwin and Prendergast 2001; Clark 2001). Promising treatment approaches for substance abusing women include comprehensive, multi-systemic treatment models (Conners, Bradley, Whiteside-Mansell and Crone 2001) and cognitive-behavioural treatment (Hall, Prendergast, Wellisch, Patten and Cao 2004).

Evaluate programming

In addition to understanding differences between men and women, we need to understand the process by which these differences are relevant towards treatment outcomes in both community and criminal justice settings (Prelissier and Jones 2005). To create truly gender-responsive services, we need a systematic examination of the theoretical and programmatic implications of our knowledge of criminal justice-involved women.

The comparatively small number of women in correctional facilities does not fully explain the current lack of knowledge regarding programme outcomes for females; even outcome studies with sufficient number of female participants rarely report outcomes by gender or focus on relevant approaches (e.g. same-sex groups) (Pelissier and Jones 2005). Outcome evaluations should certainly present their outcomes by gender and pay particular attention to promising treatment approaches. Furthermore, they should include outcome measures beyond recidivism, as incarcerated women struggle with a variety of issues that have repercussions in their families and community. Possible outcome measures could include substance recovery, housing, employment, mental health, and improved family relationships (Bloom 2000).

Conclusion

The California Department of Corrections and Rehabilitation appears to have accepted the importance of gender-responsive strategies (Hickman 2006) and has made some headway towards improving services. In the last year, CDCR has stopped allowing male guards to pat down female inmates, halted the shackling of prisoners during labour and childbirth, improved nutrition for pregnant women, and increased access to female hygiene products (Warren 2006). Furthermore, a twenty-cell wing is being built at the California Institution for Women that will allow new mothers to be housed with their newborns for up to eighteen months and then move into special community housing upon parole. Officials say they are considering changing visitation practices to enhance bonding between incarcerated mothers and their children (Warren 2006).

These changes underscore the importance of taking gender into account in regards to correctional decision-making. In these times of rising female incarceration and potential for change at the California Department of Corrections and Rehabilitation, it is particularly important to provide treatment that is responsive to the gendered pathways to criminality as well as unique health needs of women.

References

Acoca, L. (1998) 'Defusing the time bomb: Understanding and meeting the growing health care needs of incarcerated women in America', *Crime and Delinquency*, 44 (1): 49–69.

Action Committee for Women in Prison (2003) *Survey of medical care provided to women in California prisons*. California, USA: California Criminal Justice Consortium.

American Psychiatric Association (2000). Malingering or real illness: Prison staff learn difference, Psychiatric News, October, 2000, at: http://www.psych.org/pnews/00-10-20/malingering.html

Ammar, N.H. and Erez, E. (2000) 'Health delivery systems in women's prisons: the case of Ohio', *Federal Probation*, 64: 19–26.

Auerhahn, K. and Leonard, E.D. (2000) 'Docile Bodies?: Chemical restraints and the female inmate', *Journal of Criminal Law and Criminology*, 90 (2): 599–634.

Belknap, J. (2001) *The Invisible Woman: Gender, crime, and justice*. Belmont, CA: Wadsworth.

Belknap, J. (1997) 'Access to programs and health care for incarcerated women', *Federal Probation*, 60: 34–9.

Berkman, A. (1995) ' Prison health: The breaking point', *American Journal of Public Health*, 85 (12): 1616–18.

Bloom, B. (2000) 'Beyond recidivism: Perspectives on evaluation of programs for female offenders in community corrections', in M. McMahon (ed.) *Assessment to Assistance: Programs for women in community correction.* Lanham, MD: American Correctional Association.

Bloom, B. (1995) 'Imprisoned Mothers', in K. Gabel and D. Johnston (eds) *Children of Incarcerated Parents.* New York, NY: Lexington Books.

Bloom, B., Owen, B and Covington, S. (2004) 'Women offenders and the gendered effects of public policy', *Review of Policy Research*, 21 (1): 31–48.

Bloom, B., Owen, B. and Covington, S. (2003) *Gender-responsive Strategies: Research, practice, and guiding principles for women offenders.* Washington, DC: National Institute of Corrections.

Brown, V.B., Melchior, L.A. and Huba, G.J. (1999) 'Level of burden among women diagnosed with severe mental illness and substance abuse', *Journal of Psychoactive Drugs*, 31 (1): 31–41.

Bureau of Justice Statistics (2001a) *Prisoners in 2000.* Washington, DC: US Department of Justice.

Bureau of Justice Statistics (2001b) *Prison and Jail Inmates at Midyear 2000.* Washington, DC: US Department of Justice.

California Department of Corrections and Rehabilitation (2006a) *California Prisoners and Parolees 2005.* Sacramento, CA: CDCR Data Analysis Unit.

California Department of Corrections and Rehabilitation (2006b) *Online Query – Jail Profile Survey.* Sacramento, CA: Correction Standards Authority.

Casey, K. and Wiatrowski, M. (1996) 'Women offenders and "three strikes and you're out', *Three strikes and you're out: Vengeance as public policy.* Thousand Oaks, CA: Sage Publications Inc.

Clark, H.W. (2001) 'Residential substance abuse treatment for pregnant and postpartum women and their children: Treatment and policy implications', *Child Welfare*, 80 (2): 179–99.

Conners, N.A., Bradley, R.H., Whiteside-Mansell, L. and Crone, C.C. (2001) 'A comprehensive substance abuse treatment program for women and their children: An initial evaluation', *Journal of Substance Abuse Treatment*, 21: 67–75.

Corrections Independent Review Panel (2004) *Reforming Correction.* Final Report, Sacramento, CA.

Dabney, D and M. Vaughn (2000) 'Incompetent jail and prison doctors', *The Prison Journal*, 80 (2): 151–83.

Farabee, D., Joshi, V. and Anglin, M. (2001) 'Addiction careers and criminal specialization', *Crime and Delinquency*, 47 (2): 196–220.

Glaser, J.B., Warchad, A., D'Angelo, D. and Gutterman, H. (1990) 'Infectious diseases in geriatric inmates', *Review Infectious Diseases*, 12: 683–92.

Greenfeld, L.A. and Snell, T.L. (1999) *Women Offenders: Special Report*. Washington, DC: US Department of Justice, Bureau of Justice Statistics.

Hall, E.A., Baldwin, D.M. and Prendergast M.L. (2001) 'Women on parole: Barriers to success after substance abuse treatment', *Human Organizations*, 60 (3): 225–33.

Hall, E.A., Prendergast, M.L., Wellisch, J., Patten, M. and Cao, Y. (2004) 'Treating drug-abusing women prisoners: An outcome evaluation of the forever free program', *The Prison Journal*, 84 (1): 81–105.

Harlow, C.W. (1999) *Prior Abuse Reported by Inmates and Probationers*, Washington, DC: US Department of Justice, Bureau of Justice Statistics.

Henderson, D.J. (1998) 'Drug abuse and incarcerated women – Career and social adjustment', *Journal of Substance Abuse Treatment*, 15 (6): 579–87.

Hickman, R. (2006) Testimony of Secretary Hickman at Feb. 2 US Senate Oversight Hearing.

Hughes, K. (2004) *Justice Expenditure and Employment in the US 2003*. Washington, DC: Department of Justice, Bureau of Justice Statistics.

Hyde, R., Brumfield, B. and Nagel, J. (2000) 'Female inmate health care requests', *Journal of Correctional Health Care*, 7 (1): 91–103.

Ingram-Fogel, C. (1991) 'Health problems and needs of incarcerated women', *Journal of Prison and Jail Health*, 10 (1): 43–57.

James, D.J. (2004) *Profile of Jail Inmates 2002*, NCJ Publication 201932. Washington DC: National Institute of Justice.

Kane, M. and DiBartolo, M. (2002) 'Complex physical and mental health needs of rural incarcerated women', *Issues in Mental Heath Nursing*, 23: 209–29.

Krisberg, B., Craine, J., and Marchionna, S. (2004) 'Attitudes of Californians Toward Effective Correctional Policies', NCCD Focus. Oakland, CA: National Council on Crime and Delinquency.

Lindquist, C.H. and Lindquist, C.A. (1999) 'Health behind bars: Utilisation and evaluation of medical care among jail inmates', *Journal of Community Health*, 24 (4): 285–303.

Little Hoover Commission (2004) 'Breaking the Barriers for Women on Parole', Sacramento, CA.

Lockwood, D., McCorkel, J. and Inciardi, J.A. (1998) 'Effective drug treatment strategies for female substance abusers: Process, outcome, and cost effectiveness', *Drugs and Society*, 13 (1–2): 192–212.

Maeve, M.K. (1999 'Adjudicated health: Incarcerated women and the social construction of health', *Crime Law and Social Change*, 31: 49–71.

Maeve, M.K. (1998) 'Methodologic issues in qualitative research with incarcerated women', *Family and Community Health*, 21 (3): 1–15.

Maeve, M.K. (1997) 'Nursing practice with incarcerated women: Caring within mandated alienation', *Issues in Mental Health Nursing*, 18: 495–510.

Maeve, M.K and Vaughn, M.S. (2001) 'Nursing with prisoners: the practice of caring, forensic nursing or penal harm nursing?', *Advances in Nursing Science*, 24 (2): 47–64.

Marquart, J.W., Merianos, D.E., Cuvelier, S.J. and Carroll, L. (1996). 'Thinking about the relationship between health dynamics in the free community and the prison', *Crime and Delinquency*, 42 (3): 331–60.

Maruschak, L.M. and Beck, A.J. (2001) 'Medical problems of inmates, 1997', Washington, DC: Bureau of Justice Assistance.

Minkoff, K. (2001) 'Developing standards of care for individuals with co-occurring psychiatric and substance use disorders', *Psychiatric Services*, 52 (5): 597–99.

Minkoff, K. (1989) 'An integrated treatment model for dual diagnosis of psychosis and Addiction', *Hospital and Community Psychiatry*, 40 (10): 1031–1036.

Morash, M., Haarr, R. and Rucker, L. (1994) 'A comparison of programming for women and men in U.S. prisons in the 1980s', *Crime and Delinquency*, 40 (2): 197–221.

Mumola, C.J. (2000) *Incarcerated Parents and Their Children*. Washington, DC: US Department of Justice, Bureau of Justice Statistics.

National Institute of Justice (2003) *Arrestee Drug Abuse Monitoring: 2000 Annual Report*. Washington, DC.

Owen, B. and Bloom, B. (1995) *Profiling the Needs of California's Female Prisoners: A needs' assessment*. Washington, DC: US Department of Justice.

Pelissier, B. and Jones, N. (2005) 'A review of gender differences among substance abusers', *Crime and Delinquency*, 51 (3): 343–72.

Powell, M.A. and Nolan, C. (2003) 'California state prisoners with children: Findings from the 1997 survey of inmates in state and federal correctional facilities'. Sacramento, CA: California Research Bureau.

Prendergast, M., Wellisch, J. and Wong, M. (1996) 'Residential treatment for women parolees following prison-based drug treatment experiences, needs, and service outcomes', *Prison Journal*, 76: 253–74.

Radosh, P. (2002) 'Reflections on women's crime and mothers in prison: a peacemaking approach', *Crime and Delinquency*, 78: 300–15.

Reed, B.G. and Mowbray, C.T. (1999) 'Mental health and substance abuse: Implications for women's health and health care access', *Journal of American Medical Women's Association*, 54 (2): 71–8.

Richie, B.E. (2001) 'Challenges Incarcerated women face as they return to their communities: Findings from life history interviews', *Crime and Delinquency*, 47 (3): 368–89.

Roberts, C., Kennedy, S., Hammet, T. and Rosenberg, N. (2001) 'Discharge planning and continuity of care for HIV-infected state prison inmates as they return to the community: A study of ten states'. Washington, DC: Abt Associates.

Ross, P.H. and Lawrence, J.E. (1998) 'Health care for women offenders', *Corrections Today*, 60 (7): 122–29.

Shearer, R.A. (2003) 'Identifying the special needs of female offenders', *Federal Probation*, 67 (1): 46–51.

Snell, T.L. and Morton, D.C. (1994) *Women in Prison*. Washington, DC: Department of Justice, Bureau of Justice Statistics.

Sokoloff, N. (2003) 'The impact of the prison industrial complex on African American women', *Souls*, 5 (4): 31–46

Stanley, E. and Byrne, S. (2000) 'Mothers in prison: Coping with separation from Children', paper presented at the *Women in Corrections Staff and Clients Conference* convened by the Australian Institute of Criminology, October 31–November 1, 2000.

Stoller, N. (2001) 'Improving access to health care for California's women prisoners'. Sacramento CA: California Policy Research Center.

Uelmen, G., Abrahamson, D., Appel, J. and Taylor, W. (2002) *Substance Abuse and Crime Prevention Act of 2000: Progress Report*. Sacramento, CA: Drug Policy Alliance.

Vaughn, M.S. (1999) 'Penal harm medicine: State tort remedies for delaying and denying health care to prisoners', *Crime, Law and Social Change*, 31: 273–302.

Vaughn, M.S. and Collins, S.C. (2004) 'Medical malpractice in correctional facilities: State tort remedies for inappropriate and inadequate health care administered to prisoners', *Prison Journal*, 84 (4): 505–34.

Vaughn, M.S. and Smith, L.G. (1999) 'Practicing penal harm medicine in the United States: Prisoners' voices from jail', *Justice Quarterly*, 16 (1): 175–230.

Women's Prison Association. (1996) 'When a mother is arrested: How the criminal justice and child welfare systems can work together more effectively'. A needs assessment initiated by the Maryland Department of Human Resources.

Warren, J. (2006) 'Plan puts women who are incarcerated in center near families', *Los Angeles Times*, February 11.

Watterson, K. (1996) *Women in Prison: Inside the concrete womb*. Boston, MA: Northeastern University Press.

Wolff, N., Blitz, C.L., Shi, J., Bachman, R. and Siegel, J.A. (2006) 'Sexual violence inside prisons: Rates of victimization', *Journal of Urban Health: Bulletin of the New York Academy of Medicine*, 83 (5): 835–48.

Young, D.K. (2000) 'Women's perceptions of health care in prison', *Health Care for Women International*, 21: 219–234.

Chapter 10

Women prisoners and their children

Rosemary Sheehan and Catherine Flynn

Introduction

This chapter looks at what happens to the children of incarcerated women and explores how women in prison maintain their links with their children. It also looks at the key issues women face on their return to the community in terms of their family connections and parenting role. The chapter draws on a major study undertaken in Victoria, Australia over 2003–04 which interviewed women leaving prison and at intervals after prison (Trotter and Sheehan 2005). It draws also on a subsequent study of the experiences of children whose mothers had been in prison; they were children whose mothers had participated in the major study of women leaving prison (Flynn 2005). The chapter will present some background material on what is known about the extent to which women prisoners are parents with dependent children, drawing on Australian figures. What happens to the care of these children will be explored, so too will be issues of access between women and their children, views about maintaining family ties – from the families and professionals, and how policies support or hinder this, and at programmes available to women in prison that concentrate on parenting skills and maintaining family relationships.

Women as prisoners

Women form a very small part of the global prison population, yet they are a rapidly growing group (United Nations 2003; Davis 2003; Reed and Reed 1997). Australia has experienced a sharp increase in its imprisonment rates between 1994–2004, with a related increase in the number of children affected (VACRO 2006). In Victoria there has been a 58% increase in the number of women sentenced to prison between 1994–2000, compared with a 19% increase in men sentenced (Department of Justice, Victoria, *Annual General Report* 2001). In the United Kingdom, the women's prison population rose by 100% in the period 1993–1999 (Home Office 2000). In the United States the introduction of drug and mandatory sentencing laws in recent decades has contributed to a startling 210% increase in the number women who are mothers in the prison population in the years 1986-1997 (Reed and Reed 1997; Myers *et al.* 1999; Johnson and Waldfogel 2002; Travis 2005). Covington (2003: 68–69) notes that these laws and policies have prescribed 'simplistic, punitive enforcement responses for complex social problems'.

Whilst female prisoners represent approximately 7% of the prison population across Australia, they bring particular challenges, being generally young and with dependent children. The children are young with a significant proportion under six years of age (Guransky, Harvey, McGrath and O'Brien 1998). Whilst the exact number of children in Australia who have a parent in prison is unknown, in 2004 it was estimated in the State of Victoria there were approximately 4,000 children affected by parental imprisonment (Corrections Victoria 2004; Hannon 2005). In the US, almost 1.5 million children have a parent in prison with 22% of these children under five years of age (Mumola, *US Dept. of Justice Special Report* 2000). In the UK it is estimated that 8,000 children have a mother in prison each year and for fathers it is 100,000 (Brown 2001). In the European community nearly 700,000 children have a parent in prison (European Committee for Children of Imprisoned Parents 2004).

Women as parents

Imprisoning mothers has a significant impact on their children, often of greater significance than imprisoning fathers, given that mothers are more likely to be primary caregivers prior to their imprisonment. Johnston's (1995) analysis of thirty years of international research estimated that up to 75% of women in prison are mothers, and that around 60% have dependent children (typically defined as being under sixteen years of age). In New South Wales (Australia), in 1997, it was estimated that 60% of the female prison population were mothers, and between a half and two thirds of the women were sole parents (NSW Legislative Council Standing Committee on Social Issues 1997). It is estimated that 55% of women prisoners in the UK have dependent children (Home Office 2000).

Children of women who are sole parents become effectively parentless when their mother goes into prison. Caddle and Crisp (1997a) in their UK study found that in the year 1994, 61% of women in prison had dependent children under 18 years of age, and that three-quarters of these children had mostly lived their lives solely with their mother. Children of women who are prisoners endure considerable disruption in their care, often receive negligible material support and experience difficulty maintaining family ties (Farrell 1997; Healey et al. 2000; Guransky et al. 1998). Children may also be separated from their siblings if they cannot be cared for by the one carer. The care children experience is often inadequate and the stress they endure goes unrecognised as the trauma of parental imprisonment is unacknowledged (Reed and Reed 1997; Kingi 2000).

Life before prison for many women and their children is marked by unsettled housing, low incomes, substance abuse, mental health problems, family violence and child abuse and neglect (McGuigan and Pratt 2001: Humphreys et al. 2001; Stanley and Goddard 2004; Loucks 2004). Such problems create multiple stressors which complicate their role as parents (Travis 2005). Problems with mental health, substance abuse, poverty and abuse are common (Loucks 2004). A number of these children will have started their care with grandparents, prior to their parent's incarceration because of abuse or neglect, or are placed with grandparents and other relatives while their parent is in prison – whether or not they are able to effectively care for the child (Phillips and Bloom 1998; Farrell 1998). This creates financial strain, physical strain, isolation for the extended family and can strain relationships. Many women's prisons, in particular, are located in areas of geographical isolation from major cities. Issues such as distance, transport services, the cost of visiting prisons and the lack of child friendly access arrangements in the prison, make contact between children and parents difficult, and cause significant stress for all parties (Stanley and Byrne 2003).

The impact of imprisonment

Families of prisoners referred to the social stigma, isolation and ostracism that occurs; there is little public sympathy for prisoners' families (Young and Jefferson Smith 2000). The welfare, legal and justice systems do not work together and the families of prisoners do not appear to be the core business of any state or territory government departments in Australia (Woodward 2003). There are no formal channels of communication for information sharing and collaboration; in particular the child protection and justice systems have different priorities and responsibilities (Seymour 1998). Reed and Reed (1997) found that in general in the USA the child protection systems did not have a specific policy on the placement of children whose parents were to be incarcerated. This is the same in Australia where child protection services do not have protocols with the corrections system regarding the children of primary carers who are entering prison. The lack of guidelines regarding who takes responsibility for the children means the children of prisoners remain invisible, their care disrupted, and their involvement with child protection services highly likely. The life disruption for these children causes serious long-term social and emotional difficulties.

Accommodation and care arrangements for children

The incarceration of a mother usually brings considerable dislocation to the woman's children and family (Farrell 1998), given the women will generally be the primary, if not sole, carers of the children (Johnson and Waldfogel 2002; Mumola 2000; Tudball 2000; Farrell 1998; Cunningham 2001). The fragmented nature of care for children of women prisoners has significant consequences for children's stability (Sheehan and Levine 2004).

Children whose mother goes to prison will either be cared for by their other parent, or step-parent, a grandparent, or will go into care (Barnhill and Dressel 1991; Farrell 1998; Gursansky et al. 1998; Mumola 2000; Kingi 2000; Healey et al. 2001; Johnson and Waldfogel 2002). This latter outcome more likely happens for children whose families are known to statutory child welfare authorities because of child protection concerns. What is concerning is that these children more often experience one or more changes in accommodation, the result at times from little time for preparation and the need for hurried care plans (Johnston 1995; Healey, Foley and Walsh 2001). Phillips and Bloom (1998) commented on the lack of formal monitoring of the quality of care the child receives during their parent's incarceration. Moreover, caregivers for this group of children find there is no response system that is set up to help them and the children in their care. There is an invisibility about children with parents who are prisoners and the impact of the justice process on children of prisoners is not acknowledged (Young and Jefferson Smith 2000; Phillips and Bloom 1998; Gursansky et al. 1998).

Hirschfield, Katzenstein and Fellner (2002) in their study of care patterns for children with a parent in prison in New York, USA, found children with a mother in prison fared less well than those whose father was in prison: one in five women had partners who cared for their child; half of the women in prison had their children cared for by grandparents, but 20% of the women had their children in foster care. As well as adapting to changes in living arrangements, possibly moving away from schools and other familiar structures, these children have to cope with the rigours associated with prison visits, uncertainty about their parent's absence and ongoing arrangements for their care. Kingi's (2000) New Zealand study found that 20% of children had more than one carer during their mother's imprisonment and 25% of the children in the study were placed with strangers. This is particularly concerning when the great majority of women serve short sentences. Figures from the UK in 2003, show that 63% of women were sentenced to custody for six months or less (Baroness Hale 2005).

A significant contributor to the increase of women in custody, in Victoria, is the increased use of remand for women facing criminal charges. In 1993, remand prisoners constituted 15% of the women's prison population. By 2003, this was 25% (ABS 2005). The combination of short term periods in custody and the immediacy of being arrested and taken into custody intensifies the urgent and often chaotic care arrangements that are put into place when the woman taken into custody has dependent children. In Victoria, there are neither guidelines for police, or policies covering the apprehension, arrest, charging or detention of primary carers with dependent children, nor protocols about the care of the children involved (Hannon 2005:3). Thus there is no formal process that provides mothers facing incarceration with the opportunity to arrange adequate care for their children.

Barnhill and Dressel (1991) examined the impact on family who were caring for their relative's children while their mother was in prison, found that the increased financial pressures on family units, typically headed by older women, created significant stress. Travis (2005) suggests that such financial stressors could potentially contribute to more harsh or inconsistent behaviours by carers towards the children in their care. Johnston (1995) argued that the pressure on financially disadvantaged families caring for children highlighted the lack of attention given to assessing the quality and appropriateness of placements for children whose mother was in prison. Earlier research by McGowan and Blumenthal (1978) and Baunach (1985) found that where mothers had input into decisions about arrangements for their children they were satisfied with child care plans. However, the increasing numbers of women in prison and the lack of formal channels for women's input has meant women are less likely to have time to plan for their children or be part of formal care plan arrangements. There is negligible acknowledgment that the views of children about their placement are canvassed as part of any child care plans. This very likely reflects the very young ages of the children, but it is concerning that even when children are older they are not consulted (Stanton 1980).

The fragmented nature of care for children of women prisoners, in particular, who come to the attention of child protection and the Children's Court has significant consequences for children's stability (Sheehan and Levine 2004). The tentative nature of family reunification can lead a child to be reunited with their parent after prison, but if this breaks down the child is returned to care. Children experience difficulty having contact with parents whilst they are in prison, and when they are out, if their parent is transient and does not come to access. Little attention is paid in prison and post-release programmes to how families reunify successfully.

Children of imprisoned mothers

There is little known or understood about the children of parents who are in prison, or have been imprisoned, or about the impact on them of their parent's incarceration and the ways, if any, that welfare agencies respond to their special circumstances (Johnston 1995; Seymour 1998; Myers *et al.* 1999; Eddy and Reid 2003; Travis 2005). Yet it is clear that there are emotional consequences of maternal incarceration on children; Baunach's (1985) study found up to 70% of children from this cohort experienced behavioural and emotional problems. Concern is also expressed about the behaviour of these children which can place them at an increased risk of coming into contact with the criminal justice system for their own behaviours (Hagan 1996; Eddy and Reid 2003).

Kampfner (1995) examined children's reactions to their mother's imprisonment and found children expressed their distress in a range of ways, from acting out behaviours such as aggression, disruptive behaviour in school, poor academic performance to withdrawal. Seymour (1998) found withdrawal behaviour, expressed as childhood fears, sadness, anxiety and depression were common responses across this cohort of children. Kampfner (1995) found that such traumatic stress responses were similar to those of other forms of childhood loss and separation. The difference with the loss of a mother to imprisonment is found in community reactions to this loss, which are very often less sympathetic.

Maintaining contact with one's children is often a challenge for women in prison; a prison sentence can weaken or sever relationships with children (Caddle and Crisp 1997b), most particularly when the woman is serving a long sentence (Kingi 2000). Codd (2005) notes that visits between mothers in prison and their children is encouraged by the prison and corrections systems as it maintains family relationships. Visiting their mother in prison allows the child to see and communicate directly with her, to have their fears allayed about prison. Maintaining these relationships is an important support for women when they re-enter the community after prison. However, it is reported with a considerable degree of consistency across international literature that approximately half of all incarcerated parents receive no visits from their children. Codd (2005) notes that there has been a decrease in family visits, between children and their mothers, in prisons in the UK. A range of factors are seen to be influential in this: travelling distance and transport difficulties; carer unwillingness and visiting environments which are oppressive and not child-oriented (Larman and Aungles 1991; Farrell 1998; Myers, Smarsh, Amlund-Hagen and Kennon 1999; Covington 2003).

Social stigma and shame are often associated with women in prison, more so than with male imprisonment. Children who have a mother in prison try not to disclose that their mother is in prison for fear of rejection or reprisal. This secrecy is often compounded by what is referred to as 'forced silence' (Johnston 1995; Kampfner 1995; Tudball 2000; Myers et al. 1999) whereby carers actively discourage children from talking about their parent or imprisonment. Children are then unable to openly engage with, discuss and understand their feelings about their situation, thus contributing to the emotional and behavioural difficulties noted above. This silencing of children's responses was examined by McCulloch and Morrison (2002) in their study of Scottish teenagers with a family member in prison. They found the young people in their study experienced adults as reluctant to let them speak about their parent being in prison and how they felt about this. The young people believed their family and friends were afraid of the emotion they might express: 'They were scared in case we cried' (14-year-old girl in the study by McCulloch and Morrison 2002:17). This direct and indirect silencing of children is compounded by the lack of specific agencies or policies for assisting children of incarcerated parents (Codd 2005).

The extent and nature of the impact of maternal incarceration is also compounded by the lack of official statistics about the children of prisoners. Although Myers *et al.* (1999: 12) write about the US experience, noting 'no agency – local, state or federal – keeps track', the comment has international relevance. Johnston (1995) reminds that prisons have no mandate to gather such data, and not all parents want to report that they have dependent children. Yet it is key to responding to women in prison that both their role as parent, and the status of any dependent children, is known. The NSW Parliament's Standing Committee on Social Issues (1997) believes the prison system must be required to collect information about the dependent children of prisoners, otherwise these children remain invisible.

Imprisoning mothers has a negative impact on a child and how they are able to relate to their external world. The degree of impact is influenced by factors such as: the age of the child, the length of the woman's sentence, the mother's relationship with the child prior to imprisonment, the ability of the woman to sustain a relationship with the child while she is in prison, the quality of the care arrangements for the child, and what supports are used to support the woman and her child whilst she is in prison (Seymour 1998). However, as already noted, the impact of incarceration does not end with the release of the mother from prison (Stanton 1980:115). Although many women plan to, and indeed do, reunite with their children post-release, they face many social, familial, personal and financial challenges.

Women and welfare after prison: study explained

One hundred and thirty eight women with sentences of three months or more, who were due for release from Victorian prisons during 2003 were interviewed approximately four weeks before leaving prison. The women came from the two women's prisons in Victoria: a larger women's prison, housing approximately 260 women, both on remand and sentenced (Correctional Services Commissioner 2006); and the smaller minimum security prison farm, housing around 50 sentenced women at any one time. The women in the study constituted 58% of the 237 women with sentences of three months or more who were released from prison during the period in which the study was conducted. The women generally represented women in prison in Victoria, in terms of age, offences committed, sentence length, and prior periods of imprisonment. The key aim of this study was to examine women's experiences of welfare and support programmes while they were in prison. The study wanted to discover what use the women made of these programmes: psychiatric and psychological services, parenting, drug and alcohol, housing, religious programmes; and, whether or not the women found them helpful and believed they contributed to their rehabilitation, and to reducing subsequent recidivism.

As well as questions that asked specifically about the women's welfare needs, and the programmes they had participated in whilst in prison, the women were asked about family circumstances; 80 of the women had children and so were asked about parenting issues: who had the care of their children, and their plans for their children on release. Of these 80 women, 50 were sole parents, and 10 of the women had three or more children (see Table 10.1).

Eighty-eight women in the study reported that they had dependent children and spoke about who cared for their children whilst they were in prison. Twenty-five per cent of the women who were mothers reported that their children lived with their grandparents, and it was predominantly maternal grandparents who provided this care. Foster care was where 11.4% of the women's children were placed. What was concerning was that around one in seven of the women who were mothers reported that their children did not live together; they were split up and lived with a range of caregivers (see Table 10.2).

The children of seventeen women were also known to the child protection service, and were on child protection court orders that placed the children either in foster care (the children of six women) or with extended family. The women in the study whose children were known to the child protection service had little contact with the statutory child welfare service. All except two of this group of women had just one contact with the child protection service during their incarceration, despite their child or children being on court orders and the children in care or with extended family on care orders. Not surprisingly, eleven of the women found the child protection service unhelpful or very unhelpful.

Table 10.1 Family composition of participants in 'Women and welfare after prison study', Victoria, Australia 2003–04

Women and their family composition	Frequency	Per cent	Per cent	Cumulative Per cent
self & 1 child	21	15.1	15.3	15.3
self & 2 children	15	10.8	10.9	26.3
self & 3 children	42.9	2.9	29.2	
self & 3+ children	10	7.2	7.3	36.5
self & partner	10	7.2	7.3	43.8
self & Partner & 1 child	10	7.2	7.3	51.1
self & child & 2children	10	7.2	7.3	58.4
self & partner & 3 children	75.0	5.1	63.5	
self & partner & 3+ children	32.2	2.2	65.7	
self & parents	21.4	1.5	67.2	
self & parents & siblings	96.5	6.6	73.7	
self & mother & siblilngs	75.0	5.1	78.8	
self & father & siblings	32.2	2.2	81.0	
self	11	7.9	8.0	89.1
various/extended	12	8.6	8.8	97.8
other	32.2	2.2	100.0	
Total	137	98.6	100.0	
Missing	21.4			
Total	139	100.0		

Women overwhelmingly planned to have their children back in their care, and were initially generally able to achieve this. Of the 22 women whose children were in the care of the father during the mother's incarceration, 19 of the women reunited with their partner and resumed care of their children. Of the 19 women whose children were in the care of the maternal grandparents, 15 women had their children returned to their care. However, when interviewed between six and twelve months after release, the children of 5 women were in the care of their father, the children of 8 women were in the care of their grandparents, the children of 3 women were in foster care, one woman's child was in the care of their oldest sibling. The significance of grandparents is also present when women were asked about whom they had found the most helpful to them during their first year post-release: 20 of the women said it was their mother who was the most helpful (and two noted it was a daughter, two family in general), 9 women said it was their partner. However 19 women also noted it was a welfare worker who had been the most helpful.

Table 10.2 Child's place of residence whilst mother in prison (Women and welfare after prison study, Victoria, Australia 2003–04)

Child's place of residence	Frequency	Per cent	Per cent	Cumulative Per cent
father	22	15.8	16.4	16.4
maternal grandmother	18	12.9	13.4	29.9
maternal grandparents	1	.7	.7	30.6
paternal grandmother	1	.7	.7	31.3
paternal grandfather	2	1.4	1.5	32.8
aunt	4	2.9	3.0	35.8
friend	3	2.2	2.2	38.1
fostercare	10	7.2	7.5	45.5
split up/various	13	9.4	9.7	55.2
stepfather	1	.7	.7	56.0
other	10	7.2	7.5	63.4
not applicable – no children	46	33.1	34.3	97.8
Self – in prison	2	1.4	1.5	99.3
18	1	.7	.7	100.0
Total	134	96.4	100.0	
Missing	5	3.6		
Total	139	100.0		

The 28 women who used parenting programmes found them helpful and said they would use similar community-based programmes on release. However, there was more emphasis placed on treatment type services in the prison, not surprisingly perhaps given that issues associated with drug taking and drug trafficking brought many of the women into prison. Whilst there are access facilities for children to visit their mothers in prison, and weekend visits by children created significant activity in the major women's prison, there was less emphasis on working towards family reintegration, and the skills needed to achieve this. It needs to be noted however that women who are eligible can move to the prison farm prior to release, although there were no women in this category at the time of the study. The women at the prison farm may have their pre-school children live with them, to facilitate family reunification, and staff provide support services to assist with parenting and general child care.

When the women in the study were interviewed twelve months after their release from prison they were asked how they had been coping since they left prison. Women commented that returning to family life brought difficulties not expected. One woman noted that: 'it was a bit strange coming home to the children', and that whilst she was managing well enough what she found hard was 'the noise of the kids and my husband has a loud voice' (CS030).

The women with dependent children spoke about not only the difficulties they experienced reconnecting with their children but also taking on their family roles.

> I was only in for three and a half months, but still a long time-getting used to children again. Having that break from them and then having to deal again with them 24 hours a day. It's overwhelming/challenging when you come back after being isolated – can't explain or compare it. But at the same time, everything has gone back the way it was, kids/relationship routine all goes back the way it was' (CS013).

Adjusting to the routine of family life is challenging:

> 'I've got the kids – they keep me busy. It's pretty boring – the closest public transport is 40 minutes walk from here..'(CF049).

It was not just adjustment to one's children that was challenging:

> Hard being back with my partner again. Difficulty with no driver's licence. Went to get a job – need childcare – don't want to stay on Centrelink (social security) (CS022).

It could not always be assumed that the woman's children would be available to her. One woman spoke about 'child custody/access issues with ex and (his) wife' (CF005); another woman's children were now out of her care 'I went to live with my auntie – my mum got custody of the kids – then she kicked me out. I was living in my car for a while – then ... I got done for shoplifting. Broke my suspended sentence' (CF007). The fragmentation of relationships made women vulnerable to reoffending:

> Sick of all these appointments. Sick of public transport. Have a licence, but can't get a car without money. It's Catch 22. Called my parole officer – all emotional – crying – in this big house with the kids here only some of the time. I'm lonely I miss people – having lived with them for over a year. Don't see old friends ... Some days its really overpowering' (CF001).

The impact of imprisonment on women is broader than the incarceration itself. The impact on children, the extended family, on the woman's home and household is significant. It may also bring changes in family arrangements that are unexpected and unwanted.

> When you come home you feel like you don't fit, like everyone's ganging up on you, for leaving. When I got in, the house was filthy and dirty. The kids' Dad wouldn't clean up or let them clean. ... Still see the drug culture as big part of my life – they are the only people I can't talk to, the only one I can talk to now is my eldest [thirteen years] he's grown up with it ... that's sad ... taken on the carer's role with me. I wanted to leave here and start again – but I thought my eldest had been dragged around enough – went to five primary schools – and the youngest was dragged through the court with his dad and me. Wanted them to have a choice of where they didn't want to go – but when they said they wanted to stay with their Dad I was really hurt – like how could they do that to me? (CF023).

These same issues of isolation and family fragmentation resonated when women were asked what challenges they faced since their release from prison. Adapting to parenting responsibilities brought a range of challenges from the physical and practical:

> Coming back to motherhood. Was a major challenge – I slept all night in prison, now I'm looking after my eleven months old daughter [after two months away]. Her maternal grandmother looked after her while I was in prison (CS0016).

And,

> The kids had more discipline when I was at home now I have to enforce the discipline again. The noise of the kids and the house needs attention. The furniture is ruined. I'm busy getting everything fixed up (CS030).

> When I got home it was a disaster. My ex [who had been staying there with the boys] had broken every cup and dish. He hadn't dusted for eighteen months. There were fleas from the dog. My retainer went on cleaning stuff. Money – the hardest bit is not having money just to hand over to the boys when they want it because I'm not a drug dealer now (CF021).

As well as the practical aspects of household maintenance and the routine of children there were challenges with relationships:

It's hard readjusting to being home with my daughter (CF041).

I am readjusting to life – my relationship with the oldest son – he's become very chauvinistic (CF021).

Getting the kids back to normal [they don't listen to me as much – have been with their father] (CF001).

My relationship with my son – lots of things unresolved due to me having the last ten years in prison (CF002).

It was hard moving my daughter from her school. And getting around. Getting enough money [I needed to restock the house with food etc] Centrelink [social security] stuffed up my payments (CF029).

Re-gaining the role of mother was a challenge:

The challenges were mainly the kids. For the time I was away their dad had them in a good routine and everything and now I'm back they seem to be slackening off and seem to think "Mum's back now, we don't have to pull our weight as much" and all that stuff. I was sentenced to four months, which wasn't too long but it was long break from the kids ... And the kids are very demanding (CF034).

I think there should be a better way to release women into society gradually. I found it a bit much returning home with my children after being used to being alone with my baby. He was born in prison and was just a few months old when I was released. I was in eight months, a short sentence but I found it difficult to be a wife and mother again (CS029).

For some women the challenges were as much about getting access to their children as well as to housing and their usual adult roles: 'Getting back my daughter, with family, and trying to find accommodation. Going back to paying for things' (CS014).

> Sorting out access with my daughter. And getting into "today" like clothes are big challenges (CF058).

Finding housing for some women was directly related to having their children returned to their care:

> My big challenge was getting somewhere to live – I needed a place to have my daughter home. Getting my daughter back from Human Services was a big stress – I wondered what are they going to use against me so I can't have her back. I've had dramas with them for 3 years (CS012).

Persuading children to come back to the mother's care confronted some women:

> Getting my kids back is the biggest challenge. My kids are staying with friends. They don't want to come back at this stage. The house needs doing up so the fourteen year old wants to stay where she is (CS003).

Whilst some children returned quickly from foster care, others stayed with relatives because the children themselves wanted to do this or the mother wanted the children to remain stable until she had accommodation and income. Some had to go to court to argue they were now able to care for heir children. For some access to their children was very difficult:

> I can't get access to my children – they are in permanent foster care (CS036).

> I have to go to the Children's Court. My son attends a psychologist, he has behaviour problems, he is really active (CS013).

Two women whose children were living with their father, and the parents were no longer in a relationship, found it difficult to have the children visit them because the child's father was uncertain about letting the child stay at the mother's new home.

Access to children was especially problematic for women whose children were out of their care. Women in this situation spoke about sending letters and cards to their children but not hearing back either from, or about, their children. The exception to this was where the maternal grandmother had the care of the woman's children, and the woman was able to return after prison to stay at her mother's home; this greatly helped the woman regain the care of her child.

The threat of the loss of their children again was significant in the women's thinking when asked how likely they thought it was that they would commit further offences:

> What stops me is the kids. They would be the major factor. I would never want to be apart from them again. And I don't think they would forgive me if it happened a second time. It brings you to account ... one thing I hated was I wouldn't be there for my youngest son's first birthday and his first steps and his first teeth' (CS001).

> I think about my kids, my family: fifteen months is too much. I'm too afraid to think about going back there (CS042)

These findings reflect what is noted earlier on in this chapter: that financial strain, physical strain, isolation and strained relationships with children complicate the woman offender's role as mother. These factors are often combined with problems with mental health, substance abuse, housing and poverty, factors that often feature in the lives of women and their children prior to the woman's imprisonment (McGuigan and Pratt 2001: Humphreys *et al.* 2001; Goddard and Stanley 2004; Loucks 2004). Issues such as distance, transport services, the cost of visiting prisons and the lack of child friendly access arrangements in the prison, make contact between children and their mother, while she is in prison difficult, and contribute to the often unsettled relationships women have with their children when they are released from prison.

How the children perceive these issues is taken up in the next section which looks at a study of the impact of maternal incarceration on young people.

The impact of maternal incarceration on adolescent children: study findings

The study looked at the experiences of children whose mothers are in prison; these children were drawn from the study outlined above, of women leaving prison in Victoria, Australia, during 2003–04. The study aimed to discover what happens to the children of incarcerated women and explores how the children maintained their links with their mother. The study was also interested in the issues the women and children faced on the woman's return to the community. The children interviewed were aged between ten and eighteen years of age; the lower age is the age at which children are held legally responsible for their actions, the upper age is the age they cease to be legally considered children. In total, twenty-nine young people and their mothers were interviewed. A number of professionals: teachers and caseworkers, were also interviewed.

The research indicates that the placement of, and child care planning for, children whilst their mother is in prison receives little formal attention in child welfare or adult justice policy. What also emerged as a concern was the fragmented nature of care for children of women prisoners (Sheehan and Levine 2004), and the changes in school, contact with parent, the child's carer and accommodation which children were required to make when their mother went to prison. What emerged in this study was the extent to which a child might not be aware that their mother would be imprisoned. Ten of the twenty children knew beforehand – from their mother – that she would be going to prison. The woman and her children had support networks that helped them deal with impending imprisonment: a partner, parents, extended family or a designated support service. Care planning for the children varied: six children had child care plans put in place prior to their mother's imprisonment, and this plan was agreed on by the young person, their mother and the carer. Three of these children had previously experienced a number of placements with extended family prior to being placed together in a foster care placement, as their parents had previous imprisonment. Where the care plans could be negotiated it meant there could be attention to key issues that would impact on the young person: their accommodation, education, contact with mother, contact with siblings and extended family. It also meant there could be an assessment of the young person's emotional needs and what supports they required; what information they needed to know about their mother's imprisonment, what financial concerns there might be and how to maintain a young person's links with their community.

Care plans that could be developed by the young people and their mothers prior to the mother's imprisonment were more effective:

All of us decided: me, my mum and dad and my daughter. I knew I was going down before I was sentenced, so I had a bit of time to talk to mum and dad about it (Mother of 14-year-old girl).

When we got home from court I said, "Son, I'm going to prison". And that's when I started organising, you know, like the dole (social security payments) office, the house and everything around it – what my son wanted. It was always about him anyway – what he wanted to do (Mother of 10-year-old boy).

Although the young people did not always feel they had many choices:

Where else would we go? They asked us if we wanted to go back with our foster carer and we all said yes, because we'd end up getting split up if we didn't. No one else would take us all on. Mum didn't want us split up, we didn't want to be split up' (11-year-old girl).

For these young people, their mothers had some time to make plans for their children. They also had the support of at least one consistent adult, who would provide care for the young person, whether the carer was a family member or from a foster care agency. The support of family, friends or community agencies was significant:

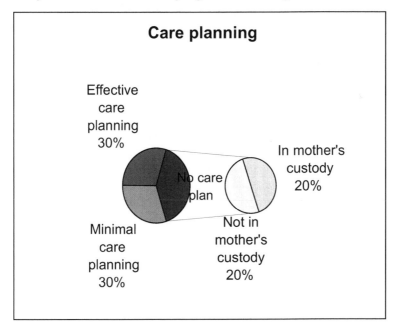

Figure 10.1 Care plans for children prior to their mother's imprisonment related to whether or not they were in their mother's care prior to prison.

> Basically, it just happened so quickly – friends just stepped in … they were close friends and obviously we spent a lot of time together anyway – I knew them well; the kids knew them……
> The kids stayed at the same school, saw friends, stayed in sporting activities…and saw brothers and sisters at weekends (Mother of five children, in the study).

> Friends that they stayed with used to bring the children visit. They organised it within themselves as to who would come (Mother of five children, in the study).

The absence of care planning

For the seven young people (35%) in this study who had no care plan in place at the point of their mother's imprisonment, the experience was very different. Four of these young people were not living with their mother when she went to prison, although all were having varying degrees of access to their mother. In three cases, the women did not believe they could negotiate with the children's fathers (from whom they were separated, and who had the care of the children) to put in place care plans that would include contact between the young people and their mothers:

> It would have just been ammunition for the father to use against me – "your mother's no good…" (Mother of 10-year-old boy).

> I didn't tell the children anything. I never do. It's always more or less, Mum, who does it, she has rung my ex-husband and told him. And I think they get told, or I know from what they've told me in the past, that they've been told that I'm like in hospital with sick, naughty people (Mother of 11-year-old girl).

These children subsequently had very limited contact, or no contact, with their mothers. One young person commented: ' … I didn't know where mum was … I felt not very happy because everyone else had their mum around them and I wanted my mum … I would like to see her in person in prison. Anything, as long as I know she's still caring about us' (11-year-old girl in study).

The impact was also significant for the mothers of these children:

> I had three visits over a twelve month period. I phoned two to three times a week; and sent letters – never got no replies though ...I thought they had to have contact visits as part of the orders and I brought it up with my solicitor. He said my ex-husband was probably thinking of the best interests of the children – worried about the environment and that. The visit centre's not that bad – there's a playground and stuff (Mother of 10-year-old girl).

The remaining three young people had no care plan in place. They were living with their mothers prior to their mother's imprisonment. Their mothers were sole parents who were arrested and remanded in prison:

> She was just gone. I was at school and the police came around … I came home and there was no one here, and I rang around. One of mum's friends came around and told me (16-year-old girl).

One mother had no support person to call on:

> I couldn't contact anyone – I was in the cells for three weeks. I got the Salvation Army to ring my Mum and check on the kids after a week.

Overall there was minimal care planning for young people whose mother was going into prison. This meant little attention could be paid to the key areas identified earlier: accommodation, education, contact with mother, siblings and extended family, finances, maintaining the young person's links to the community, ensuring emotional support. These young people had less knowledge about their mother's circumstances, had negligible involvement in negotiating plans about their care, and experienced changes in their accommodation. In fact, three young people did not know their mother was in prison. Two young people remained in their family home; the third had stable accommodation because his mother had arranged this, but she did not tell the young person that living arrangements had changed because of her imprisonment. The four young people who knew that their mother would be going into prison did not have adequate care plans in place to support them.

The women who struggled to negotiate anything more than a minimal care plan for their children in these circumstance, had significant personal problems: with substance abuse (five women) and mental illness (two women) and had minimal supports to assist them.

Factors that impact on women's ability to negotiate care planning

What emerges in this study is that women very often have little time to put plans in place for their children. Women who are arrested and immediately placed in custody are unable to negotiate arrangements for their children, and depend very much on family and friends to care for their children. Police arrest procedures provide no guidelines about how to deal with children whose primary carer is arrested. Where women are sole parents this is particularly problematic, as some of the statements above reflect. In this study 25% of the women were immediately remanded in custody on arrest. The increased use of remand in Victoria increases the group of children for whom there may be less than adequate care arrangements while their mother is incarcerated. In Victoria, in 1993, women on remand for criminal offences comprised 15% of the female prison population. In 2003, they comprised 25% of the female prison population. The criminal justice system largely ignores the female offender's role as mother and her parenting responsibilities:

> The lawyer pleaded with the judge when I was being sentenced to give me a few extra days – to come back on Monday – to have time to organise childcare. He said "No". I was devastated. I had to rely on the lawyer to make all the calls and organise the kids... I also couldn't organise and pack up the transitional house I'd been in... (Mother of six children, in the study).

The personal circumstances of women who go to prison often impede their parenting responsibilities and capacity to plan for the care of their children. They are more likely to be sole parents, and have difficult relationships with their children's fathers. Problems with substance abuse, mental illness, family violence and social isolation characterise this group of women (Loucks 2004). Their incapacity to make adequate care arrangements for their children reflects 'anxiety or chaos in the lives of parents due to crime, heavy drug and alcohol use and poverty' (Healey, Foley and Walsh 2000: 15)

Women who had the time, personal resources and supports were able to develop care plans for their children that were of important mutual benefit. The presence in the woman's life of at least one positive adult support person was significant in assisting women to mobilise resources to plan care for their children. What was clear however was that there needs to be greater system recognition of the parenting roles and responsibilities of women before the court and that impact of the decisions of the criminal justice system on the children of these women.

Concluding comment

The impact of parental imprisonment on children is qualitatively different for women who go to prison, most particularly when women are the sole carers of their children. The nature of this impact is conveyed above in the findings from the two studies that are key to this chapter. What overwhelmingly emerges is the need for greater awareness and acknowledgement in court proceedings of women's family circumstances. A family impact statement should be submitted to the court in proceedings where the defendant is a primary carer of dependant children. This should be supported by court-appointed children's support workers, who can co-ordinate care arrangements for the children of women being sentenced, and who can liaise with the statutory child welfare agency where necessary. It is clear that child-centred practices must be introduced into the adult criminal justice system when women who are parents face going to prison. This is not to diminish the independence of the judiciary, nor the appropriateness of disposition matching the nature of the crime. It simply recognises the breadth of impact on family members when a woman with dependent children goes to prison. It does ask the criminal justice system to look more carefully at the need to remand women in custody or sentence women to prison, and to view this as the disposition of last resort.

References

Australian Bureau of Statistics (2004) *Prisoners in Australia*, Catalogue: 4517.0, Canberra, ACT: Australian Bureau of Statistics.

Australian Bureau of Statistics (2005) 'Women in Prison', *Year Book Australia – Crime and Justice*. Catalogue: 1301.0, Canberra, ACT: Australian Bureau of Statistics.

Barnhill, S. and Dressel, P. (1991) *Three generations at risk*. Atlanta, GA: Aid to Imprisoned Mothers.

Baunach, P.J. (1985) *Mothers in Prison*. New Brunswick, Canada: Transaction Books.

Brown, K. (2001) *No-one's ever asked me – Young people with a prisoner in the family*. London, UK: Federation of Prisoners' Families Support Groups.

Caddle, D. and Crisp, D. (1997a) *Mothers in Prison*. Home Office Research Findings No. 38. London, UK: Research and Statistics Directorate, Home Office.

Caddle, D. and Crisp, D. (1997b) *Imprisoned Women and Mothers*, Home Office Research Findings No. 162. London, UK: Research and Statistics Directorate, Home Office.

Codd, H. (2005) 'Prisoners' Families and Resettlement: A critical analysis'. Paper presented at *European Deviance Group Conference*, April 2005, Preston, England.

Correctional Services Commissioner (2006) *Statistical Profile and the Victorian Prison System 2000–01 to 2004–05*. Victoria, Australia: Department of Justice.

Corrections Victoria (2004) *Mother and Child Interim Policy*. Victoria, Australia: Department of Justice.

Covington, S. (2003) 'A Woman's Journey Home: Challenges for female offenders', in J. Travis and M. Waul (eds) *Prisoners Once Removed: The impact of incarceration and re-entry on children, families and communities*. Washington DC: The Urban Institute Press.

Cunningham, A. (2001) 'Forgotten families – the impacts of imprisonment', *Family Matters*, Winter, 59, 35–38.

Cunningham, A. and Baker, L. (2003) *Waiting for Mommy: Giving a voice to the hidden victims of imprisonment*. London, Ontario: Centre for Children and Families in the Justice System.

Davis, A. Y. (2003) *Are Prisons Obsolete?* New York: Seven Stories Press.

Department of Justice, Victoria (2001) *Annual General Report 1999–2000*. Melbourne, Australia: Department of Justice.

Eddy, J.M. and Reid, J.B. (2003) 'The Adolescent Children of Incarcerated Parents: A developmental perspective', in J. Travis and M. Waul (eds) *Prisoners Once Removed: The impact of incarceration and re-entry on children, families and communities*. Washington DC: The Urban Institute Press.

European Committee for Children of Imprisoned Parents (2004) *Who are we?* http://www.eurochips.org

Farrell, A. (1997) 'Policies for incarcerated mothers and their families in Australian corrections', *Australian and New Zealand Journal of Criminology*, 31 (2): 101–18.

Farrell, A. (1998) 'Mothers Offending Against their Role: An Australian Experience', *Women and Criminal Justice*, 9 (4): 47–67.

Flynn, C. (2005) 'Who's minding the children? Care planning with young people whose mothers are incarcerated', paper presented at *What works with Women Offenders: A cross-national dialogue about effective responses to female offenders*, Prato, Italy, June 20–22, 2005.

Flynn, C. (2006) 'Factoring motherhood into the judicial process: How we can better meet the needs of young people whose mothers are in conflict with the criminal justice system', paper presented at World Congress of the International Association of Youth and Family Judges and Magistrates, Belfast, N. Ireland, August 27–September 1, 2006.

Gibbs, C. (1971) 'The Effect of the Imprisonment of Women upon their Children', *British Journal of Criminology*, 11, 113–30.

Gursansky, D., Harvey, J., McGrath, B. and O'Brien, B. (1998) *Who's Minding the Kids? ... developing coordinated services for children whose mothers are imprisoned'*. Adelaide: Social Policy Research Group, University of South Australia.

Hagan, J. (1996) 'The Next Generation: Children of prisoners', *Journal of the Oklahoma Criminal Justice Research Consortium*, 3: 19–28.

Hale Baroness, Brenda Hale QC (2005) 'The sinners and the sinned against: women in the criminal justice system', The Longford Lecture 2005, in association with the Prison Reform Trust, London.

Hannon, T. (2005) 'Children: Unintended victims of legal process', Paper presented at: *What works with women offenders: A cross-national dialogue about effective responses to female offenders*, Monash University Centre, Prato, Italy, 20–22 June, 2005.

Healey, K., Foley, D. and Walsh, K. (2000) *Parents in prison and their families: Everyone's business and no-one's concern*. Brisbane, Australia: Catholic Prisons Ministry, Brisbane.

Hirschfield, P., Katzenstein, S. and Fellner, J. (2002) 'Collateral Casualties: Children of incarcerated drug offenders in New York', *Human Rights Watch*, 14, 3, G, June 2002.

Home Office (2000) *Statistics on Women and the Criminal Justice System*. London: Home Office.

Hounslow, B., Stephenson, A., Stewart, J. and Crancher, J. (1982) *Children of Imprisoned Parents*. Sydney, NSW, Australia: NSW. Department of Youth and Community Services.

Humphreys, C., Mullender, A., Lowe, P., Hague, G., Abrahams, H., and Hester, M. (2001) 'Domestic Violence and Child Abuse: Developing sensitivities and guidance', *Child Abuse Review*, 10, 183–97.

Johnson, E.I. and Waldfogel, J. (2002) 'Parental Incarceration: Recent Trends and the Implications for child welfare', *Social Service Review*, 76 (3): 460–479.

Johnson, T.K. (2005) Unpublished PhD thesis, 'Hidden Voices: The life experiences of African American adolescent girls with mothers in prison'. Texas, USA: The University of Texas at Austin, Texas.

Johnston, D. (1995) 'Effects of Parental Incarceration', in K. Gabel and D. Johnston (eds.) (1995) *Children of Incarcerated Parents*. New York: Lexington Books.

Kampfner, C.J. (1995) 'Post-Traumatic Stress Reactions in Children of Imprisoned Mothers', in K. Gabel and D. Johnston (eds) (1995) *Children of Incarcerated Parents*. New York: Lexington Books.

King, D. (2002) *Parents, Children and Prison: Effects of parental imprisonment on children*, Dublin, Ireland: Centre for Social and Educational Research, Dublin Institute of Technology.

Kingi, V. (2000) 'The Children of Women in Prison: A New Zealand Study', paper presented at *Women in Corrections: Staff and clients conference*, Australian Institute of Criminology, Adelaide, Australia: 31 October–1 November, 2000.

Larman, G. and Aungles, A. (1991) 'Children of Prisoners and their Outside Carers: The invisible population', in P. Weiser Easteal and S. McKillop (eds) *Women and the Law*, Proceedings from the Australian Institute of Criminology Conference, Canberra, 262–70.

Loucks, N. (2004) 'Women in Prison', in G. McIvor (ed.) *Women Who Offend*. New York: Jessica Kingsley.

McGowan, B.G. and Blumenthal, K.L. (1978) *Why Punish the Children? A study of the children of women prisoners*. Hackensack, NJ: National Council on Crime and Delinquency.

McGuigan, W. and Pratt, C. (2001) 'The predictive impact of domestic violence on three types of child maltreatment', *Child Abuse and Neglect*, 25, 869–83.

McCulloch, C. and Morrison, C. (2002) 'Teenagers with a family member in prison'. Glasgow, Scotland: Scottish Forum on Prisons and Families, Glasgow.

Mumola, C. (2000) 'Incarcerated Parents and Their Children', Bureau of Justice Statistics Special Report, US Department of Justice, at: http://www.ojp.usdoj.gov/bjs/

Myers, B.J., Smarsh, T.M., Amlund-Hagen, K. and Kennon, S. (1999) 'Children of Incarcerated Mothers', *Journal of Child and Family Studies*, 8 (1): 11–25.

NSW Parliament Standing Committee on Social Issues (1997) *Report into children of imprisoned parents*, Report No. 12, July 1997, Sydney, NSW, Australia: Parliament of New South Wales Legislative Council.

Office of the Corrective Services Commissioner (1996) *Women Prisoners in Victoria*, Melbourne, Victoria, Australia: Department of Justice.

Phillips, S. and Bloom, B. (1998) 'In whose best interest? The impact of changing policy on relatives caring for children with incarcerated parents', *Child Welfare*, 77 (5): 531–41.

Reed, D.F. and Reed, E.L. (1997) 'Children of Incarcerated Parents', *Social Justice*, 24 (3): 152–69.

Seymour, C.B. (1998) 'Children with Parents in Prison: Child welfare policy, program and practice issues', *Child Welfare*, 77 (5): 469–93.

Sheehan, R. and Levine, G. (2004) 'Parents as prisoners: maintaining the parent-child relationship', *15th ISPCAN Congress*, Brisbane, Australia, 19–22 September, 2004.

Standing Committee on Social Issues, (1997) *A Report into Children of Imprisoned Parents*, Report No. 12, Sydney, NSW, Australia: Parliament of New South Wales Legislative Council.

Stanley, E. and Byrne, S. (2001) 'Mothers in Prison: Coping with separation from children', paper presented at *Women in Corrections: Staff and clients conference, 31 October–1 November 2000*, Adelaide, Australia: Australian Institute of Criminology.

Stanley, J. and Goddard, C. (2004) 'Multiple forms of Violence and Other Criminal Activities as an Indicator of Severe Child Maltreatment', *Child Abuse Review*, 13, 246–62.

Stanton, A.M. (1980) *When Mothers go to Jail.* Lexington, Massachusetts: Lexington Books.

Travis, J. (2005) *But They All Come Back: Facing the Challenges of Prisoner Re-entry.* The Urban Institute Press, Washington, DC.

Trotter, C. and Sheehan, R. (2005) 'Women after prison', paper presented at *What Works with Women Offenders: A cross-national dialogue about effective responses to female offenders*, Prato, Italy, June 20–22, 2005.

Tudball, N. (2000) *Doing it Hard: A study of the needs of children and families of prisoners in Victoria.* Melbourne, Victoria, Australia: VACRO.

United Nations (2003) *The Seventh United Nations Survey on Crime Trends and the Operations of Criminal Justice Systems 1998–2000:* http:\\www.unodc.org/unodc/en/crime-cicp-survey-seventh.html

Victorian Association for the Care and Resettlement of Offenders (VACRO), in conjunction with Flat Out (2006) *Children: Unintended victims of legal process- A review of policies and legislation affecting children with incarcerated parents*, Discussion Paper, prepared by Terry Hannon, VACRO, Victoria, Australia: June 2006.

Woodward, R. (2003) 'Families of Prisoners: Literature review on issues and difficulties', *Occasional Paper 10*, Canberra, Australia: Government Department of Family and Community Services.

Young, D.S. and Jefferson Smith, C. (2000) 'When moms are incarcerated: The needs of children, mothers and caregivers' *Families in Society: The journal of contemporary human services*, 81 (2): 130–47.

Chapter 11

Barriers to employment, training and education in prison and beyond: a peer-led solution

Caroline O'Keeffe, Paul Senior and
Valerie Monti-Holland

Introduction

Women ex-offenders face numerous seemingly insurmountable barriers when attempting to access employment, training and education (ETE) following a prison sentence (see for example Dowling 2001; Hamlyn and Lewis 2000; O'Keeffe 2003). Moreover, for this cohort of women the process of attempting to 'better themselves' through ETE, following a criminal conviction, is often experienced as extremely disempowering. This chapter uses the Supporting Others through Volunteer Action (SOVA) 'Women into Work' programme[1] to showcase empirical evidence of the successes of 'peer led' approaches, to both research and service delivery, in overcoming barriers to ETE for women ex-offenders.[2]

The chapter begins with a description of what is meant by 'peer approaches' and an outline of the specifics of how this particular programme was facilitated and implemented. This is followed by a broad overview of the findings of the peer research element of the programme in order to outline the barriers to ETE faced by women ex-offenders both when in custody and on release. We then examine the ETE opportunities which were presented to women ex-offenders as a result of their engagement with the peer research programme. This leads to the second element of the Women into Work programme which involved building on the peer research by adopting peer approaches to service delivery in pilot projects set up to address the key barriers identified. Interwoven throughout the chapter is reflection upon the considerable challenges raised by this innovative programme of work, in particular, the interesting questions around the ex-offender 'identity' and the ways in which it 'shifts' as a result of peer working. In summary, this chapter provides a unique understanding of the potential and pitfalls of 'peer' working in overcoming ETE barriers for women ex-offenders.

What is peer research?

Peer research is a relatively new and innovative type of research, which has developed from the traditions of 'participatory', 'action' and 'empowerment' research (Foote Whyte 1991; Coghlan and Brannick 2001; Trueman *et al.* 2000). Despite subtle differences between these approaches a common characteristic of them all is that they represent a shift away from 'top down' research where those with the most power in organisations decide how the research should be conducted. Instead, they offer a 'bottom up' approach where those individuals who are going to be directly affected by the outcomes play an active role in the research process. Participatory approaches to research stress the importance of community involvement and involve shifting the power base and ownership of the research process to 'non experts' thus reducing the 'academicism' of research. It is a means of:

> preventing an elite group from exclusively determining the interests of others, in effect of transferring power to those groups engaged in the production of popular knowledge (Sohng 1995: 3).

This approach to research reflects changes in working practices in service planning and delivery in the social care arena where there has been increasing awareness over the past couple of decades of the potential for involving service users/members of the community (Beresford and Croft 1993). In relation to peer approaches to service delivery within the criminal justice arena, there is an increasing trend towards enabling offenders to support their peers (e.g. listening schemes in prison,[3] peer advisors at the St Giles Trust.[4] This trend also has a history internationally (e.g. the Kris 'buddy' scheme in Sweden;[5] in New York, the Women's Prison Association peer mentoring programme[6]).

User participation in research and service delivery has largely been concerned with 'disadvantaged' groups with a particular emphasis on using participation in research as a tool of empowerment.

Empowerment as a term has become increasingly popular within various arenas during the last few years (psychology, mental health, management and political science). Interestingly, despite the huge amount of rhetoric on empowerment there remains no agreed definition of the term (Walters, Lygo-Baker and Strkljevic 2001). However, the term is largely concerned with the application of democracy and the acquisition or withdrawal of power (Walters *et al.* 2001). Empowerment is also concerned with recognising our own abilities to act and become involved in productive processes for the benefit of both ourselves and others (O'Keeffe 2003).

Peer research may usefully be called the 'ultimate participatory research methodology'. Participatory research approaches ask those who have direct experience of the research area to participate in the research process in a real and meaningful way. This may involve for example, gaining an input into research design or enabling people to have a say in how research findings will be used. In a peer research programme service users are fully engaged with all aspects of actually conducting the research, from design to data collection, to writing up results. Thus the SOVA Women into Work programme actively sought out women ex-offenders to employ as researchers.

Facilitating the peer research process

In order to facilitate the peer research process three full-time paid 'peer researchers' were employed for twelve-months, one of whom was serving a custodial sentence. Their main roles were to design and deliver the peer research in addition to assisting in the recruitment, training and co-ordination of 'trainees'. In addition to the three full-time workers eleven sessional workers ('trainees') were employed to assist in conducting the research and to represent their peer group at meetings of the overall Women into Work programme. Of these, eight were in custody. Trainees were paid on a sessional basis, depending on the amount of work they were able to do.

The peer researchers received seven days training in the practicalities of conducting research, research design and qualitative data analysis. In addition, the peer researchers attended and helped to deliver a training programme to trainees. All workers received ongoing advice, support and guidance from the programme manager and the research manager for the programme. The peer researchers also received formal supervision from the programme manager. In addition, the peer researchers adopted the role of 'mentor' for the trainees and trainees also received ongoing support from prison staff or community organisations with which they were involved. Semi-structured in-depth interviews (both one-to-one and focus group interviews) were chosen as the method of data collection for this study. Thus, a main feature of the role of both peer researchers and trainees was to interview fellow women offenders about their experiences of accessing ETE. In total 243 women in custody were interviewed and 103 in the community.

Peer research findings

The findings of this research have clearly demonstrated that although women (ex)offenders showed desire and motivation to access ETE, numerous barriers existed which prevented this from happening in many cases. A fuller analysis of the findings can be found elsewhere (O'Keeffe 2003). However some of the key findings are presented below.

Importance of ETE for women (ex)offenders

Research participants perceived getting into ETE as important for a variety of reasons. To many women breaking out of old lifestyle patterns and earning their own money represented a sense of freedom and overall well-being, offering the opportunity to escape from an offending lifestyle and to have a so-called 'normal lifestyle' incorporating routine, stability, independence and taking responsibility for themselves and their family.

> I want normality. I want to be steady. I want stability and routine and … I'm sick of all the things I've done in the past. It gets boring. (Focus group participant)

> The fact that you can get up every morning and earn a living … you know you feel a sense of worth. But if you don't have it then the next thing you do, you start thinking of getting into drugs or … (Focus group participant)

Women speak of their involvement in ETE as part of their 'rebuilding process' following a conviction, on both a practical and emotional level. In particular, the increased confidence that women get from

ETE whilst in custody enables them to cope with reality in the outside world more effectively. ETE is also an important factor in re-establishing (or in some cases gaining for the first time) a sense of self-worth.

> I think people warm to you more if they know that you're working ... you know, if you're on the dole or whatever, it's 'oh bloody layabout' ... it's trying to get back into that kind of ... scenario again and it's hard, it really is. (Focus group participant)

> At the moment the part time driving I am doing its helping me to build myself back up again ... I feel that bit more confident about interviews and facing people. (Focus group participant)

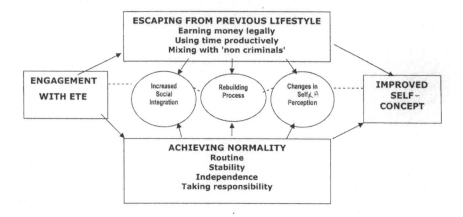

Figure 11.1 The importance/centrality of ETE in the lives of women ex-offenders

ETE within the prison environment

Interestingly, many participants viewed prison as the ideal opportunity to engage with ETE. There existed a high level of motivation to engage in ETE amongst the study sample and there were a number of motivating factors. These included:

- to help women 'get through' their prison sentence, offering a sense of purpose in a seemingly purposeless existence;

- having the opportunity to engage in ETE in a focused manner, without external distractions such as drug taking, childcare responsibilities;
- providing a 'stepping stone' to bettering themselves on release;
- having increased choices on release may prevent returning to a previous criminal lifestyle.

In this sense women speak of having gained rather than lost out as a result of coming to prison. However, although many women spoke of a positive experience of ETE whilst in custody, the level of satisfaction varied somewhat between establishments and the study data shows that experiences are not uniformly positive. Some of the limitations of ETE in prison included:

- an over-emphasis on basic skills level education within prisons and a lack of opportunity to progress to higher level courses;
- lack of available staff and resources;
- a lack of communication/consistency between establishments in ETE provision;
- a lack of tailoring ETE provision to individual need;
- a lack of available information regarding the opportunities which are available;
- lack of integration between work and education.

Women state that, to a certain extent, the ETE offered in prisons is 'tokenistic' and about 'being able to tick the right boxes'. The diverse needs and aspirations of women tend not be addressed thus women feel that it is the prison itself rather than them as individuals who are benefiting from it. Women also claim that ETE is not tailored towards the job market outside of custody and does not necessarily equip them with skills and experience, which would be attractive to potential employers. Women feel frustrated when the work, which they undertake, appears mindless and boring:

> They do need to offer more courses because when it gets to the position that I'm in there is absolutely nothing for me to do. So it's like I've hit a brick wall. I'm not getting any further no matter how hard I try. I just can't get to the next step. (Focus group participant)

> I ended up re-sitting exams that I'd already done before, just for the hell of it, because there was nothing else to do. (Focus group participant)

It doesn't really give you much incentive or enthusiasm. It's like me working the gardens. All your whole time's spent putting in plants, then pulling them up, putting them back in again and pulling them up and that goes on for whole, that's all I did for a whole fourteen months. (Focus group participant)

I think we've got quite a lot of needs. I think they need to really look at what is necessary to go out there in the job market. At the moment it's just general education. (Focus group participant)

Also, women serving short sentences may be particularly disadvantaged in terms of ETE opportunities. Not only do they find it difficult to receive useful sentence planning and access to courses but the short time they are in custody often means that there is little change in their mindset thus such women may be at a higher risk of simply returning to their previous lifestyle.

Issues of disclosure

An additional significant barrier to ETE for female ex-offenders was disclosure of convictions and perceived or actual attitudes of employers (these two issues are very closely linked). Confusion existed around disclosing convictions when applying for a job. Also the decision about whether or not to disclose is a difficult one for women to make. Disclosing is considered to be a very high-risk strategy but similarly not disclosing is a risk as failure to do so may 'backfire on them'. It was felt by some women that dishonesty would just reinforce negative views of offenders that employers may have and also would prove stressful for women to have 'skeletons in the cupboard' in their work environment.

However some women did feel that they would be justified in not disclosing their conviction(s) due to the perceived prevalence of stereotyping and discrimination among employers. Within the research data there emerges a strong sense of it being a 'no win situation' with employers as, no matter what, women perceive that their conviction(s) would always override the range of skills and experience which they may be able to offer the employer. For many women, the thought of having to disclose their conviction(s) provides a huge disincentive to getting back into work.

It's just putting down about my criminal record that puts me off ... I get to the bottom and it's always at the bottom and I think oh I might as well chuck it in the bin because I mean you never get a reply. (Focus group participant)

I have to say that I would hate to have to go into a job centre and apply for a job simply because I would just dread what you do. Do you lie or do you not lie? (Focus group participant)

The requirement for disclosure creates a huge stumbling block in terms of moving forward and shedding an old, undesirable identity. Women's ideas around how they are viewed by potential employers are tied up with issues of mistrust, un-desirability and an inability to change. Women feel that their entire identity is bound up with their criminality ('just a criminal') and employers fail to see the person behind the crime. Women with a criminal background feel they are viewed as a homogenous group, sharing the same negative characteristics ('smack heads', 'scum', 'losers', 'thieves'). Additionally it is felt that employers do not appreciate the diversity of women in the prison population and the variety of backgrounds and experiences, which they have. Society has a certain image of ex-offenders as somehow different from 'normal' people:

Obviously they are going to be biased because the first thing they see is a criminal, they don't see the person behind it. They don't see a person that has made a mistake and regrets what they've done and just wants to do whatever they can to prove that they are not a bad person. (Focus group participant)

You will often find that people in society would never think that prisoners would look like normal people. Most of them think that they will be distinctive. (Focus group participant)

Managing the transition from 'in to out'

Women in the study report numerous difficulties when making the transition from being in prison to resettling into the community. The difficulties involved in managing this transition are highly significant because they demonstrate that from the moment of their release women are faced with numerous difficulties and struggles which take priority over accessing ETE. It is clear that women will need support with these issues before they will be in a position to start thinking about ETE.

In direct contrast to commonly held societal perceptions about being incarcerated, women speak of prison as a 'safe environment', which provides welcome protection from the outside world. Women quickly adjust to the routine of prison and the security of knowing that their routine is dictated to them, thus negating the necessity to think and provide for themselves.

> In jail you've got that security. You've got three meals a day. You've got no bills. Everything's provided for you. (Focus group participant)

> Sometimes its harder to live outside than it is in here, you know? Everything's so compact in here but out there you've got your own decisions to make. (Focus group participant)

The extent to which institutionalisation occurs will greatly influence the way in which women experience the transition from in to out and the level of difficulties they may encounter. Those issues which are likely to priority over accessing ETE once released from prison include:

- Obtaining accommodation
- Rebuilding family relationships

Fighting a losing battle

Life 'on the out' is a struggle for women and each small step taken can seem like having 'a mountain to climb'. As a result of being faced with so many barriers and with so few resources to overcome them, women feel like they are 'fighting a losing battle'. It is very apparent when reading through the research data that this cohort of women feel incredibly powerless. This is reflected in the kinds of metaphors, which they used during the interviews, often speaking of having things 'done to them' rather than being able to take control themselves:

> It's going to be hard. You're in here, you're cocooned. It's your sanctuary. When you go on your resettlement visits everything's

just so loud and everyone's in your face and everyone's pulling you. (Focus group participant)

The self-perception of offenders as powerless needs to be overcome if women are to believe that they can succeed and that it is in their power to effect change for the future. It is clear that women need to be supported in regaining some control over their lives and need to be encouraged to believe that they can succeed.

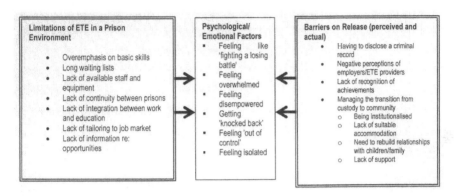

Figure 11.2   Barriers to ETE experienced by women ex-offenders

Overcoming barriers through peer research

The women ex-offenders who were involved in conducting this research were able to overcome many of the barriers outlined above. Peer researchers and trainees had the opportunity to work on a well-resourced programme which was not limited by the constraints of prison budgets. As a result of participation in the programme, peer researchers were offered interesting ETE opportunities which were wholly different from those limited options available within the prison regime. The training and work offered was varied and interesting and often a world away from previous ETE experiences. Peer researchers were also offered the opportunity to engage with OCN accredited training in Peer Research Methods as well as other training courses such as Presentation Skills and Report Writing. Also, there was direct linkage between the training and work elements of the programme.

Peer researchers had a large degree of autonomy over their work and a say in which work areas they wanted to be involved. They also quickly gained a sense of ownership of, control over, and identification with, the research process. The comprehensive support package offered to peer researchers resulted in a reduced 'fear factor' in undertaking ETE in a new area. Throughout the programme there existed an acknowledgement of the difficulties faced by women who were in custody and those who had recently left prison. For those peer researchers still in custody, every effort was made to enable them to obtain the appropriate licences for day release when necessary.

The opportunity to work outside the prison in a supportive environment assisted women in making the transition between 'in' and 'out' thus helping them to prepare for release. Indeed, some women reported that one of the most valuable aspects of involvement in the programme was being able to distance oneself from the prison and mix with a variety of professionals from different backgrounds.

Crucially, all research posts were specifically advertised as being for women with experience of the Criminal Justice System and this eliminated anxiety around disclosure. Indeed it was made clear throughout the process that women's experience of the Criminal Justice System was highly valued in terms of being able to effectively inform the research process and in this sense peer researchers were able to view this experience as having a positive outcome, often for the first time in their lives. In addition engagement in the programme provided a space where women ex-offenders were valued, listened to and given the opportunity to influence change in relation to ETE.

Peer researchers reported a very positive experience of the world of work, characterised by trusting and open working relationships. In addition they reported an increase in confidence and positive feelings about their capacity to contribute in a work setting. Most importantly, involvement in the project also contributed significantly to their future employability and new job opportunities. In the words of one peer researcher:

Its allowed me to step on that ladder and now I'm on it I'm not getting off...no one's kicking me off either. (peer researcher)

Peer approaches to service delivery

The next phase of the Women into Work programme was to commission pilot projects based on the findings of the research. The 'peer' ethos was carried through this next phase with a total of seven women ex-offenders being employed in two of the five projects which were commissioned. One such project was community based[7] and one prison based[8] but both were set up to offer ETE support and guidance to women. A further project recruited six peer volunteer workers.[9] Within these posts women were able to draw on their life experiences to support and empower their 'peers' in the resettlement process. Although their job titles varied, they are referred to here as peer support workers (PSWs). As with the peer researchers, the posts were explicitly targeted at women who had experience of the Criminal Justice System. The following sections explore the ways in which the service delivery element of the Women into Work programme continued with the ethos of peer working in order to offer women ex-offenders further opportunities to overcome some of the barriers to ETE outlined earlier.

Training and support

As in the research element of the programme, peer support workers were offered a comprehensive training and support package. On a practical level they were enabled to access a number of training courses including:

- NVQ 3 Advice and Guidance
- Benefits and Welfare Knowledge
- Communication skills
- Diversity and Cultural Awareness
- Presentation skills.

Project managers facilitated an 'all encompassing' support system which recognised the reality and totality of women's lives. Inherent in this is recognition of the potential impact which 'outside' issues could have on PSWs experience of the world of work. It became apparent that managing the support needs of PSWs was somewhat different and more demanding/challenging than more traditional line management arrangements, not least because PSWs may potentially have similar needs to the client group that they are working with:

> I haven't even got a bed ... I'm in a bedsit so I need a bed so I said just so long as I can get one room comfortable I don't mind then starting on the rest cause I'd rather do that anyway but so long as I can get one room settled (PSW, SOVA Project)

Regular formal one-to-one supervision was conducted with PSWs. However the informal support which PSWs gave each other between meetings was also highly valued. Key to this was a recognition and sharing of each others' skills and knowledge. Such informal support networks proved extremely empowering and enabled truly effective team working:

> We get on brilliant you know we have a right good laugh ... we always talk to each other on the phone as well if we need to know anything and it's in their areas or we've just had an idea, we just phone each other and talk. (PSW, SOVA Project)

As stated by a project manager:

> They've got to explore their own abilities and stuff and it's recognising 'okay I can do that, I can do this' that's when they become empowered. (project manager, SOVA Project)

Personal development

Despite having to overcome a number of hurdles (both personal and professional) during the course of their employment, PSWs reported increased empowerment and self confidence in addition to the practical skills and knowledge they acquired:

> I can remember like when I'd first go into meetings like with Women Into Work I was like ... I used to be so nervous and not speak a word and now I'll talk. (PSW, Norfolk Project)

> It's great when I get comments from girls and their appreciation of what I've done for them and they tell me 'Oh, you've done a brilliant job' and whatever. It's empowering for me and I'm giving them empowerment as well. It's like empowerment bouncing off each other! They're getting empowered and I'm getting empowered and more confident as I go along. All of it is just great. (PSW, NACRO Project)

Their employment enabled PSWs to experience considerable personal growth; specifically, 'peer working' stood them in good stead for future employment in different fields:

I've got the record there still, but I've proved myself to be trusted and whatever because I've been allowed back in an establishment which is the best proof I could have ... so I think I'll be more confident going for another job after. (PSW, NACRO Project)

On a more personal level one PSW outlined how being able to support women ex-offenders in a professional role has played a crucial role in her own resettlement:

I'm still resettling myself now three years later and I think the one thing that has kept me from going over the edge is the focus I've had on my job and the responsibility I felt ... getting feedback from the girls was the most amazing high, you feel such a sense of achievement and if you help just one person if you can stop one person from going back, if you can give one person self-esteem and the chance of entering a job ... that in itself means you have achieved something and that means it [peer support] works. I really do find that by throwing myself into it ... I know it sounds madness ... but it heals me at the same time. (PSW, NACRO Project)

Prison staff on the whole reacted very positively to the PSWs, treating them as normal colleagues and with respect. For one PSW the experiences of revisiting prisons where she had once resided was overwhelmingly positive, offering an opportunity to reaffirm feelings of self-acceptance and show to others how far she had come:

Yes it's brilliant I love going back into prison. Even some of the officers recognise me and say 'ooh you used to be in here' but then they ask me what I'm doing and have I got a job and I just tell them you know I'm not ashamed of what I used to be because now I've put it to good use. (PSW, SOVA Project)

Shifting identities from offender to professional

Adopting the role of PSW involved significant 'shifts' in identity. This initially posed some practical problems for PSWs as financial constraints made it difficult for them to purchase clothes appropriate for duties expected of them (e.g. attending meetings, delivering presentations). It proved extremely disempowering for the PSWs to go into a meeting where people were smartly dressed in suits and carrying brief cases and immediately created an obvious gulf between themselves and the 'professionals'.

> It's obvious that these are the women that are PSWs because you can spot the way that they're dressed and that is what they feel and its added to because they now have to give a presentation. (SOVA Regional Director).

> There was a big problem being more presentable like presentation wise because with me only being released in September and having to start again like trying to build up a decent wardrobe. (PSW, SOVA Project).

In addition, dilemmas were evident regarding PSWs readiness to re-enter prison establishments where they had once resided in order to conduct their work duties:

> She was too fresh, she knew some of the ladies here, she knew a lot of the staff her ... you could certainly look maybe 3 or 4 years down the road if somebody had left and there was a change of staff and there was a change of regime and a change of culture as we all expect, and that would have made it easier ... both for their sake as well as the sake of the establishment. (Principal Prison Officer)

There is also a need to consider the potential cost to the PSWs of expecting them to reveal their offending background within their professional role:

> I went in to ask them you know New Hall prison and as a formality I was requested or I was asked to by my line manager to inform them of my previous background ... that's not a problem although I don't want to keep doing it, you know. Do I have to keep disclosing, you know? I'm in there within a role and when I spoke to the Head of Resettlement I think he was more interested in how prison affected me or what I got out of the prison or what the prison service did for me than my role as on this project. (PSW, SOVA Project)

Thus the 'professionalisation' of PSWs was shown to be a complex issue and the following questions need careful consideration when undertaking an innovative peer approach:

254

- Do PSWs see themselves as professionals?
- How long does this process take?
- At what stage do PSWs accept themselves as professionals or ex-offenders?
- At what stage do PSWs become accepted by others as professionals
- At what point does it become unacceptable to expect women to disclose their backgrounds in their professional role?

Relationships between peer workers and beneficiaries

The benefits of a peer led approach to service delivery were multi-layered and offered numerous ways of overcoming barriers to ETE for both peer workers and beneficiaries of services (i.e. the women who accessed peer support service). A degree of shared background and experience facilitated increased rapport, openness and a strong interpersonal connection between PSWs and beneficiaries:

> If a normal person went in – and I'm not saying I'm not normal – but if someone went in from another agency and whatever, the girls ain't going to interact as much because the person's not going to understand as I understand. (PSW, NACRO Project)

PSWs were also able to provide positive role models and inspiration for beneficiaries which was likely to encourage them to engage with ETE more readily than if accessing a more traditional service:

> Because she's only just left and she's in this position now and you can see she's doing so well for herself – especially in a women's prison and she's a black woman as well – and for me that has kind of 'Well, if you can do it, in that short space of time, then I can do anything! (Beneficiary, NACRO Project)

> I think it's because she's been where I've been. You know, she's served time, but she's done something positive with that and that's what I'm looking for. That's what I've been striving for. (Beneficiary, SOVA Project)

Peer support workers' commitment and dedication to their role is immediately proven in the mind of beneficiaries by virtue of their decision to come back to work in the prison environment post-release. This was perceived as hugely impressive by beneficiaries and undoubtedly contributed to effective relationships. They felt it provided evidence of genuineness which is vital for building trust:

> I mean (PSW) seems like an absolutely wonderful person anyway and to have come out of prison and want to come back into the prison environment anyway, that's just like ... that shows complete dedication. You only meet people like that every now and then that are willing to give themselves totally. (Beneficiary, NACRO Project)

Beneficiaries felt they were heard by peer workers in a way that does not occur within more traditional services. Being heard is characterised by acknowledging experience and feeling and being prepared to act on what is said:

> She can hear what we're saying. I'm a really educated woman, it's just that I'm not given the chance to prove myself ... it's really holding me back and none of the staff are hearing me. Do you understand? You can talk till you're blue in the face in here. They're not hearing you. (Beneficiary, NACRO Project)

One of the more obvious benefits is increased rapport and identification with clients and enabling clients to remain in their comfort zone whilst still getting the help that they need:

> It is easier for them to talk to me because they know that I'm not going to judge them in any way they can use words you know just like swear words that they can just relax and talk to me ... I know what they are going through and I know what's like to be locked behind a door at night and not have nowhere to live and to be on drugs and so on. (PSW, SOVA Project)

Efficiency of service

There is evidence to suggest that employing PSWs may result in a more efficient service due to the increased knowledge of PSWs when guiding and supporting beneficiaries. There is an inherent value for beneficiaries in being able to learn from the direct experience of project workers who are able to provide a personal reference for services:

I wouldn't have known the exact places to go … the hostel that I was in before I came into prison was dreadful … and like [project workers] spoken to me and said there's hostels that are ok … I mean the one that she's in at the moment is just like a flat share. (Beneficiary, NACRO Project)

Knowledge of prison processes and protocols and how to work effectively within the prison system was also appreciated:

She's been through it all already and she must know the red tape … and where you can't go and she knows the ways to get around things, which maybe someone who hasn't been in prison wouldn't know. (Beneficiary, NACRO Project)

Personal experience of trying to get things done in a prison environment offered a unique insight into how to form effective relationships with staff and colleagues which a non-peer worker would not have. This meant that PSWs can be particularly effective in their negotiations with staff and this will impact upon the effectiveness of service which they are able to deliver:

I think my experience of being a prisoner helps me because it has given me the patience and it has given me the insight and it has given me that look on my face that says 'that's okay not a problem I will come back when it's convenient for you' and just to you know, try and calm the girl (beneficiary) down as well and say 'look you know this is how you've got to play it', you know it's a bit like a game, you have to play a game. (PSW, SOVA Project)

Although peer workers can play a key role in motivating beneficiaries and increasing confidence, their own experiences of being released from prison meant they were able to offer a realistic perspective on the difficulties which beneficiaries may be faced with:

I don't try and pretend to the girls that it's easy I want them to know that coming out of prison is actually worse than going in because you look through that window through rose tinted glasses. You think to yourself 'I am going to do this when I get out, I am going to do that' … there was no one there to explain to me or warn me that's why I think it is so, so important that you know not just for getting them into work and that but for the whole peer support thing to explain that whilst freedom is your dream the reality is that it's just like another prison but the rules are harder. (PSW, NACRO Project)

Resistances to peer working

As with any innovative way of working which goes against the status quo there is the potential for resistance among certain staff members, particularly those who feel they have little influence over decisions made to implement such initiatives. To a small extent this appears to be the case in this instance:

The resistance here I think was maybe, you know, half a dozen people predominantly on the ground floor with no managerial influence, who expressed a negative view of the ladies who'd been selected to deliver the programme ... and the difficulty with that of course is that they network with others. The resistance was probably because some staff had the knowledge that one of them actually had served some time here. That was difficult. (Principal Prison Officer)

At times this resentment was evident in the behaviour of individual officers towards project staff:

One day I wanted to get through the gate and he didn't want to let me through and made me wait, there was three of them stood there and I was just stood at the gate waiting but I don't let them know that they're upsetting me ... he was talking the way screws talk to cons'. (PSW, SOVA Project)

This was certainly the exception rather than the rule. However, it is still important to recognise the very negative impact which this may have on workers and the potential for negative past experiences to resurface:

You're in **that place** again ... its hard to sort of ... I haven't said owt to anybody but I felt like you're in that place, you're in that police station and ... you're going in there prepared for the job, you want to do it, you want to do it properly you know what I mean and somebody like that you know. (PSW, SOVA Project)

Discussion

The SOVA Women into Work programme offered a unique, innovative approach to overcoming barriers to ETE for women ex-offenders. Within the programme both peer researchers and peer support workers were offered a positive experience of the world of work where their experiences of the Criminal Justice System were utilised and valued. The opportunities presented to women ex-offenders on this programme increased their self confidence and ultimately their future employability. In addition the beneficiaries of peer led support services may expect to gain from an increased rapport and closeness with their support workers which may facilitate a less daunting transition in the world of ETE. Although the benefits of peer working are numerous, the process may also prove resource intensive as the training and support needs of workers are likely to be higher than those for non-peers. In addition, the shift in identity which may occur during peer-led employment (i.e. from offender to professional) may be experienced as both liberating and problematic and so the process also needs to be carefully managed and supported. In summary, the Women into Work programme has clearly demonstrated the potential for peer led solutions to be more effective in overcoming barriers to ETE for women ex-offenders than more traditional approaches, not least because of their empowering and holistic emphasis.

Notes

1 Funding from the EQUAL stream of the European Social Fund was secured for the programme in 2001 by SOVA in partnership with 12 voluntary and statutory sector agencies. The aim of the programme was to work towards combating discrimination and inequality experienced by women who have been disadvantaged, particularly by their experiences of the criminal justice system. The Hallam Centre of Community Justice at Sheffield Hallam University have been responsible for conducting all the research and evaluation elements of the programme and have also been involved in dissemination activity. For all our relevant work relating to the programme see www.hccj.shu.ac.uk

2 'Ex-offenders' is the chosen term for the SOVA Women into Work Programme. This term applied to women who were still in custody and those who had left custody. An important aspect of the Women into Work Programme was to address discrimination of women with criminal convictions. The term was adopted to avoid burdening women with an 'offender' label which no longer applies in many cases.

3 The first prisoner Listener scheme in England & Wales started in 1991 at Swansea prison in Wales. The scheme was developed with the recognition that the most powerful influence on a prisoner's induction into prison, however hard staff work, is fellow prisoners. The prisoner Listener scheme aims to harness that peer group support in a positive way by training prisoners to offer emotional support to their fellow prisoners.

4 St Giles Trust are a London based voluntary organisation who work with prisoners to train them to give advice and guidance to other prisoners, enabling prisoners to help each other to break the cycle of prison, unemployment, poverty and reoffending.

5 The organisation known as KRIS (Criminals' Return Into Society), was formed in Stockholm in 1997 on the initiative of four individuals with a long history of involvement in crime and drug abuse. The basic idea was to form an association of people with similar experiences, which could provide a supportive network for individuals wishing to leave a life of crime and drug abuse behind them.

6 WPA's Peer Training Institute employs women with histories of criminal justice involvement as peer mentors to help women recently released from state and city correctional facilities. After their 9 month employment with WPA, peer mentors are well equipped to secure full time employment or expand their educational opportunities.

7 The Peer Mentoring Support and Resettlement Pilot managed by SOVA

8 The 'Going Straight to Work' Project managed by NACRO

9 The Norfolk Women into Employment and Training Project managed by the Women's Employment Enterprise and Training and Unit.

References

Beresford, P. and Croft, S. (1993) *Citizen Involvement: A practical guide for change*. Basingstoke: Macmillan.

Coghlan, D. and Brannick, T. (2001) *Doing Action Research in Your Own Organisation*. London: Sage.

Dowling, C. (2001) *Making the Education Connection: Women, prison and education*. London: Women in Prison.

Foote Whyte, W. (1991) *Participatory Action Research*. CA: Sage.

Hamlyn, B, and Lewis, D. (2000) *Women Prisoners: A survey of their work and training experiences in custody and on release*. London: Home Office.

O'Keeffe, C. (2003) *Moving Mountains: Identifying and addressing barriers to employment, training and education from the voices of women (ex)offenders*. Sheffield: SHU Press.

Sohng, S.S.L. (1995) Participatory Research and Community Organising, Paper presented at *The New Social Movement and Community Organising Conference*, University of Washington, Seattle, WA, November 1–3, 1995.

Trueman, C., Mertens, D.M. and Humphries, B. (2000) *Research and Inequality.* London: UCL Press.

Walters, N., Lygo-Baker, S. and Strkljevic, S. (2001) *Empowerment Indicators: Combating social exclusion in Europe.* Bristol: The Policy Press.

Chapter 12

Employment: offending and reintegration

Tracie McPherson

Introduction

This chapter looks at the importance of employment in the successful reintegration of women offenders into the community. It discusses findings from the Correctional Service Employment Pilot Program (CSEPP), funded by Corrections Victoria, and considers the strengths and limitations of the programme. It describes also the contribution made by the 'Employment Expo', a forum that introduced employer agencies to women in prison.

Female prisoners experience significant barriers to gaining employment on release from prison (Cox 2001). Such barriers may include mental and physical health issues, lack of stable accommodation, low levels of educational attainment, poor or limited vocational skills, lack of networks that would assist them to find employment, discrimination due to their criminal conviction, lack of recent work experience and, lack of motivation and self-confidence. Other barriers for female prisoners are their limited vocational skills, which reduces their access to employment (Cox and Carlin, 1999). This is demonstrated statistically in Victoria where 78.1% of women have not completed high school and the unemployment rate upon reception to prison was 59% in 2004 (Corrections Victoria 2005).

Holzer, Raphael and Stoll (2003) recognised that employment plays a significant role in the reintegration of offenders into the community and a reduction in reoffending. Jucovy (2006) found that when on leaving prison and returning to the community ex-prisoners are typically faced with an immediate need to find employment, to both earn an income and implement some structure in their lives. Individuals leaving prison are confronted with many issues: housing, health, community and family reintegration, any or all of which might hinder maintaining employment.

In order to address these issues it was proposed to introduce a comprehensive employment programme into the prisons. The Correctional Service Employment Pilot Program (CSEPP) was introduced by Corrections Victoria as an employment assistance programme for prisoners and offenders. The review of the corrections system in Victoria in 2002 led to a new emphasis on the reintegration of prisoners into the community, to enable them to become active members of the community. Corrections Victoria's *Long Term Management Strategy* (Office of the Correctional Services Commissioner 2001) aimed to reduce reoffending through significant investment in rehabilitation and prison diversion programs. It was recognised that prisoners and offenders require intensive support for a wide range of needs for which they require specialist assistance. It was also recognised that such support would need to be long-term – with the likelihood of slow and intermittent progress and the need for basic skill development as part of pre-employment preparation. There would also be a need for other services to be involved: housing, health and personal support services. The lack of skills development including low levels of numeracy and literacy, limited education and poor employment skills significantly disadvantages this client group in the employment market.

The Correctional Service Employment Pilot Programme (hereafter referred to as CSEPP) commenced in June 2002 as a pilot programme for two years. A further two years of the programme was subsequently funded, commencing in July 2004 and finishing in June 2006. The findings, which are reported here, are from the four years of this pilot programme, and have contributed to the key policy formulated for women offenders by Corrections Victoria, known as *Better Pathways* (Corrections Victoria 2006). CSEPP was a reintegration programme with two key objectives: employment and reduction in re-offending. The primary goal of CSEPP was to provide employment assistance to an overall population of 2,500 male and female prisoners and offenders who were at medium or high risk of reoffending, and who were assessed as having high support needs. There was a need to place 450 members of this group in full-time sustained employment (thirteen weeks continuous employment) within a two-year period. The findings in this chapter are the culmination of the four-year CSEPP pilot program. Whilst the programme was funded by Corrections Victoria, the women's service was administered by Melbourne Citymission, a non-government agency in Victoria that has a long history of working with marginalised women.

The CSEPP programme commenced with women six months prior to their release, continued throughout the period of their parole and was maintained for a further twelve months. Assisting the entry of ex-prisoners into employment is a complex process with issues of housing, health and family reintegration taking priority. These issues need to be managed before linking the individual to employment. The individual ex-prisoner generally needs significant assistance to guide and prepare them as job seekers to meet the expectations of potential employers. Holzer, Raphael, and Stoll (2002) identified how well the prospective employee presents was the key factor that influenced employers hiring workers in low-wage and low-skill employment settings, such as factory and the hospitality industries. In reality, most employers seek applicants who are willing to work and demonstrate communication and interpersonal skills. This required extensive vocational counselling and encouraging the women to explore their long-term future. This proved challenging because most women indicated that they had never thought about much beyond their day-to-day survival where their priorities were to maintain housing and meet basic living needs. (Graffam, Shinkfield, Lavelle and McPherson 2004).

The programme outlined

The women's component of CSEPP was conducted in Victoria's two women's prisons: the Dame Phyllis Frost Centre is a maximum-security prison that has the capacity to incarcerate 240 women. This prison is for remand and sentenced prisoners. Tarrengower prison is a minimum-security prison and has a capacity of 52 prisoners. The majority of women at Tarrengower are either first time offenders or have achieved a minimum security rating at the Dame Phyllis Frost Centre. CSEPP incorporated work with the women both in the community and in the prison setting. The Employment Expo project was implemented in the prison.

The strengths of the programme provide an important insight into what is effective in terms of employment and facilitating integration into the community after prison. The *length of time in the programme* is the first key factor to examine. Women were able to participate in the programme for the six months prior to their release, during the term of their parole and for twelve months after the conclusion of their order. This length of time meant the women developed a strong rapport with the programme, and strong working relationships with programme providers. This was evident when women who might have lost contact with the programme soon after release made contact again once they had settled. Women could remain linked with the programme whilst attending to pressing issues such as obtaining housing and working on family reconciliation. These were issues, as identified earlier that very often needed to be addressed before women could look to employment; when resolved they would return to the programme to gain employment assistance. The pre and post aspect meant that workers did not have to continually talk about their offending history, and this allowed the worker to focus on employment and vocational training needs.

Job readiness and job search training

Job search training was developed to prepare the women for the rigours of searching for employment. The training included common job-search training tools such as handouts about interview skills, assisting with resume development and application writing. What was different in working with this group of women, from working with the general population, was that the training was either one-on-one or in conducted in small groups of two or three. The individual focus meant the material could be adapted to the meet the women's learning abilities and gave them the opportunity to explore future possibilities in a non-threatening environment. Job search training conducted with large groups in the prison setting might mean women had to disclose their past employment experiences in an environment in which they were less than comfortable, possibly resulting in reluctance to explore their employment options as thoroughly. In the prison environment, women tend to reveal very little about themselves or their past; job-search training gave them the opportunity to return to some normality upon release. Key to the job-search training was the development of a manual: starting with goal setting and finishing with the job interview process, which included how to approach legal requirements to disclose one's criminal record to a future employer. The manual was designed to enable the woman to work at her own pace, to explore how she felt about gaining employment and what she might do to gain more work experience. The job-search training programme allowed the women to monitor their own progress and establish their own goals in a non-judgemental manner.

Continuity of service

Women who commenced the programme when in prison were transferred on release to a *community-based* employment consultant based in the area in which they were going to live. The CSEPP program provided these services across seven sites in metropolitan Melbourne and two sites in rural Victoria. Ideally the community-based employment consultants, prior to their release, would visit the prison to meet their client. Release from prison was often a daunting experience for the women, as it required balancing reintegration into the community with meeting their parole obligations, and requirements for counselling and other services. Being able to build a relationship with the employment service prior to release eased this transition. Dialogue between the prison and the community consultants gave the consultant the opportunity to follow up women who might be struggling with the transition from prison into the community.

Individual action plan

The programme provided an *individual action plan* for each woman. It set out specific goals, taking into account issues around housing, childcare and family reunification. As already noted, these were issues that needed to be addressed before women could concentrate on employment. The individual action plan would consider access visits to children, or childcare needs or the need to look for employment during children's school hours. It was essential these issues were canvassed so that women could meet the demands of parole, job search and family reconciliation. The action plan incorporated the requirements of the first three months of parole; including the appointments and counselling that were statutory requirements.

Self-esteem and motivational workshop

Central to the CSEPP program was a workshop that looked at both *self-esteem and motivation*; it addressed the women's feelings of self-doubt and dealt with the isolation they experienced whilst in prison. In working with the women, it became clear that one of their biggest fears on release was that everyone would know by looking at them that they had been in prison. It was important to challenge these thought patterns prior to their release to allow the women to deal with their perceived fears. Working with the women in a one-on-one situation the worker would explore the different scenarios the women might face upon release. The women were encouraged to think about what obstacles they would confront as they sought to reintegrate into the community. The aim was to develop cognitive strategies that would help them to cope with such situations. The women face tremendous barriers upon release but with some work within the employment programme, they were able to start looking for solutions to these barriers. The workshop was successful because it prepared the client for the difficulties they might encounter upon release, and gave them tools to overcome the issues they had identified as they arose.

Transitional model

The CSEPP programme included a *transition to employment* approach. This meant that upon release from prison, the women were able to maintain contact with the prison employment services until they had settled and were ready to engage with the community-based employment consultant. This was particularly successful for clients being released to crisis or temporary accommodation as it gave them time to find more settled accommodation. It also gave the clients a contact within the service if they needed assistance with reintegration back into the community such as referral to housing or other support services.

Positive working relationships with education facility and prison programme staff

The success of the programme depended on building *effective working relationships* with other key stakeholders. The programme developed a solid reputation in the prison by consistently being present on the days it said it would be at the prison, and by always following through with queries about employment and vocational training opportunities. The programme developed a collaborative with the education facility which provided both educational and vocational training and assistance to prisoners as required. The education service's building allowed CSEPP to use their facilities and work with the educational provider around implementation, funding and assistance with some vocational and short-term courses. The programme's presence in the educational provider's building allowed programme staff to become familiar with the women in a different way. The education environment was more relaxed and unstructured, compared with the more structured requirements in which the CSEPP programme was delivered, which was on an appointment only system. When the service was based in the education facility the programme offered a more flexible approach. Women could be seen when they requested, to complete one-on-one job search training and to have an opportunity to have an informal discussion about their future employment needs.

Trained staff

The community-based consultants who were employed by the programme had previously either worked in the community service sector or the employment services sector. The prison-based employment consultants who were employed to work in the programme had all previously worked with offenders, homeless or disadvantaged people within the community. The employment consultants who worked in the community were experienced in basic community service work and had *extensive experience* in working with highly disadvantaged groups within government funded employment services and programmes. The staff working in the programme met monthly to exchange information about what worked best in their work with the women clients seeking employment. These meetings were important because a large percentage of the consultants' work was performed in isolation, and the exchange of information gave staff the opportunity to share experiences and develop strategies to better assist their clients.

A major strength of the programme was that the staff employed, whilst having varying experience and education levels, were committed to social justice principles and wanted to make a difference for ex-prisoners. As a group, staff demonstrated a good knowledge of prisoners and offenders as a client group. They demonstrated the ability to build rapport and trust, and the ability to motivate their clients whilst being mindful of their personal circumstances. They worked closely with prison staff and had a good working knowledge of the corrections system. They were supportive of their clients but also maintained clear boundaries.

Voluntary programme

The women who came to register with the programme were told at the outset that their participation was *voluntary*; undertaking the programme had no bearing on parole outcomes or decisions to breach orders that might be made by either community corrections officers or welfare agencies. The women were free to terminate their participation in the programme at anytime. The voluntary nature of the programme was significant because it meant the women could discuss issues and concerns without the fear that this could impact on their parole.

Financial resources

The programme provided *funding* to women assist them on their release with the purchase of items they needed to help them with job-seeking. These items included prepaid mobile phones – which meant the women could be contacted by potential employers, clothing to wear to interviews, travel tickets and phone cards. Funds were also allocated so that the employment consultants could pay for vocational and short-term courses, which would enhance clients' skills for employment.

Post-placement support

Women who gained community-based employment were provided with intensive *post-placement support* by an employment consultant for the first thirteen weeks, which included telephone and face-to-face contact. This gave the woman the opportunity to talk about the process of reintegration into the workforce, any issues they faced regarding workplace behaviour, time management and provided for discussion about conflict resolution skills. The importance of post-placement support was that if the woman lost her job she could reconnect to the service and commence job searching again.

Programme limitations

There were however a number of limitations to the programme. The initial aim of the programme was to engage employers and seek their co-operation in providing employment for women leaving prison. This goal however was unrealistic at the time even though the staff had extensive experience in community service the programme had negligible knowledge about the client group of women offenders and the issues they faced with reintegration into the community and gaining employment. Even when an employer had a job available, the programme did not always have a suitable candidate, and so the opportunity would be lost. Awareness training was implemented to assist the programme staff to further understand the expectations of employers. It became clear to the workers in the programme that just because jobs were available they may not be the best opportunities for the client group. It was also clear that prior to engaging employers, programme staff needed to be aware of issues such as access to the employment by public transport, the work conditions and hours of work, as these might become barriers for the women trying to maintain work. It has already been noted that the programme developed a brochure, which advised the client group about legal obligations surrounding disclosure of one's criminal record; The brochure offered some strategies about how women approach this, and how, if required to make these disclosures, they could do this within a safe context, recognising that a criminal record could discriminate against a client.

No funding for recognition of social outcomes

There was a significant amount of work the external consultants needed to do before the client was ready for employment. They needed to look at the availability of housing, how to facilitate community reintegration, and what material aid was needed and the possibility of family reunification. The key performance indicators for the programme did not however recognise the additional resourcing the consultants needed to do before they could link a client to employment. Assistance with, and referrals to, housing, material aid and crisis services, took away from their core objective, which was to place clients in employment.

High caseloads for community-based employment consultants

The high level of demand on the community-based services, and the need to respond to client issues, meant the time required to prepare the client group for employment was not always available. This put enormous pressure on the workers, and at times the programme did not meet the high expectations of the client group. For example, there were times of instability in the programme when staff moved to other employment and either replacing staff, or providing short-term additional staff, had not been factored into the contract. This meant the clients were without a service until a replacement staff member was found. This could have been overcome by training more than one staff member in each agency in the programme operation.

Demands made by other pre-release programmes

Women getting ready for release have a range of expectations to meet and programmes to maintain, and this can get in the way of having the time needed to prepare for seeking employment. Women at the pre-release stage have a seemingly endless list of assessments and meetings to attend to prepare them for release. To make this more manageable for the women, the prison employment consultant developed links with other programmes such as housing and support services, and would ensure appointments coincided, to reduce the demands on the women to continually attend for appointments.

Clients not contactable after prison

It was often difficult to make contact with women who were living in crisis or temporary accommodation after their release from prison. Whilst the prison employment consultant went to great effort to maintain links with the women, it was very difficult to locate and engage clients who did not have permanent accommodation. However, if the woman and the prison employment consultant had established a strong working relationship then the woman would eventually make contact when she had settled into more stable accommodation

The Employment Expo

The US Crime Prevention Institution and the Bureau of Prisons developed the Employment Expo project from a programme operating in the male prison in Texas, USA. These programmes were initiated between 1992 and 1996 to provide prisoners with the opportunity to participate in job interviews with actual employers from companies operating in the community (US Federal Bureau of Prisons 2003). The Texas programme attracted an increase in participating companies as it proved to be successful, thus enhancing work opportunities for those leaving prison.

Pre-release or transitional programs, such as CSEPP, provide general job information and job search training, which includes resume development. The Employment Expo adds an extra element to the pre-release preparation by giving prisoners a realistic experience in which they can practice and improve their job seeking skills. It gives the clients an opportunity to practice their interview skills and discuss employment options upon release. It was envisaged that this opportunity not only built on the tangible skills that a prisoner required for the job market, but also increased confidence and self- esteem. It lessened the fear of the job seeking experience that comes from being out of practice and disconnected to the community. Most women expressed concern about their lack of current employment history and skills, and the fact that their criminal record would hinder their possible employment. The Expo set out to lessen these concerns by providing the opportunity to discuss their future options and find out about what training would increase their chances of employment.

The objectives of the Employment Expo were to offer real pathways to employment by providing clients with an opportunity to test their interview skills and learn how they may be further developed; empowering clients to feel confident and motivated about re-entering the work force; and giving the clients a 'first hand' experience of employer expectations and industry requirements. It's dual aim to challenge employers' perceptions of prisoners by allowing them to interact in a non-threatening environment and to experience the women as they were now, not what they had been. It also hoped to increase the likelihood of employers hiring ex-offenders after being exposed to the prison and the prisoners.

The outcomes of the project were extremely successful with both prisoners and employers giving overwhelming positive feedback

The seriousness with which the women prisoners took the mock interviews was fantastic and their obvious enthusiasm certainly surprised me and made me come back to work raving about how beneficial the whole thing was. The women were so excited to be able to discuss their future options, and most asked about education and vocational courses, which was fantastic. (Comment from an employer)

Job interviews have always scared me, now even though I would still be nervous, I know what to expect'. (Participant's comment)

While it was not possible to predict whether or not the Employment Expo would in the long term increase the likelihood of the women securing employment on release from prison or reduce their likelihood of reoffending. However, a follow up of the participants by the Employment Expo Project Worker showed the long-term benefits (see Table 12.1). The Expo in the short term did meet the original objectives of giving women information about real work opportunities and skill development for employment when they were released from prison.

Programme outcomes

The CSEPP Project interviewed the women who attended the first Employment Expo at the Dame Phyllis Frost Centre (the main women's prison in Victoria) in October 2004 to see how effective the Expo was in terms of gaining employment after their release from prison. The women were interviewed either by telephone or in

Table 12.1 Post-release outcomes for women who attended Employment Expo, October 2004

Post-release status	No. of women	%
Employed	10	41.60
Unemployed/Pregnant	5	20.80
Reoffended after release	4	17.00
New charges prior to release:		
never released	4	17.00
Unable to locate	1	3.60
TOTAL	24	100%

person, at two months, four months and six months after release. Of the twenty-four women who were in this first cohort, all except one woman – who could not be located – were interviewed.

The success of the Employment Expo is illustrated below in the experiences of one woman who had been in prison:

> Prior to this sentence, I was, in a way enjoying the whole gaol experience, having no responsibilities and nobody missed me on the outside. Back in my second sentence, my parents practically disowned me, and moved interstate, so I felt like I had no reason to stay out. Towards the end of 2004 a friend asked me to join her in going to the 'Employment Expo' in the prison. I was reluctant, but I said yes for her.

> On the day of the Expo I couldn't imagine how beneficial it would be. The best part was the mock interviews, which for me was more about just talking to people. They gave me many tips and ideas on how to do the work I wanted and I really think their being positive towards me made me realise, for the first time in ages, that I was worth more than drugs and gaol. I had goals, and because of them it gave me a reason not to use when I got out of prison.

> It was suggested to me to do a course in massage. I knew I couldn't afford it so the employment worker offered to pay, which again, was someone showing faith in me. The whole experience was all so positive for me. I got out of gaol and enrolled to do a Basic Massage Course at a local University. As promised, the programme paid for it.

> If it wasn't for the experience of the "Employment Expo", who knows where I'd be today, because prior to it I had no immediate intention of changing my lifestyle. I didn't feel there was any reason to. I am now drug free and on my way to becoming a professional masseur (Kylie's story. She was at the time serving her sixth sentence).

The Employment Expo project became an integral part of the employment project. It raised the profile of the employment programme with the women in prison and within the Corrections sector, and benefited greatly the women it set out to help. Furthermore, it gave employers an opportunity to participate in a different approach to working with potential job seekers and it challenged their perceptions about offenders and their attitudes to, and willingness for, work.

Conclusion

The women in this study wanted to be employed after they were released from prison so they had sufficient income to support themselves and their families. Taxman, Young and Byrne (2002) found that, in reality, when women in this position did find work it was generally in unskilled or lesser-skilled employment. They often struggled financially on low incomes with little recognition by the community and fragmented reintegration. These difficulties were compounded by: less than positive employer attitudes to the women seeking work; their lower literacy levels and lack of occupational skills; and, difficulties they might have finding stable accommodation (Heinrich 2000). The CSEPP programme offered a different experience. It provided a forum that confronted the challenges of finding work. It offered life skills preparation, placement in employment and skills in retaining employment, as well as assistance with broader issues associated with reducing reoffending and reintegration into the community (Graffam, Shinkfield, Lavelle and McPherson 2005). The timeframe of the programme (the length of the corrections order plus twelve months) enable the women to access these services over a longer period of time. This provided the opportunity to build on employment success and look at long-term employment sustainability.

The Queensland Government, in Australia, introduced similar employment programmes in 2001–02, on a trial basis, as part of a post-release employment programme. This programme provided support for only two months prior to release from prison and two months post-release. However, its introduction was limited to two regional areas in Queensland, and it is difficult to generalise about outcomes in such a limited context (Cox 2001). The CSEPP Programme in Victoria provided a state-wide service. It offered links to employment services for women who were return to live in areas that were not covered by the pilot programme. This meant every woman who participated in the programme whilst in prison could benefit from commencing the programme in the prison and being linked to a local service when they were released.

Programmes that are similar to CSEPP are being introduced in other countries, given the success of CSEPP. They are generally smaller programmes that are being implemented primarily to facilitate the reintegration of offenders into the community. The US Crime Prevention Institution (CPI) and the US Bureau of Prisons (BOP) projects in Texas prepare prisoners for job interviews, but do incorporate the other the transitional aspects of CSEPP such as linking the individual to an external employment consultant and assisting them with the transition to work, factors that emerged as strengths of the CSEPP model.

Within the United Kingdom programmes such as *Women to Work* in London offers training to ex-prisoners who act as mentors to newly released prisoners. In the USA, the *Ready4Work* initiative links male and female prisoners to a mentor prior to their release, to provide support and practical assistance with post-release employment and reintegration into the community. The Florida Offenders Employment Programme offers apprenticeships to people leaving prison; this is supported by the Florida Corrections Commission (Field-Pimms 2004). These programmes have all had success, albeit varied and perhaps narrow in focus. The CSEPP Programme overcame the significant limitation of making links for women between prison and the community; the programmes ensured women were supported from release to resettlement in the community. This was a major achievement as it is often difficult to make links between services located in the metropolitan region with services in regional and rural Victoria.

Lawrence, Mears, Dubin and Travis (2002) found that participation in prison-based treatment programmes and community-based treatment programmes was positive; it led to lower recidivism rates for women who had previously been in custody – in June 2005, there was a 41.2% reduction in return to custody by women in Victoria (Corrections Victoria 2005). Within the first two years of the CSEPP pilot programme, there was a 27.2% reduction in reoffending rate by women registered with the programme (Job Futures 2004). Interviews with female ex-prisoners by Solomon and Waul (2001) affirmed that a critical element to success in reducing re-offending was the individual's readiness or resolve to change. If the individual had this resolve then they were motivated to make use of the range of transition and support services available in prison and on release. The importance of the woman's readiness for employment has particular relevance to both job acquisition and retention (Graffam, Shinkfield, Lavelle and McPherson 2005).

The CSEPP pilot programme gained extensive experience in

responding to the employment needs of female prisoners. It became clear that employment is a necessary element for the successful reintegration of women into the community, and that a programme such as CSEPP improved their self-esteem and long-term employment prospects. Whilst CSEPP finished as a programme in June 2006, the knowledge gained led to the development of the 'Women For Work' programme as a key element of the new Correction's Victoria, *Better Pathways Strategy* (Department of Justice 2005) 'Women for Work' is a specific employment programme for women exiting prison or women on correctional orders, with a major focus on training and employment. 'Women For Work', unlike CSEPP, has been implemented using one service provider, which provides better continuity and a more streamlined approach to assisting women in the transition from prison to community and has a more clearly defined employer engagement strategy.

References

Corrections Victoria (2005) *Statistical Profile of the Victorian Prison System 2001–01 to 2004–05.* Victoria, Australia: Victorian Government Department of Justice.

Cox, R. (2001) *Post-release employment assistance program.* Queensland, Australia: Department of Corrective Services.

Cox, R. and Carlin, A. (1999) *Review into the delivery of vocational education training in Queensland.* Queensland, Australia: Department of Corrective Services.

Department of Justice (2005) *Better pathways: An integrated response to women's offending and reoffending.* Victoria, Australia: Victorian Government Department of Justice.

Federal Bureau of Prisons (2003), *The Mock Job Fair Handbook: Delivering the future.* Washington, DC: Department of Justice.

Field-Pimm, M. (2004) *Theory and Practice in Offender Employment Programs.* Victoria, Australia: Job Futures (unpublished).

Graffam, J., Shinkfield, A., Milhailides, S. and Lavelle, B. (2005) *Creating Pathways to Reintegration.* Deakin University, Victoria: The Correctional Services Employment Pilot Programme.

Heinrich, S. (2000) *Reducing recidivism through work: Barriers and opportunities for employment of exoffenders.* University of Illinois, Illinois, USA: Great Cities Institute.

Holzer H.J., Raphael, S. and Stoll, M.A (2003) *Employer demand for ex-offenders.* Los Angeles, USA.

Job Futures (2004) *Toward social inclusion for ex-offenders through employment.* Melbourne, Australia: Victorian Council of Social Services.

Jucovy, L. (2006) *Just Out, Early Lessons form the Ready4Work Prisoner Re-entry Initiative.* Pennsylvania, USA: Field Report Series, Public and Private Ventures.

Lawrence, S., Mears D.D., Dubin. G. and Travis J. (2002) *The practice and promise of prison programming.* Washington D.C.: USA Urban Institute Justice Policy Centre.

Office of the Correctional Services Commissioner (2000) *Strategic Plan July 2001–June 2004.* Melbourne, Australia: Victorian Department of Justice.

Solomon A.L., Gouvis C. and Waul, M. (2001) *Summary of focus groups with ex-prisoners in the district: ingredients for successful reintegration.* Washington, DC: Urban Institute Justice Policy Centre.

Taxman, F.S., Young D., and Byrne, J.M. (2002) *Offenders views of re-entry: implication for process, program and service.* Maryland, USA: Bureau of Governmental Research, University of Maryland.

Chapter 13

Housing and support after prison

Sally Malin

Introduction

This chapter explores the importance of housing, and linked support, for women ex-offenders. Drawing on a research project conducted between October 2003 and December 2004 which reviewed the impact of the UK government's £2.8 billion Supporting People (SP) programme, the chapter summarises UK evidence on the housing and support needs of women ex-offenders, and assesses the extent to which the SP programme has succeeded in improving planning and provision for this group. Local case studies are used to illustrate both the potential and the challenges so far evident in the implementation of the SP programme, and comparative perspectives from Paris, France, and Canada highlight the need for further reflection on models for the social inclusion of women ex-offenders.

The research was funded by the Griffins Society Visiting Research Fellowship Programme, and undertaken through the Social Policy Department at the London School of Economics and Political Science.[1]

Context

This section of the paper outlines the context for the research, outlining characteristics of the UK prison population (and in particular of the female prison population), detailing the role of housing in resettlement of women offenders, and introducing the Supporting People programme.

Characteristics of the prison population in England and Wales

In autumn 2003, when this research project began, the prison population in England and Wales stood at 74,055, an increase of 2% on the number in November 2002. Of these, 4,417 were female, an increase of 1% over the year, and 69,638 male, an increase of 2% over the year (Home Office, 2003). Both the growth and the absolute numbers in prison reflected a high rate of imprisonment in England and Wales by comparison with most other Western European countries (International Centre for Prison Studies, King's College, London, 2006).

All the research indicates that the majority of both the female and male prison populations in England and Wales come from backgrounds of significant disadvantage. The government's Social Exclusion Unit (2002) found that, compared with the general population, prisoners are thirteen times more likely to have been in care as a child; thirteen times as likely to have been unemployed; ten times as likely to have been a regular truant or excluded from school; and five times more likely to have been in receipt of benefits (Social Exclusion Unit, 2002).

Many young prisoners come from unstable living conditions and the majority are out of work (Social Exclusion Unit, 2002). Mental health problems, drug and alcohol abuse are common amongst young adult prisoners. They are more likely than adults to suffer from mental health problems, and are more likely to commit suicide than both younger and older prisoners (Singleton *et al.* 2000).

In addition, the number of people in prison as a direct result of drugs is high and still growing. However, many prisoners have never received help with their drug problems. The Social Exclusion Unit report estimated that in one prison 70% of prisoners came into gaol with a drugs misuse problem, but that 80% of these had never had any contact with drug treatment services (Social Exclusion Unit, 2002).

Many prisoners have significant mental health problems. Some 72% of male and 70% of female sentenced prisoners suffer from two or more mental health disorders. These figures compare with just 5% of men and 2% of women in the general population (Singleton, *et al.* 1998). Neurotic and personality disorders are particularly prevalent: 40% of male, and 63% of female, sentenced prisoners have a neurotic disorder, over three times the level in the general population. A significant number of prisoners suffer from a psychotic disorder: 7% of men and 14% of women, equating to respectively fourteen and twenty-three times the level found in the general population.

Women prisoners, however, are significantly more vulnerable than their male counterparts. One study found that some 15% of sentenced women prisoners had previously been admitted to a psychiatric hospital, and 37% had previously attempted suicide (Singleton *et al.* 1998).

Female prisoners with severe mental health problems are also often not diverted to more appropriate secure provision. A study which looked at 44 women from HMP Holloway, a women's prison in north London, who were seeking mental health care provided outside the prison found that half were turned down for a range of reasons. A shortage of beds, and of expert mental health professionals, were key factors. Compared to those who were allowed to have beds in mental health unit, the rejected women were more likely to have harmed themselves, to have suffered childhood abuse, to have committed serious offences and to be seen as violent or dangerous. The study concluded that 'inadequate service provision' both in scope and skills was a factor in determining whether or not such women could be transferred (Gorsuch, 1998).

Furthermore, women prisoners are much less likely than the general population to be able to call on the support of a stable relationship, but more likely to have childcare responsibilities. Although figures are not collected centrally on the number of women in prison who are mothers[2], Home Office research indicates that 66% of female prisoners are mothers, and each year it is estimated that 17,700 children are separated from their mother by imprisonment[3] HM Prisons Inspectorate found that 25% of women prisoners had their children's father or a spouse or partner caring for their children; 25% were cared for by their grandmothers; 29% were cared for by other family members or friends, and 12% were in care, with foster parents, or had been adopted (HM Prison Inspectorate, 1997). And, strikingly, just 5% of women prisoners' children remain in their own home once their mother has been sentenced (Prison Reform

The role of housing in resettlement

The importance of housing in the resettlement of offenders is long established. In 2002 the Social Exclusion Unit reviewed criminological and social research on the evidence of the factors that influence reoffending, and identified housing as one of nine key factors: drug and alcohol misuse; mental and physical health; attitudes and self-control; institutionalisation and life skills; housing; financial support and debt; and family networks.

The SEU report noted evidence that around one in three prisoners are not in permanent accommodation prior to imprisonment; as many as a third of prisoners lose their housing on imprisonment; around a third of prisoners about to leave prison said that they had nowhere to stay and noted that a recent study had indicated that around one in every twenty prisoners claimed to have been sleeping rough immediately prior to imprisonment.

The report also identified a number of specific housing issues facing women prisoners on release, many of which flow from the characteristics of the female prison population discussed above. Thus the greater proportion of single women means that there are fewer partners to maintain housing in their absence. Fewer women's prisons means that women are more likely to be held far from home – making it harder to maintain effective contact with housing providers. And although half of all women prisoners have dependent children, on release many are unable to regain their children from care without suitable accommodation, and cannot get access to housing appropriate for a family without first regaining custody of their children.

The Social Exclusion Unit report then explored areas where policy change on housing could make a positive impact on resettlement. Three key areas were identified: housing benefit policy meant that homes unoccupied due to imprisonment of the tenant in turn led to a loss of benefit, and consequently loss then of housing, as did poor communication with housing providers; difficulties in accessing housing on release, including limited supply of hostel accommodation; and patchy practice within prisons in the provision of housing advice to prisoners. These areas need to be seen in the wider context of the SEU's overall view that any successes in tackling offending behaviour and reducing reoffending were often achieved against the odds given a lack of capacity, unclear lines of accountability, insufficient joint working, and a lack of innovation.

Given the characteristics of the prison population, it is evident that for many ex-prisoners housing is a necessary but not sufficient element of resettlement. Indeed, the levels of disadvantage and vulnerability experienced by many ex-prisoners suggest that without additional support, securing and then retaining housing will be extremely difficult. The Supporting People programme was explicitly envisaged by the SEU report as playing a key role in delivering such support.

Housing and reoffending: solutions and Supporting People

The UK Government proposed a number of responses to the housing problems of offenders in England and Wales which had been identified in the SEU report.

Firstly, the Government's National Accommodation Strategy, as part of the National Rehabilitation Strategy led by the Home Office, will seek to ensure that prisoners do not initially lose their homes as a consequence of being in custody.

Secondly, the Homelessness Act (2002) made changes to the homelessness legislation which prevent the blanket exclusion of particular groups, including prisoners. The Homelessness (Priority Need for Accommodation) (England) Order 2002 extends the category of homeless applicants who have a priority need for accommodation to include, among others, those vulnerable as a result of having served time in prison. The Order, which applies only in England, does not however mean that all released prisoners will automatically have priority need for accommodation – it is for the housing authority to decide whether an individual applicant is vulnerable.

The third key response of the government to the housing issues identified by the SEU has been the Supporting People (SP) programme. SP is a government programme which took effect in April 2003, bringing major changes to the planning and funding of housing related support for around 1 million people, including both ex-prisoners and people at risk of offending. The programme brings together the main partners of health, housing, social services, probation and local authorities, to plan strategically and to commission services that are cost effective, reliable, transparent, needs-led and client-based. For 2004–5, the total Supporting People grant for the UK was £2.8 billion; for England, £1.8 billion.

The UK Government's Office of the Deputy Prime Minister (ODPM) has the main responsibility for the Supporting People programme. It allocates a Supporting People grant to administering authorities and monitors their performance. Administering authorities (unitary authorities, and counties in two tier areas) are then responsible for implementing the programme within their local area. The administering authorities contract with providers and partner organisations for the provision of Supporting People services. A commissioning body (effectively a partnership of local housing, social care, health and probation statutory services) sits above an administering authority and plays a key role in advising and approving a Supporting People strategy. Negotiation and consultation is also required with all housing and support service providers, other statutory service providers, the private sector and voluntary organisations both to plan and to commission support services to meet identified needs.

The Supporting People programme brings together considerable existing funding streams including transitional housing benefit, which has paid for the support costs associated with housing during the implementation phase; the housing Corporation's Supported Housing Management Grant; and the Probation Accommodation Grant Scheme into a single resource to be administered by 150 administering local authorities.

The intention was for the SP programme to enable stronger joint planning and a greater diversity of provision, better tailored to individual (and especially unmet) needs across a wide range of client groups. For example:

- Support services for vulnerable older people who wish to live independently, including those in sheltered housing;

- Temporary hostel accommodation, including probation hostels and those providing support for women fleeing domestic violence;

- Floating support to a range of vulnerable people including young people leaving care;

- Home Improvement Agency services whose work includes providing practical support to older owner occupiers to enable them to live independently;

- Support services for people with mental health problems, or learning difficulties;

- Support services for people from black and minority ethnic communities whose specific needs had often gone unrecognised or unmet.

The Supporting People programme therefore has considerable relevance for released women prisoners. It offers the possibility of providing support which could both strengthen access to housing, and the likelihood of successful retention of that housing.

However, there have been concerns, particularly at local level, about the ambitious scope and pace of the initiative. In particular, concern has been expressed about a shift from the previous national and rights-based system, to a cash limited and locally administered funding system. Would cash-strapped local authorities seek to shift responsibility for expensive community care clients with high levels of need to the new Supporting People budget? And if so, would provision for other groups suffer: particularly groups such as ex-offenders, who are often seen by local communities as less deserving of financial (or any other) support?

It was therefore unclear to what extent Supporting People was likely in practice to create more – and better – housing related support for women ex-prisoners. Nor was it clear whether a local authority based planning system would have the strategic capacity to plan effectively for such a diverse and challenging client group.

The research explained

I wanted to explore the impact of Supporting People on planning and provision for women ex-offenders. Methodologically, this was a challenge: Supporting People was at the time of the research project a relatively new programme which had been implemented at considerable speed; it encompassed 150 local authorities; and its remit for women ex-offenders needed to be seen against the broader canvas of the many other client groups it seeks to serve.

The research sought to meet the challenge through a three-strand approach: national, local and comparative. I wanted to know what, from a national perspective, were the aspirations for Supporting People, what was seen to be working well, and what less well. I then wanted to know whether national hopes were mirrored by local reality. Finally, a comparative perspective was sought in order to provide a broader – if opportunistic – 'paradigm check': might there be something to learn from approaches outside the UK to provision for women ex-offenders?

For the national perspective, semi-structured interviews were undertaken with representatives from key national agencies involved in implementing Supporting People: the Office of the Deputy Prime Minister; Home Office; Prison Service; and the National Probation Directorate.

The research then moved on to explore local perspectives of the impact of Supporting People at local level. Interviews were undertaken with key players in the London Boroughs of Camden and Islington, and in Leeds. In practice, the opportunity to interview key local personnel was severely constrained by other demands on potential interviewees' time. This means that the local case studies reflect a narrow spectrum of views, and conclusions from data collected can only be tentative.

To supplement the local case studies, a review of Audit Commission inspections of local authority Supporting People programme was undertaken. This provided a broader picture of some of the challenges involved in implementing Supporting People, although it should be noted that data collected relates to all ex-offenders and not solely to women ex-offenders.

Contact was also made with a number of 'prime movers' – individuals and projects identified by earlier interviewees as promoting innovation and development. In practice, this led to some blurring of the original research design, with data collected not only about initiatives funded through Supporting People, but also from other housing initiatives. However, the information collected did highlight some good news of potential relevance to women ex-offenders.

The final stage of the research sought to provide a comparative perspective through study of 2 community-based initiatives for ex-offenders outside England and Wales: community chaplaincy in Canada, and a French project, Soleillet, based in Paris.

Findings and discussion: National perspectives

In this part of the research, I wanted to find out how key national agencies in England saw the potential of Supporting People to address the needs of women ex-offenders. Interviews were held with representatives of the Office of the Deputy Prime Minister (ODPM), the Home Office, the Prison Service and the National Probation Directorate.

It should be noted that the individuals interviewed gave their individual perspectives on Supporting People, which should not therefore be read as the official views of the agencies concerned.

It should also be noted that interviews were carried out against a fast moving background. Key national developments relating to Supporting People during the research project (October 2003 – December 2004) are summarised at the end of this section

Key themes identified from the national interviews related to the political challenges involved in using SP as a means to improve planning and provision for women ex-offenders; issues relating to partnership working; and processes for ensuring appropriate needs assessment of women ex-offenders.

Supporting People has offered the possibility at local authority level of a better match between need and resource. However, this has inevitably been accompanied by a heightened profile of provision for ex-offenders within the local arena, against a background of wide public concern about crime and considerable hostility to ex-offenders. Securing shifts of resource from existing beneficiaries to a politically unpopular group was widely acknowledged as a difficult task

The outlook for the Supporting People programme was seen as largely dependent on successful inter-agency partnerships at local level. Civic leadership and sustained work to secure front-line integration of services were seen as key to successful partnerships. Developing and sustaining good working relationships with the voluntary sector was also seen as vital to ensure innovation, and dynamic links into local communities.

The national aspiration for Supporting People at its outset was for better individualised programmes of support, made possible by improved needs assessment. At national level there was recognition that while some local authorities had good track records with regard to the needs of women ex-offenders, many other authorities had limited knowledge, and could see women ex-offenders as low priority, given the absolute low numbers accruing to any one authority. Economies of scale were seen as possibly indicating the need for sub regional, rather than local authority, planning and provision for women ex-offenders.

National developments during the research

From very early in the life of the Supporting People programme, concerns were voiced about the rapidly escalating cost of the programme. While the 1998 White Paper outlining proposals for the SP programme had estimated costs of some £350–700 million across Great Britain, estimates and costs rose so steeply that the 2003–4 allocation for England alone was £1.8 billion.

In response, the ODPM and Her Majesty's Treasury in October 2003 commissioned Robson Rhodes to lead an independent review to gauge the true picture of how the Supporting People funding was being utilised. The review was published in January 2004.

A number of findings and recommendations emerged from the Robson Rhodes review. Local authorities had been required to implement Supporting People from very varied platforms of existing provision, and the Review recommended that an improved allocation formula be developed better to reflect population, need and cost. The evidence base for commissioning was often weak, and more effective tools for local needs assessment and service review were recommended. Particular attention was recommended for both floating and generic support services. Significantly, the review identified difficulties in securing an adequate level of resource for less popular groups, including ex-offenders, and recommended that the ODPM with others should give early consideration to measures to establish and protect an adequate level of funding and provision for the least popular vulnerable groups. Concerns were also voiced about the capacity of individual local authority SP teams to conduct specialist strategic reviews, and recommended that more strategic reviews be conducted across larger groupings of local authority SP teams.

The Robson Rhodes review was reviewed by the ODPM Select Committee in July 2004. The Committee endorsed many of the Review's findings, expressed concern about the implementation process of SP, and urged the ODPM to establish clear criteria as to what SP monies could properly fund and if necessary ring fencing funding for less politically popular groups such as ex offenders.

Also in July 2004 the government published Reducing Reoffending: National action plan, which built on the 2002 SEU report. The two key themes of the Action Plan were greater strategic focus, and better joined up working.

Finally, in December 2004 the ODPM announced a 2005 consultation on the revised needs-based distribution formula which would provide the basis for allocating Supporting People grant in the future, with likely significant changes to existing patterns of allocation between authorities.

Local perspectives: local case studies

As with the national interviews, it should be noted that interviewees were providing individual perspectives on Supporting People, not the official view of their respective organisations.

The two London case studies, in the Boroughs of Camden and Islington, have many common characteristics in terms of populations. Both are inner city areas with very diverse populations in terms of income, ethnicity and culture. However, Camden with a population of 198,020, had a SP allocation for 2004–5 of around £40 million, and Islington, with a population of 175,797, had a 2004–5 SP allocation of around £17 million.

On a positive note, Supporting People was seen for women ex-offenders to have enabled a closer focus on need, and potential reduction in stigma on accessing services; scope for a better joint agencies response to high-risk ex-offenders; and room to develop floating support services better able to meet both generic and specialist needs. New scrutiny and inspection regimes were seen to have potential to drive up the quality of services provided.

More negatively, local SP teams had struggled to meet what felt like ever changing demands from central government, and links with local prisons had proven hard to sustain. Acute local political pressure was anticipated as resource was scheduled to transfer to less popular groups such as ex-offenders. Housing for women ex-offenders remained in extremely short supply, reflecting London wide shortages of affordable accommodation , and one hostel reported having a 'short stay' resident with them for over 5 years. The low absolute numbers of women offenders within each authority meant that women ex-offenders were often seen as a lower priority than other larger, or more vocal, care groups.

The third local case study was undertaken in Leeds, a regional English city, which has a population of 715,401, and a 2004–5 SP allocation of around £35 million.

Two features stand out from the Leeds case study: firstly, a long standing emphasis on robust qualitative needs analysis as the premise for service development, including SP; secondly, the need for strong partnership arrangements both between statutory agencies, and with the voluntary sector.

The Leeds research produced a sophisticated analysis of need and current gaps in provision. In particular, issues for women ex-offenders have been identified, including the experience of child sexual abuse, prostitution, motherhood and an increased in custodial sentencing for women. It has been recognised that the female peak offending age is younger than that of men, and risk factors for women (particularly young women) have often been overlooked. The scarcity of bail hostel provision appropriate for women has also been identified.

Women ex-offenders' preferences were generally for social housing with flexible housing related support. Having a proper home of one's own was seen as a key goal. Support was often being received from agencies not funded through Supporting People, such as the specialist agencies for women involved in prostitution. Some of these agencies felt that they themselves were on the fringes, and that better co-ordination between the statutory and voluntary sectors would be required so that multi-agency packages of support could meet their clients' needs more effectively.

If, from a central government perspective, key aims for SP were to enable better needs assessment, more effective joint working, and innovative forms of service provision, the local case studies appear to indicate that none of the 3 local authorities studied had succeeded on all counts. Rather, the picture emerging would seem to be one of patchy progress, at times achieved against considerable odds.

The Audit Commission Review of the Supporting People programme

The UK Government's Audit Commission has been charged with carrying out inspections of all Administering Local Authority (ALA) areas across England for Supporting People within a five year period. The timetable also provides for re-inspections where serious concerns over performance arise, and for inspections at the direction of the Secretary of State where the ODPM has concerns over progress and performance.

The Housing Inspectorate has lead responsibility for this work, Inspections are carried out with the Social Services Inspectorate and the Home Office's Probation Inspectorate. Each inspection team also includes a service user inspector.

Reports follow a standard format. However, as might be expected from a programme of such wide scope and recent implementation, there is considerable range in the focus of key findings. Not all reports make specific comment on services for ex-offenders, although comment on strategies and on provision for other care groups may in some cases either include or have relevance for ex-offenders. It was therefore impossible to tabulate findings for the purposes of this research project.

Positive examples came, inter alia, from Manchester City Council which was commended for good service user involvement, including hard to reach groups, and effective leadership to partner agencies; Richmond upon Thames which has developed a range of positive services for hard to reach groups, including offenders and women fleeing domestic violence, and has also led effective joint working across agencies to identify services for those who pose a risk of harm to the public; and Northamptonshire County Council, which was commended for the development of a comprehensive Supporting People strategy which linked with wider strategies relating to crime and disorder, and for development of an information sharing protocol for high risk offenders. It is interesting to note that there appeared to be no clear correlations between positive practice and, for example, either political party leadership, or a rural or urban population.

From the perspective of women ex-offenders, less positive news came (again, inter alia) from Somerset County Council, which had made limited progress in its work with probation and developing services for offenders; London Borough of Enfield, where links between the vision for Supporting People services and the priorities and plans for some other strategic groups such as probation and health were not seen to be robust; and Wokingham District Council, where existing provision was almost all for older people, people with learning disabilities and people with mental health problems, and less that 9% of funding going to other groups, with consequent unmet need for other groups including offenders. Again, there appeared to be no clear correlation between slow progress and political party leadership, or a rural or urban population.

Findings from the Audit Commission inspections appear therefore to corroborate those from the 3 local case studies: across the range of client groups, some progress, often against the odds; for ex-offenders, rather more limited progress, and no clear correlation between progress and either political party leadership or population type.

Findings from other 'prime movers'

A number of projects and initiatives were identified through the research. Two striking examples were the New Bridge Project, Liverpool (in a deprived part of northern England), and East Potential's Time for Youth Project in (a similarly deprived part of) East London.

The New Bridge Project was established in 2004 to run for 2 years with funding from the ODPM and Liverpool City Council. The project seeks through two workers – 'Liverpool experts' – to ensure that local Merseyside prisoners being released from prison have information and access to community-based resettlement services available to them both pre and post release, thus preventing vulnerable individuals from getting lost in the 'maze' of services and then returning to crime.

At any one time, North West prisons hold over 11,000 offenders of whom 800 are women; 1500 women are released from North West prisons each year. With an initial focus on HMPs Liverpool and Styal (the latter is a women's prison) the project has aimed to target those with a right to settle in Liverpool and who were sentenced to twelve months or less in prison.

East Potential's Time for Youth project works with young people aged 16–24 in East London, Harlow and surrounding communities. The project works with young people who have convictions, those offending who have not been convicted, and those at risk of offending. It built on the French concept of 'foyer' accommodation which had in France led to a network of 'foyers pour jeunes travailleurs' (hostels for young workers). In the UK foyers had then developed as a means of integrating responses to youth unemployment and youth homelessness, becoming closely associated with the provision within a hostel environment of employment and training services.

At the Time for Youth project foyer accommodation is available, as is also floating support. This latter is support not attached to residence in foyer accommodation, and means that young people successfully resettled into permanent housing, evicted, or taken into custody, can still access Time for Youth support. It is unusual in providing support to the higher age of 24, allowing more vulnerable young people a longer period to make the transition to adulthood.

The Home Office's Accommodation Plus Group has also used Time for Youth as a pilot to examine the impact of successful interventions with young women offenders, and given the project funding for gender specific work with young women. This will support examination of those factors that make young women in particular more likely to offend.

It is, I suggest, apparent from the above that the impact of Supporting People at local level has been immensely varied. To date, there is limited data on its impact on provision for ex-offenders, including women ex-offenders. The mammoth scale of the task which local authorities have been set is all too clear both from the review of Audit Commission inspection reports, and from the local case studies. Needs assessment remains of a variable quality, with limited evidence of the kind of individualised and service-user led practice which had been envisaged. Partnership remains problematic at both strategic and operational levels. Innovation through effective links with the voluntary sector has been patchy. Political difficulties in securing or sustaining transfer of resources to less politically popular groups are evident.

However, there are also signs of hope. The Leeds case study demonstrates an imaginative approach to needs assessment, and provides one of the very few sources for hearing from women ex-offenders themselves the kinds of services they would find helpful. A number of the Audit Commission inspection reports demonstrate effective joint working between key agencies, and, perhaps, a growing local awareness of the need to ensure effective planning and provision for ex-offenders, despite the political challenges involved. The New Bridge project in Liverpool demonstrates an imaginative and replicable response to the mismatch between Prison Service areas and local authorities, and Time for Youth a strong example of the scope offered through 'floating support' better to meet the complex needs of young offenders.

Comparative perspectives: why comparative perspective?

There has been growing interest in recent years in the changing relationships between national cultures or traditions in criminal justice, and the ways in which crime control policies and practices now flow within and between nation states. Indeed, such interest was one impetus behind the June 2005 *What Works with Women Offenders?* Conference at the Monash University Centre in Prato, Italy, in which this book has its origins.

My purpose in including two comparative perspectives in the research project was rather more modest. I would suggest that government thinking about criminal justice policy in England and Wales has got stuck, particularly when considered in relation to social policy. There is therefore merit, I propose, in looking at examples of two projects from other jurisdictions to cast fresh light on what is, within England and Wales, taken for granted. I suggest that the project from France highlights an emphasis on the citizenship of ex-offenders, and that the project from Canada – which has now attracted considerable governmental and Prison Service interest here in England and Wales – suggests the potential for using faith communities to develop social inclusion of ex-offenders.

Soleillet Project, L'Aurore, Paris[4]

L'Aurore was founded in 1871 in response to the needs of former prisoners who had been incarcerated because of their participation in the 1871 Paris Commune, and its initial Board of Management included high status individuals such as senators, lawyers, military personnel and civil servants from the War Ministry.

The organisation has a formal commitment to the values of humanism, secularism and solidarity. From its initial work with ex-offenders, and then with the mentally ill, it has now developed to address all aspects of social exclusion through a three pronged approach:

- To deal with medical, social and care issues, so that clients are welcomed as human beings and members of a community of citizens, with due respect being paid to their rights and their dignity, and adequate financial support being provided by the public purse;

- To develop political and civic strategies, in order that governmental structures pay attention to the issues that concern both individuals and social groups within the care of the association;

- To remain pragmatic, so as to maintain effectiveness within the prevailing realities and constraints.

In 1977 L'Aurore was approached by colleagues in the criminal justice and social services systems, and asked to work with them to explore the possibilities of setting up facilities geared to caring for both single women and mothers coming out of prison. In response, Soleillet was set up in 1984. The project can now accommodate 37 women, children, and in some cases a couple with children, and has access to a further fourteen flats in the social housing estate very near the Soleillet centre.

Community chaplaincy[5]

Community chaplaincy has been active in Correctional Services, Canada, for over twenty years, and now provides support to some 11,000 individuals (offenders and their families) each year.

Community chaplaincy ministries are organisations within the faith communities with whom Correctional Services Canada has contracts. Practical, emotional and spiritual needs are met. Offenders using community chaplaincy services come from a range of ethnic and faith backgrounds, with some key regional differences. In the Prairies region 45% of the individuals accessing community chaplaincy are aboriginal, of whom 15% state that they are practising native spirituality. The black community is strongest in Halifax and Toronto, and St John's, Newfoundland, has a number of Inuit in its community.

Interest in community chaplaincy is now developing in the UK. In 2001 the Salvation Army provided two officers to the ecumenical Churches' Criminal Justice Forum with a remit to explore the scope for developing community chaplaincy in England and Wales.[6]

Pilots using the community chaplaincy model appropriately tailored to local circumstances have since been established in prisons in Swansea, Gloucester, North Staffordshire and Preston, and at the time of the research, were being developed in Feltham, Brixton, Low Newton, Manchester, Dorchester, Leeds, Nottingham and Cardiff. A national community chaplaincy network was also emerging.

Discussion: Policy and politics

Supporting People is an ambitious government initiative which has sought to improve housing related support for a very broad – and diverse – group of people. In order to achieve this goal, Supporting People introduced a new integrated funding framework and necessitated stronger cross agency partnerships.

For ex-offenders, Supporting People has constituted one key strand of the government's response to the housing issues identified in the 2002 SEU report. Stronger identification at local authority level of both need and resource has offered the possibility of spend better aligned to individual need and local possibilities than the predecessor Probation Accommodation Grant system.

However, Supporting People has also heightened the political profile of provision for ex-offenders within the local arena, against a background of wide public concern about crime and considerable hostility to ex-offenders. Securing appropriate resources and development of new needs-based provision for women ex-offenders has also proven additionally problematic given the absolute low numbers of women accruing to any individual local authority.

The comparative case studies from France and Canada, with their respective emphases on citizenship and community, serve as helpful reminders of other ways of envisioning the social inclusion of women ex-offenders. There is a need now for further consideration of the values base of 'what works', particularly with regard to women ex-offenders, and of models for the social inclusion of women ex-offenders.

Practice

At a practical level, the SP programme involves some 150 authorities, over 6000 providers, and approximately 37,000 individual contracts. It was therefore not surprising to learn from both the national and local data collected for this research that local authorities entered Supporting People from very different starting points.

Some local authorities already had substantial supported housing provision in their patch, and high levels of spend on a range of client groups. Other local authorities saw Supporting People as an opportunity to secure valuable additional funding, sometimes to the benefit of their own directly managed provision, sometimes to that of voluntary and independent sector providers. Some new provision, in particular generic floating support, may have been of questionable relevance to client need. Approaches to needs assessment and gap analysis have been varied, particularly for hard to reach groups with complex needs, such as women ex-offenders. User involvement in service review and planning has been equally patchy.

The Robson Rhodes review and Audit Commission inspections lend weight to all these findings. Although the government put in place a number of measures to address these issues, the findings of this research indicate that further specific attention to women ex-offenders may be required in order to ensure their housing support needs are met effectively through Supporting People.

Partnership

The success of Supporting People must rely heavily on effective inter-agency partnerships at local level. This research suggests that commitment to, and experience of, effective inter-agency partnership has been extremely varied. Despite both central government insistence and much local good will, it has in practice been very difficult to secure both the civic leadership and front-line integration required. The Probation Service in particular seems to have struggled in many areas to sustain a place at the planning table, and involvement of the voluntary sector has been uneven. In consequence, there have perhaps been too few advocates for women ex-offenders.

Promoting innovation

The voluntary sector has the potential to play a key role in promoting innovative provision for ex-offenders through Supporting People. The Liverpool New Bridge project, for example, demonstrates an imaginative response to the geographical mismatch between the prison estate and prisoners' local authorities. Similarly, the Time for Youth project illustrates a model that can provide support when and where the young people need it.

However, strong control of Supporting People from central government combined with formidable operational challenges at local level have meant that this potential of the voluntary sector has not yet been fully realised. There do not seem to be readily available channels for information exchange about SP funded voluntary sector projects for ex-offenders, and the process for securing funding through Supporting People for new voluntary sector projects can be unduly complex.

Conclusion

This research project aimed to explore the impact of Supporting People at an early stage in its life on planning and provision for women ex-offenders. It is evident from the research, firstly, that comprehensive information to support a robust evaluation of its impact on this group is not yet available.

From the information collected, it would appear that SP has had a positive impact in its introduction of a new integrated funding framework and the strengthening of cross agency partnerships. However, variance in pre-existing provision, and the heightened political profile of provision at local level, have created widespread problems in securing appropriate resource for ex-offenders. For women ex-offenders, this has been compounded in many local authorities by poorly developed approaches to needs assessment (in particular with regard to women), by the absolute low numbers of women ex-offenders accruing to any one local authority, and the lack of arrangements to share good and innovative practice for this group.

If the Supporting People programme is to meet its potential and to make a real contribution to meeting the housing and support needs of women ex-offenders in the UK, the following now need to be developed as a matter of urgency: best practice and gender sensitive models of needs assessment; collaborative arrangements across local authorities, and with the voluntary sector; and strengthened civic and professional leadership with and on behalf of women ex-offenders.

Notes

1 The Griffins Society is a voluntary organisation working for the care and resettlement of female offenders including those with a history of mental illness and violent behaviour. The Society was set up in 1966. At that time there was little residential provision for women offenders and the Society concentrated its efforts on filling that gap by providing specialist hostel and move on accommodation. Those residential projects were transferred to another voluntary organisation in 1997 and the Society decided to alter the focus of its activities. This change of emphasis included establishing the Griffins Society Visiting Research Fellowship programme in the Social Policy Department at the London School of Economics and Political Science (LSE) in 2001. For further information see www.thegriffinssociety.org

2 Hansard, House of Commons written answer, 28 April 2003.

3 Hansard, House of Commons written answer, 16 May 2003.

4 For more information, see http.//www.aurore.asso.fr/etablissements/hebergement/solleillet–1.htm

5 For more information about community chaplaincy in Canada, see http.//www.csc-scc.gc.ca/text/prgm/chap/pro06-3_e.shtml

6 For more information about community chaplaincy in the UK, see http.//www.ccjf.org

References

Home Office (2003) Prison Population Brief. London: Home Office

International Centre for Prison Studies, http://www.kcl.ac.uk/depsta/rel/icps/worldbrief/europe.html

Social Exclusion Unit (2002) Reducing Reoffending by Ex-Prisoners. London: Office for National Statistics.

Singleton et al. (2000) *Psychiatric morbidity among young offenders in England and Wales*. London: Office for National Statistics.

Singleton et al. (1998) *Psychiatric morbidity among prisoners in England and Wales*. London: Office for National Statistics.

Gorsuch, N. (1998) 'Unmet need among disturbed female offenders', *Journal of Forensic Psychiatry*, 9 (3).

HM Prisons Inspectorate (1997) Women in Prison: A Thematic Review by HM Chief Inspector of Prisons for England and Wales. London: Home Office.

Prison Reform Trust (2000) *Justice for Women: The need for reform*. London: Prison Reform Trust.

Chapter 14

What does work for women offenders?

Rosemary Sheehan, Gill McIvor and Chris Trotter

This book – and the conference upon which the contributions to it were based – was prompted by a concern to harness the growing body of international knowledge and experiences in relation to women caught up in the criminal justice system. The volume editors had been alerted to the difficulties faced by female offenders at each stage in the criminal justice process through their own involvement in a range of research studies examining women's experiences, needs and access to services and supports and through awareness of the expanding international literature on what has been, relatively speaking, an ignored area of criminological exploration and analysis. However, an understanding of how and why women offend, the processes through which women desist and the barriers to desistance can inform strategies to improve services to women who offend. This book has, therefore, drawn upon a range of international contributions from academics and practitioners to identify common experiences and key challenges.

A starting point, of course, that provides the context for most of the contributions to this volume is the unprecedented increase in women's imprisonment that has occurred in western jurisdictions in recent years. The scale of the problem and its implications in terms of prison conditions, prison overcrowding and women's access to health and other services have prompted policy attention in some jurisdictions to reducing the use of women's imprisonment through the availability of more and better resources in the community.

As McIvor argues in Chapter 1, policy commitments to reducing the use of women's imprisonment receive support from the observation that the types of offences most women commit are relatively minor and could not be construed as posing a significant public risk. Moreover, although there is an international trend towards the imposition of longer custodial sentence (without any attendant increase in the seriousness of female offending) the majority of women who receive custodial sentences are imprisoned for short periods of time. Short prison sentences are unlikely to achieve much in terms of addressing women's problems, meeting their needs and assisting their reintegration into the community, but the disruption to women's lives – and those of their children – can be immense.

As Sheehan and Flynn observe in Chapter 10 of this volume, male-centred approaches to corrections fail to take into account the parenting and family responsibilities of prisoners. Little emphasis is placed on programmes that facilitate family reintegration. Imprisoning mothers has a significant impact on their children, often of greater significance than imprisoning fathers, given that mothers are more likely to be primary caregivers prior to their imprisonment. Children of women who are prisoners endure considerable disruption in their care and they and their mothers experience great difficulty maintaining family ties. The impact imprisoning mothers has on their children provides powerful support for the diversion of women offenders from the criminal justice system.

Developing gender-appropriate community-based provisions

A key message from this book, therefore, is the need for services and supports that enable greater use to be made of non-custodial disposals for women who offend. The form these resources should take needs to be informed by an understanding of *why* women offend and *how* they might be encouraged and assisted to lead law-abiding lives. It is now generally accepted that women tend to have different pathways into offending from men and that services for women need to resonate with their experiences and needs. Simply adapting programmes, interventions or services that have been developed for male offenders is unlikely to suffice. Instead, gender appropriate services need to be developed that engage with issues linked to women's offending and that are delivered in a context that encourages and supports women in the process of change. As Gelsthorpe concludes in Chapter 3, developing gender-appropriate provision is 'an important prerequisite to promoting social justice, social inclusion and citizenship and the responsibilities and relationships which flow from them which may enhance offenders' reintegration and help promote their desistance from crime'.

There has been increasing academic attention of late to the concept of desistance-focused practice, which advocates a strength-based approach to supervision that aims to work alongside and support the process of desistance from crime (e.g. McNeill 2003; 2006). As Monica Barry indicates in Chapter 2 of this volume, there is growing evidence of the importance of social capital – both its accumulation and opportunities for its expenditure – in helping offenders to desist. Opportunities for 'generativity' and the assumption of responsibility for others appear to be particularly relevant in this regard (see also McNeill and Maruna 2007) highlighting the relevance of a strong relational dimension to effective services for women that his been highlighted by a number of commentators in this volume and elsewhere (Gilligan 1982; Bloom and Covington 1998; Covington 1998). This would appear to demand an approach to the supervision of women who offend that extends well beyond the relatively narrow focus on cognitive behavioural methods that has tended to characterise the development of offending-related provision for men and that has received additional impetus from the establishment in several jurisdictions (including Canada, England and Wales and Scotland) of formal systems for programme accreditation. As Gelsthorpe and McIvor (2007:340) have argued 'in the face of evidence from programmes which have focused on women's needs, it is unlikely that accredited programmes alone will be sufficiently holistic in nature to address the complex needs of women'.

In Chapter 5, Malloch and Loucks question whether cognitive skills programmes which focus on changing ways of thinking are likely to be effective for women and – reinforcing Pearce's argument in Chapter 6 that interventions for women need to be tailored to their experiences and needs – point to certain features which the research suggests are important in programmes for women. These include the use of women only groups, multi-agency co-operation – particularly involving integration of mental health and substance abuse services – and, individualised treatment following a thorough assessment. Malloch and Loucks discuss an innovative holistic approach in Scotland to dealing with women offenders who have problems with drug and alcohol. The aim of the 218 Time Out Centre is to provide holistic services to women on a residential and non-residential basis, with a number of different services – including drug treatment, heath care and psychiatric services – provided through a single access point. The initial results reported are promising, with most of the women saying that their drug use had reduced or stopped. It is services such as this that received enthusiastic support in the Corsten report into vulnerable women in the criminal justice system in England and Wales (Home Office 2007).

A key element of the 218 Time Out Centre is the positive, supportive relationships that are developed between the staff delivering services and the women who access them. O'Keefe, Senior and Monti-Holland also discuss the importance of relationship oriented approaches to women offenders in Chapter 11 in the context of an innovative 'Women to Work' programme which involved prisoners and offenders in the community in peer support. The women in the programme felt they were listened to and heard by peer workers and showed evidence of increased self-confidence and employability. O'Keefe, Senior and Monti-Holland also discuss the value of holistic services that offer personal support to women and deal with a wide range of problems that are defined from the woman's perspective. They argue that an holistic approach seems to work best both in terms of the opinions of the women who receive it and according to the limited empirical studies on recidivism.

Trotter writes in Chapter 7 about probation and parole services for women. He discusses what works in the supervision of women particularly those released on parole, while acknowledging that much of the knowledge in this area has been developed with male or at best mixed cohorts. Nevertheless, he suggests that a recent study of women offenders undertaken in Australia pointed to the success of relationship-oriented holistic programmes, whether they were offered in prison or following release from prison. Not only were the women happy with these type of programmes but they were also related to lower recidivism rates for the women in the study. The women also did better if they received parole and they did better if the parole officers adopted a holistic focus. The women themselves reported that they gained a lot, both in prison and after prison, from services which addressed all of their problems rather than focusing on one or two issues. They were particularly positive about the holistic relationship support services offered by voluntary agencies and religious organisations. Women who received these types of services also had low recidivism rates.

While these chapters provide consistent support for holistic approaches and for supervision which focuses on the whole person rather than on individual problems or needs, there is less agreement among the authors in terms of the values of case management systems. For example, Malloch and Loucks emphasise the value of providing many services under one roof and the benefits of multi-agency co-operation. Trotter, on the other hand, questions the value of case management systems which provide women with many workers and suggests that individual support workers might take greater responsibility for working with a range of issues, such as drug use, finances, family issues or peer group relationships, depending on which are of most concern to individual women at any given time.

In addition to holistic services being more effective Trotter refers to a number of practice principles which appear to be effective with both men and women. In particular he suggests that pro-social modelling is relevant to supervision with women although he sounds a note of caution in relation to the use of confrontation in the supervision of women. He also highlights the importance of supervision which deals with the issues facing women from their own perspective and points to a number of studies which have suggested that women may benefit from parole supervision. Women face particularly severe problems on release from prison and parole, it seems, may help to link them into support services which those released into the community without the benefit of supervision may not receive. In reaching these conclusions the chapter draws upon a study undertaken in Australia which found substantially reduced recidivism rates for women given parole.

Pearce in Chapter 6 discusses a risk and need assessment instrument – OASys – that has been developed for, and used by, the probation and prison services in England and Wales. The instrument aims to identify 'criminogenic' needs of offenders, which – as several other contributors to this volume acknowledge – often differ between women and men. On this basis, she suggests that treatment targets for women should be different from those of men and more directly focused on issues of victimisation and issues of past abuse, relationships and emotional well being. Such a conclusion receives support from the study by Severson, Berry and Postmus (Chapter 4) that explored protective factors relating to histories of physical and sexual victimisation reported by women offenders, focusing upon the differing needs and risk factors among women offenders in comparison to women in the community. They found that incarcerated women were more likely to have histories of alcohol and drug use, physical and sexual victimisation in childhood and in adulthood including violence perpetrated by intimate partners. Incarcerated women tended to have fewer social supports in the community and were more likely to have maladaptive coping skills. Incarcerated women also had less education, had their children earlier and were more often welfare dependent. The study found that women from both groups had experienced very high rates of violence even though this was more prevalent among incarcerated women.

Providing services to women in prison

As Sheehan and Flynn argue in Chapter 10, maintaining contact with their children is often a challenge for women in prison; a prison sentence can weaken or sever relationships with children. Parenting programmes and visiting programmes can work to restore and improve these relationships, yet do not appear to be seen as core prison-based programmes. Yet, having these relationships is an important support for women when they re-enter the community after prison. However, many incarcerated parents receive no visits from their children. Issues such as distance, transport services, the cost of visiting prisons and the lack of child-friendly visiting arrangements in prison, make contact between mothers and children difficult. Sheehan and Flynn found that the lack of care planning for young people whose mother was going into prison, meant little attention could be paid to key areas of accommodation for children, their education, contact with their mother, siblings and extended family, and finances. What is clear is that there needs to be greater system recognition of the parenting roles and responsibilities of women before the court and of the impact of the decisions of the criminal justice system on the children of these women.

Wolf, Silva, Knight and Javdani in Chapter 9 point to the increasing number of women drawn into the criminal justice system in the US because of drug-related crime. Despite drug abuse being a strong predictor of crime, prison systems in the US fail to address women's substance abuse problems, or the health problems that flow as a consequence. Women leave prison still struggling with substance abuse, with little or no community supports, or incentives to bring them in from the margins. Wolf, Silva, Knight and Javdani argue that pathways into crime are linked to health issues for women. The drug related offences that bring women into prison in the US have health needs associated with substance abuse, mental illness and infectious disease, as well a range of untreated health concerns – among them, sexually transmitted diseases, high blood pressure, asthma and diabetes. They note that women come into prison with years of neglected health needs to which the prison finds it difficult to respond. The lack of gender-appropriate services that respond to the distinct and distinctive health needs of women, combined with the priority given to custodial concerns, means little attention is paid to how to deliver effective and responsive health services to women in prison. Wolf, Silva, Knight and Javdani argue that overcrowding in prisons in the US, reduced programmes, male-centred models of staffing and services, a lack of expertise in managing substance abuse, all undermine women's abilities to manage their health concerns, which is particularly important once they are released.

Ogloff and Tye in Chapter 8 point to similar concerns about the mental health of women in prison, given the high rates of mental disorder and distress in women prisoners. They argue the need for diversion from the criminal justice system to deal with mental illness, as well as removing less serious offenders from the system. They emphasise that transitional health care is essential, especially given the interrelation between physical health, substance absue, mental health issues and recidivism. They propose a model for the treatment of mental illness among women in custody that recognises their particular needs, and screens for urgency in the assessment process. Their model is based on comprehensive assessment and treatment, as well as institutional and post-release community planning. It is a model that involves all prison staff in its implementation. They note that it is essential to maintain services commenced in prison, on release, given the difficulties involved in transition to the community and high recidivism rates. The model is an holistic approach that recognises the parallel importance of issues related to housing, employment and family together with mental health care to ease transition to the community.

Supporting resettlement

The use of diversion and community-based orders, or decarcaeration (Carlen 2002), allows women to remain in their communities. Women's recidivism is highly dependent on their success after returning to their communities, yet Wolf, Silva, Knight and Javadni argue that the provision of negligible services and the lack of gender-responsive programming fail to support community re-entry and jeopardise rehabilitation. While Severson, Berry and Postmus suggest in Chapter 4 that women's assumptions that their problems will go away or that they can handle them themselves may act as barriers to accessing services, a final broad theme which can be identified from the contributions to this volume concerns the practical barriers to effective reintegration and resettlement. Women face particular barriers in their transition to the community: organising housing, finding a job, and reuniting with their children. Given that most women serve short sentences, it is suggested that community-based approaches offer better efforts at offence prevention and access to services. Where women are incarcerated it is argued that community linkages must be established to provide women that link them with community-based organsiations prior to their release.

O'Keefe, Senior and Monti-Holland (Chapter 11) found that there are a number of barriers for women offenders or ex-offenders in seeking employment and training. There was often an over emphasis on basic skills in prison-based programmes, a lack of staff, few individually tailored programmes, and a lack of integration between prison-based and community-based programmes. Disclosing previous offences proved to be a barrier for most women along with negative attitudes towards offenders. Often also obtaining accommodation and rebuilding family relationships distracted women from seeking training and employment. They suggest however that many of the women in their peer support programme were able to overcome these barriers as a result of the support they received.

In Chapter 12 McPherson argues that employment is key to reintegration. Her evaluation of an employment programme introduced into the women's prison in Victoria found this actively helped reduce recidivism. However, it needed to be long-term and linked between custody and community. The women needed to meet, prior to their release, with workers with whom they would be working in the community and the programme had to link to housing, health and personal support services. Employment however had to be meaningful and sustainable, and housing, health and family issues needed to be managed before linking the woman to employment. The strength of this programme was that women commenced in it six months before release and could stay in it twelve months after release, providing continuous links to service providers, who were based in the area to which the women were returning to live. The programme provided an individual action plan for each woman, incorporating parole conditions into plans for housing, family reconnection and employment. The programme emphasised self-esteem and motivation, and the development of skills to enable women to have a sense of control over their life circumstances.

It is difficult to obtain accurate estimates of the accommodation needs of women who offend partly because they may tolerate abusive relationships to prevent themselves from becoming homeless.

307

This, combined with the small numbers of female offenders who are recognised to be in need of accommodation, makes provision of services and planning for provision of services especially problematic. Yet there is ample evidence that accommodation is a common problem, especially among women leaving prison (MacRae *et al.* 2006; Trotter *et al.* 2006) and that the accommodation obtained by female ex-prisoners is often characterised by its instability. For example, three months after release a third of the female ex-prisoners in Morris *et al.*'s (1995) study were not living in the address they had expected to return to following their release. As Malin argues in Chapter 13, imprisonment impacts disproportionately upon women in terms of their accommodation needs on release. This is because imprisoned women are less likely than imprisoned men to be living with a partner who can maintain tenancy of their home while they are serving a custodial sentence. In the UK, women with children who are looked after by social services while they are in prison may also find themselves in an invidious 'catch 22' situation following release, being unable to assume responsibility for the care of their children without suitable accommodation and being ineligible for priority accommodation unless they have responsibility for dependent children. The prioritising of ex-offenders in the context of the UK government's 'Supporting People' initiative may be construed as representing an improvement upon previous arrangements, however as Malin observes, implementation of the initiative has been patchy and it is not yet clear whether ex-offenders will be disadvantaged in comparison to other more 'deserving' groups.

Concluding observations

Each of the authors in this book highlights the needs of women in the criminal justice system and point to the fact that women offenders have multiple problems. The backgrounds of the women in prison are characterised by experiences of abuse, drug misuse, poor educational attainment, poverty, psychological distress and self-harm. While men often share many of these characteristics, problems amongst female prisoners are generally more acute even though their offending presents less of a threat to public safety. Female prisoners are more likely to have a history of physical or sexual abuse and more likely to face issues relating to the care of their children. They are also more likely to be convicted of acquisitive crimes and less likely to be convicted of violent crimes in comparison to men.

Whether the aim is to assist women's resettlement following a prison sentence or to provide resources in the community that encourage the courts to impose non-custodial sanctions on women in the knowledge that their needs and problems (including those linked to their offending) may be addressed, the contributions to this volume highlight the importance of women having access to what Worrall (1996: 74) has referred to as 'the structural pre-conditions of social justice – housing, employment and health facilities ... without which ... they have no chance of reconstituting their own lives and those of their "families", however they choose to define that term'.

What overwhelmingly emerges is the need for greater awareness and acknowledgement in court proceedings of the impact of imprisonment on women, and the use of dispositions that keep less-serious offenders out of prison. This is not to diminish the independence of the judiciary, nor the appropriateness of disposition matching the nature of the crime. It simply recognises the breadth of impact on a woman when she goes to prison, that this impact is qualitatively different from that of male imprisonment, especially when the woman is the primary carer of dependant children. It does ask the criminal justice system to look more carefully at the need to remand women in custody or sentence women to prison, and to view this as the disposition of last resort.

The recent UK report by Baroness Jean Corsten (Home Office 2007) into women with particular vulnerabilities in the criminal justice system has many synergies with the chapters of this book. We strongly support many of the comments and directions recommended in her report. In particular she suggests that women can be described as victims as well as offenders. She comments on the 'catastrophic' impact of women's imprisonment on children, the inappropriate use of imprisonment for many women and the multiplicity of problems which women face. She argues for a 'seamless continuation of care' both inside and outside prison and for a focus on their accommodation needs. She suggests that problems leading to women's offending will respond far more to casework, support and treatment in the community rather than imprisonment. The chapters of this book suggest that the pursuit of her recommendations by government would provide great benefits to women in the criminal justice system and the wider community.

References

Bloom, B. and Covington, S. (1998) *Gender-Specific Programming for Female Offenders: What is it and why is it important?*, Paper presented at the Annual Meeting of the American Society of Criminology, Washington, DC.

Carlen, P. (ed.) (2002) *Women and Punishment: The struggle for justice*, Collumpton, UK: Willan Publishing.

Covington, S. (1998) 'The relational theory of women's psychological development: implications for the criminal justice system', in R. Zaplin (ed.), *Female Offenders: Critical perspectives and effective intervention*. Gaithersburg, MD: Aspen Publishers.

Gelsthorpe, L. and McIvor, G. (2007) 'Dealing with diversity.' In L. Gelsthorpe and R. Morgan (eds) *Handbook of Probation*, Collumpton, UK: Willan Publishing.

Gilligan, C. (1982) *In a Different Voice*, Cambridge MA.: Harvard University Press.

Home Office (2007) *The Corston Report: A report by Baroness Jean Corston of a review of women with particular vulnerabilities in the criminal justice system.* London: Home Office.

MacRae, R., McIvor, G., Malloch, M., Barry, M. and Murray, L. (2006) *Evaluation of the Scottish Prison Service Transitional Care Initiative*. Edinburgh: Scottish Executive Social Research.

McNeill, F. (2003) 'Desistance-focused probation practice.' In W-H Chui and M. Nellis (eds) *Moving Probation Forward: Evidence, arguments and practice*, Harlow: Pearson Longman.

McNeill, F. (2006) 'A desistance paradigm for offender management,' *Criminology and Criminal Justice* 6 (1): 39–62.

McNeill, F. and Maruna, S. (2007) 'Giving up and giving back: Desistance, generativity and social work with offenders.' In G. McIvor and P. Raynor (eds) *Developments in Social Work with Offenders*, London: Jessica Kingsley.

Morris, A., Wilkinson, C., Tisi, A., Woodrow, J. and Rockley, A. (1995) *Managing the Needs of Female Prisoners*. London: Home Office.

Trotter, C., Sheehan, R. and McIvor, G. (2006) *Women After Prison*, report to the Catholic Social Services Management Committee and Australian Research Council, Melbourne, Victoria: Monash University Department of Social Work.

Worrall, A. (1996) 'Gender, criminal justice and probation.' In G. McIvor (ed.) *Working with Offenders: Research highlights in social work, 26*, London: Jessica Kingsley.

Index